Please remember that this is a library book,
and that it belongs only temporarily to each
person who uses it. Be considerate. Do
not write in this, or any, library book.

"Reading aloud is a joyous experience for child and for parent. *The Read-Aloud Handbook* offers useful hints as to why the experience is so mutually rewarding and how to make it work."
—Arthur Schlesinger

"Fresh, vital, and inspirational . . . bravo for Trelease! I urge everyone who cares about literacy—and that should include people without children—to read this book."
—Digby Diehl, *Los Angeles Herald Examiner*

"Not only contains wise advice on introducing children to books, but it contains an excellent annotated list of . . . books to which children truly respond."
—*The San Diego Union*

"Little sensible advice has been offered parents on how they can go about it in a practical way, or at least how to get beyond the Richard Scarry–Berenstain Bear syndrome. Jim Trelease has filled this vacuum with a book that is a wonder of success in its completeness of down-to-earth, yet intelligent, approaches to reading aloud."
—*Family Journal*

PENGUIN BOOKS

THE NEW READ-ALOUD HANDBOOK

Jim Trelease works full-time addressing parents, teachers, and professional groups on the subjects of children, literature, and television. A graduate of the University of Massachusetts, he was for twenty years an award-winning artist and writer for *The Springfield* (MA) *Daily News*. His work has also appeared in the Sunday book review sections of *The New York Times* and *The Washington Post*.

Initially self-published in 1979, *The Read-Aloud Handbook* has had three American editions along with British, Australian, and Japanese editions.

Despite a lecture schedule that carries him to every part of North America, Mr. Trelease is still a regular visitor to classrooms near his home in the Connecticut River Valley, sharing with children his career as a writer and a love of children's books. The father of two grown children, he lives in Springfield, Massachusetts, with his wife, Susan.

Jim Trelease's lectures are available on 16mm film and on 90-minute audiocassette. For information, write Reading Tree Productions, 51 Arvesta Street, Springfield, MA 01118.

Jim Trelease

The
New Read-Aloud

Handbook

penguin

books

PENGUIN BOOKS
Published by the Penguin Group
Viking Penguin, a division of Penguin Books USA Inc.,
375 Hudson Street, New York, New York 10014, U.S.A.
Penguin Books Ltd, 27 Wrights Lane, London W8 5TZ, England
Penguin Books Australia Ltd, Ringwood, Victoria, Australia
Penguin Books Canada Ltd, 2801 John Street, Markham, Ontario, Canada L3R 1B4
Penguin Books (N.Z.) Ltd, 182–190 Wairau Road, Auckland 10, New Zealand

Penguin Books Ltd, Registered Offices: Harmondsworth, Middlesex, England

The Read Aloud Handbook was first published in the United States of America
in Penguin Books 1982
First revised edition published 1985
This second revised edition published 1989

10 9 8 7 6 5 4

Portions of this work were
originally published in pamphlet form.

Library of Congress Cataloging in Publication Data

Trelease, Jim.
The new read-aloud handbook / Jim Trelease.
p.   cm.
Rev. ed. of: The read-aloud handbook. 1985.
Bibliography: p.
Includes index.
ISBN 0 14 046.881 1
1. Oral reading.   I. Trelease, Jim. Read-aloud handbook.
II. Title.
LB1573.5.T68   1989
372.6—dc20   89-31925

Printed in the United States of America
Set in Bembo
DESIGNED BY FRITZ A. METSCH
PHOTOGRAPHS BY JOANNE RATHE

To Elizabeth and Jamie—
the best audience a reader-aloud could hope to find.

And to Alvin R. Schmidt,
a ninth-grade English teacher who found the time
twenty-seven years ago
to write to the parents of one of his students to tell
them that they had a talented child. The vote
of confidence has never been forgotten.

Contents

Acknowledgments   *x i*

Introduction   *x i i i*

1   Why Read Aloud?   *1*

2   When to Begin Read-Aloud   *19*

3   The Stages of Read-Aloud   *41*

4   The Dos and Don'ts of Read-Aloud   *79*

5   Read-Aloud Success Stories   *86*

6   Home and Public Libraries   97

7   Television   116

8   Sustained Silent Reading: Reading-Aloud's   139
    Natural Partner

9   How to Use the Treasury   148

10 Treasury of Read-Alouds   153
        Predictable Books   153
        Wordless Books   154
        Reference Resources   156
        Picture Books   157
        Short Novels   202
        Novels   217
        Poetry   250
        Anthologies   256

    Notes   265

    Bibliography   278

    Subject Index   283

    Author-Illustrator Index to the Treasury   286

Acknowledgments

This book could not have been written without the support and cooperation of many friends, associates, neighbors, children, teachers, and editors. I especially wish to acknowledge my everlasting gratitude to Mary A. Dryden, principal of New North Community School in Springfield, Massachusetts, for beginning it all by convincing me to visit her class twenty-two years ago, when she was teaching fifth grade.

I am deeply indebted to the editors of *The Springfield* (MA) *Daily News* for their long-standing support of staff involvement with the community's schoolchildren. It was this policy which provided the early impetus for my experiences in the classroom. At the same time,

I am particularly grateful to Associate Editor Jane Maroney of *The Springfield Morning Union,* whose guiding hand helped shape the initial concept of this book; Ruth Danckert, then children's book editor of *The Springfield Sunday Republican;* and George R. Delisle of *The Daily News.*

For their assistance in preparing the photographs used in this edition I am grateful to the following: Joanne Rathe; Kristen Hallahan; Mary Lynn Mathews; Katie, Meghan, and Jean McFarlin; Christa, Clark, and Susan McCarthy-Miller; Kathy Nozzolillo and her students at White Street School in Springfield, Massachusetts; Principal Thomas P. O'Neill Jr. and the students at Samuel Lewenberg Middle School in Matapan, Massachusetts; Vonetta and Myra Smith; Bridget, Greg, Jeanne, and Brian Trelease; Kathryn Van Avery; Matthew, Kerry, and Peggy Weber; Larry Greene, Tommy Lynch, and Rachel and Victoria Diaz.

For the many clerical and manuscript needs that accompany a revision, I thank Kelly Botta and Linda Long of my staff.

In addition, I would like to thank my neighbor Shirley Uman, whose enthusiasm for my idea spilled over at a family reunion ten years ago within hearing distance of a fledgling literary agent, Raphael Sagalyn, who carried it home to Penguin Books; Bee Cullinan of New York University for her early encouragement and painstaking advice; and my editor at Penguin, Kathryn Court, who, as a new mother, brings a new dimension to this edition's editing.

And, finally, I thank my family—my wife, Susan, and our grown children—for their patience under the avalanche of books and papers, as well as their understanding during the long absences required for each revised edition.

Introduction

If we would get our parents to read to their preschool children fifteen minutes a day, we could revolutionize the schools.
—Superintendent of Chicago
Public Schools (1981)

In the first Penguin edition of this book, back in 1982, I began with an anecdote about a sixth-grade teacher in my home city, Springfield, Massachusetts, who began each school year by reading aloud to her class. Seven years later the anecdote is still worth repeating because no other incident better exemplifies the purpose of this book.

On that first day of school, Karen Chartier began by reading aloud to the class. Her wide-eyed students listened attentively as she finished the first page and turned to the second.

At that moment, Johnny, a student in the front row, raised his hand and told her she'd forgotten "to show us the picture on that first page."

"Oh, I didn't forget," she explained. "It's just that this book doesn't have any pictures."

Johnny frowned for a second, before he asked, "Then how are we going to know what the people look like in the story?"

Johnny had a problem. He was going blind in his mind's eye. He had seldom, if ever, been read to in school or at home, had read little on his own, and was suffering from an underdeveloped imagination that required the daily hypodermic of television's moving images in order to function. His teacher was trying to cure that addiction, massage his withered imagination, and educate him by expanding his world. And *that* is what this book is about.

A large part of the educational research and practice of the last twenty years confirms conclusively that the best way to raise a reader is to read to that child—in the home and in the classroom.

This simple, uncomplicated fifteen-minute-a-day exercise is not only one of the greatest intellectual (and emotional) gifts you can give a child; it is also the cheapest way to ensure the longevity of a culture.

At the very start, you should understand the costs involved. Public library cards are free and therefore the most expensive and beautiful children's books in the world are yours, free for a lifetime. There are no fancy teaching machines to buy for your home or classroom, nothing to plug in, no lesson plans or flashcards. Nor do you need a college or high school diploma to do it. For those who believe it cannot be valuable unless you can order it from a catalogue or buy it at a mall, you're going to be disappointed. The only cost is your time.

It also might be helpful for you to know this is two books in one. The first half is the evidence in support of reading aloud, when to begin, and how to make it work—supported by personal experiences. It also addresses the subject of television, the largest stumbling block to reading enjoyment and achievement, and suggests how families and schools can cope with its pervasive influence.

The second half of the book is the Treasury of Read-Alouds, a beginner's guide to recommended titles, from picture books to novels. The listing is intended to take the guesswork out of reading aloud for busy parents and teachers (many of whom were never read to in their own childhoods) who want to begin reading aloud but don't have the time to take a course in children's literature. Since the Treasury is annotated with age and grade levels, it does not have to be read all at once. Before using the Treasury, however, you will find it helpful to read Chapter 9 (How to Use the Treasury).

For those readers who wonder how this edition differs from previous ones, I assure you that none of the fundamentals has changed. Statistics have been updated, and exciting new research and many experiences added, along with new patterns in learning and parenting. Nearly 8,000 new children's books have been published since the last edition and I've collected what I hope are some of the best read-alouds and added them to the Treasury. I have also removed those titles that are now out of print.

My foremost perspective is that of a parent—because that is how I came to write this book in the first place. Back in the 1960s, I was a young father of two children and working as an artist and writer for a daily newspaper in Massachusetts. I was also reading to my daughter—and soon my son—each night, unaware of any cognitive or emotional benefits that would come of it. I read for one reason: *not* because of any education courses I took in college (I'd taken none as an English major), and *not* because the pediatrician told me to (he hadn't). I read because *my* father had read to *me*. And because he'd read to me, when my time came I knew intuitively there is a torch that is supposed to be passed from one generation to the next. And through the countless nights of reading I began to realize that when enough of the torchbearers—parents and teachers—stop passing the torches, a culture begins to die.

As a school volunteer in Springfield, Massachusetts (I'd been visiting classrooms on a weekly basis for several years, discussing my careers as artist and writer), I was invited one day to speak to a sixth-grade class.

After spending an hour with the class, talking about newspapers, illustrations, and cartoons, I gathered my materials and prepared to leave, when I noticed a book on the shelf near the door. It was *The*

Bears' House, by Marilyn Sachs, and it caught my eye immediately because I'd just finished reading it to my daughter.

"Who's reading *The Bears' House?*" I asked the class. Several girls' hands went up.

"I just finished reading it," I said. Their eyes lit up. They couldn't believe it. This man, who had just told them stories about how he got started in newspapers, this man, whose drawings and stories they had been clipping out of the paper for the last month— this man was reading one of *their* books?

So I explained about my children, Elizabeth and Jamie, and how I read to each of them every night. I told them how, when my children were little, they were most interested in the pictures. That was fine with me because I was an artist and I was interested in the pictures, too. I told them how much I'd loved Maurice Sendak's *Where the Wild Things Are* because of how he drew the monsters. I loved to scan the Little Tim books to see how Edward Ardizzone drew the ocean and *Make Way for Ducklings* to see how Robert McCloskey drew the ducks.

"And did you know," I said, when I saw them perk up at the mention of the *Ducklings* classic, "that Mr. McCloskey had a dreadful time trying to draw those ducks? He finally brought six ducklings up to his apartment in order to get a closer look. In the end, because they kept moving around so much, do you know what he did? You may find this hard to believe, but I promise you it's true: in order to get them to hold still, he put them to sleep by getting them drunk on champagne!"

The class clapped and cheered their approval of McCloskey's unorthodox approach.

I went on to explain that as my children grew older, our read-aloud stories became longer and I began to realize that not only were the pictures beautiful in children's books but the stories were, too. "Now those books have become my hobby. We hated so much to return our favorites to the library, we decided to buy copies for ourselves. Today we have hundreds and hundreds." Again the eyes widened in wonder.

Then we talked about *The Bears' House:* what it was about (for those in the room who had not read it); what the students liked about it; and what else they had read by the same author. I asked the rest of the class what they had read lately. There was an avalanche of hands and a chorus of books. It was forty-five minutes before I could say good-bye. I stepped out into the corridor, where the teacher thanked me for coming. "But most of all," she said, "thank you for what you said about the books. You have no idea what it means for them to hear it from someone outside the classroom."

In the days following the visit I pondered what had happened in that classroom. The teacher subsequently wrote to say that the children had begged and begged to go to the library that afternoon in order to get some of the books I'd talked about. I wondered what it was that I had said that was so different. I had only talked about my family's favorite books.

All I was doing was giving book reports. As soon as I called it that I realized what was so special about it. It probably was the first time any of those children had ever heard an adult give not only a book report but an unsolicited book report—and that's the best kind. How many of them had ever heard a teacher say, "You'll have to bear with me today, class, I'm a little fuzzy-headed this morning. I stayed up until three o'clock this morning reading the most wonderful book. I just couldn't put it down. Would you like to hear what the book was about?" Of course they would!

I had talked animatedly about the characters, dramatically about the plots, warmly about the authors. I'd teased the children's interest by giving them a book report. But an even better description of it would be "a commercial." I'd started by selling them on newspapers and a career. And I'd concluded by selling them on books and reading.

From that day to this, I've never visited a class without asking: "What have you read lately?" Between 1968 and 1982, I spoke in hundreds of classrooms, exchanged book reports with thousands of children, and out of those years and numbers certain patterns emerged:

- Beginning with the late 1960s there was a dramatic decline in the number of books read by the children in those classrooms. Each year they'd read less and less.
- The decline was so sharp that by 1979 when I asked, "What have you read lately?" the children were naming their classroom textbooks. That happened not once but numerous times.

- Lack of interest in reading was apparent in both public and private schools, in suburban as well as urban locales. In one private school, the entire sixth grade couldn't name more than five books they had read in the last three months. Either ignoring or ignorant of the reading problem at her school, the principal confided to me later that the school had begun to turn the corner—there was now a waiting list for enrollment. I shuddered and wondered if prospective students really knew what they were waiting for.
- While the decline was general, it was not all-inclusive. Some classes overwhelmed me with their responses; they loved books and read voraciously. In each case that contagious enthusiasm was a direct result of a teacher's attitude. He or she loved books and shared that affection by reading aloud and talking to the class about books.
- In many cases, when teachers and parents witnessed the children's responses to my "commercials," they asked for a list of "good read-alouds." Some had tried reading aloud previously and had been stung by a dull book: the children were bored, the reader was bored, and the book was put away along with the whole idea of reading aloud.

When I thought about my personal experiences and those I was witnessing in classrooms, I soon understood the link between children being read to and how well they were able to read alone. I looked at the read-aloud research sitting on the shelves of college libraries and found it backed my theory completely.

In the late 1970s, when I realized there was nothing generally available for parents and teachers on reading aloud, not even book lists (except brief ones included in children's literature textbooks), I decided to compile my own. Because I worked for a newspaper at the time and I had access to modern typesetting equipment, the task was relatively simple: I'd write a short how-to booklet on reading aloud to children, half the book being a list of recommended titles. To be candid, I never imagined the events that were to follow. Initially, it was a modest self-publishing venture (it cost me $650— the family vacation money one summer—for the first printing), with local bookstores taking copies on consignment. Within three years the booklet sold more than 20,000 copies in thirty states and Canada. By 1982, Penguin Books had seen a copy and asked me to expand it into the first edition of the book you are reading now. Since then there have been two more American editions, as well as British, Australian, and Japanese editions.

I share that background with you not in a self-congratulatory way but rather as evidence in support of a major thesis of this book: The literacy problems of ten years ago are still with us; we know how to cure much of it; and you can help. I propose that you—one parent, one grandparent, one teacher, or one librarian—can make a lasting difference.

Just as one angry mother made a significant difference in the drunk-driving laws of this country (MADD—Mothers Against Drunk Driving), so too one man affected an entire state in the 1980s by founding Read-Aloud Delaware; and one principal (dedicated to read-aloud) made a difference in a Boston middle school that he changed from one known as "the loony bin" to one with the highest reading scores and the longest waiting list in the city. (I'll give you their stories in later chapters.)

A lot has happened since that first edition back in 1979. My children are grown now and I no longer work for a newspaper. Instead, I work exclusively with parents and teachers, doing 150 programs a year on the importance of reading aloud. Sometimes, when I stop to think about that, it saddens me. How does the most educated country in the world come to the point where people have to be reminded to do something as important and commonsensical as reading to children? Maybe it's because common sense is not as common as we'd like to believe.

There have been other changes, as well. That teacher, Karen Chartier, is still teaching, still reading aloud—but in a different school. Indeed, American education has changed. During the last ten years, the U.S. Department of Education—alarmed by the growing number of "Johnnys" among its 45 million students—issued its famous 1983 report calling America a "nation at risk" unless reforms took place.

Reform suddenly became the education buzzword and that report was followed by literally three hundred more in the next five years, touching every corner of the classroom, from preschool to university. In the last five years, the majority of states have raised both graduation requirements and teacher salaries, toughened curriculums, strengthened teacher-training programs, some instituted competency testing for teachers, and fifteen began spending tax dollars to educate four-year-olds.

As report findings became public, grass-roots movements grew among educators, parents, and the business community demanding everything from all-day kindergartens to delayed schooling, from excellence to equality. Ignorant of the school dropout rates of the past (76 percent in 1940, 90 percent in 1900), some even called for a return to the curriculum of the good old days.

Yet another heated debate has arisen among reading professionals about the best way to teach reading. Though the three camps (basal, whole language, and literature-based) occasionally sound like accusatory TV evangelists, the results so far have been a breath of fresh air instead of stale chalk dust. Adapting to change, textbook publishers have begun to choose the best from all camps to build new curriculums.

Seeking immediate results in the wake of national education reform, too many schools have embraced a philosophy of "Don't teach it in the morning unless you can test it in the afternoon." Thus it becomes easy to lose sight of the fact that teaching is not an exact science and these are not Chryslers and Toyotas. They are children.

Among the things we must teach little human beings if we are to remain civilized are love, justice, courage, and compassion. These essentials cannot be taught and then measured *immediately* on paper. The long-term process of reading literature is one of the best ways to teach them.

In the intervening years since the first edition there have been dramatic changes on Johnny's side of the class as well. Ten years ago, most of Karen Chartier's students had not attended preschool or day care. And most came from homes where Mother did not work outside the home. There was no video rental store nearby and there was no cable TV. In one childhood's time, all that has become common experience, affecting childhood, learning, and reading.

Any wholesale change in society will always be reflected in its children and thus the society's future. Any society (like ours) that offers either so many distractions or negative role models that two out of three children can't read, won't read, or hate to read is going to suffer as a result. It will suffer in the choices those children eventually make in the voting booth, how they choose to spend their time and money; how they raise their children; what they adopt as a value system; and whom they emulate.

A hopeful sign is the growing interest on the part of new parents—not just in education but in the parenting process. Born in the rudderless sixties and seventies and better educated than their predecessors, many young parents seem determined to correct the mistakes of their own parents by devouring many of the three hundred parenting books now in print. To the relief of educators who watched PTAs decline for twenty years, membership has been rising since 1983.

There are two rubs in this. First, parents most in need of help (the ones who bring the largest number of at-risk children into schools)—young, poor, undereducated mothers and fathers—either won't or can't avail themselves of these tools; and second, a growing number of affluent, fast-track parents are using education as a pressure cooker to produce an instant adult.

The challenge posed by both kinds of parent is addressed here. As for those parents (and educators) bent on raising "superbabies," I offer this immediate disclaimer: This is not a book on teaching your child *how* to read; it is a book on teaching him to *want* to read. The four-year-old who is forced into reading might be a gifted child. *Might* be. More likely the child is the product of a pushy, insecure parent intent on impressing the neighborhood or office with a four-year-old reader. I will explain the difference between children who arrive at reading naturally as a result of being read to and those who arrive prematurely as a result of "hothousing."

Suffice it to say, the business of childhood is play; the prime purpose of being four is to enjoy being four—of secondary importance is to prepare for being five. What the pressuring parent needs to do is read Dr. David Elkind's two books, *The Hurried Child* and *Miseducation: Preschoolers at Risk,* which clearly document the dangers of what many principals call "suburban child abuse." It is sobering research and common-sense reading.

If you really want to help your child, send for "Getting Ready for School." More than 3,000 kindergarten teachers identified the

105 most desirable skills children could have *by the time they start school*—not by three years of age. To obtain a copy, mail a self-addressed envelope with forty-five cents' postage to: "Getting Ready for School," World Book, 510 Merchandise Mart Plaza, Station 99, Chicago, IL 60654.

For those busy parents willing to concede the importance of reading to children but unable to find the time to do it, I remind you: We're only talking about fifteen minutes a day (unless you and the child opt for more). Surely you can afford *that*. With the passing of the forty-hour work week, the American worker has never spent less time on the job or had more free time. The question is: How do we spend that time? Male and female adults each spend an average of six hours a week shopping[1], and each averages thirty hours a week watching television. Contrast those figures with the 1986 study that found working mothers spending an average of only eleven minutes of quality (one-on-one) time with a child daily (thirty minutes on weekends). Working fathers devoted even less—eight minutes daily and fourteen minutes on weekends. Mothers at home hardly improved the scores, devoting only two minutes more each day.[2] If there's a time shortage, guess who's getting the short end.

The problem is not time. With few exceptions, it is simply a matter of priorities. Most find the time to put in a full workday, take a full complement of coffee breaks, eat lunch, dinner, read the newspaper, watch the nightly newscast or ball team, do the dishes, talk on the phone for thirty minutes (mostly about nothing), run to the store for a pack of cigarettes or a lottery ticket, drive to the mall, and never miss that favorite prime-time show. Somehow they find the time for those things—important or unimportant as they are—but can't find time to read to a child.

You don't have to be an astrologer to predict certain parts of the future. In twenty years, the ball teams will still be winning or losing, you'll have twice, even three times as many malls to shop in, your favorite soaps will be rerunning on one of 150 different channels, and the dishes and dustballs will still be waiting. But your little boy or little girl will not. They'll be all grown up, with lives of their own. You get only one shot at it.

There is one particular group I wish a word with in this introduction—fathers. While I confess to having a special feeling for them, too often the feeling is one of disappointment. One of my personal goals is to convince as many fathers as possible of their powerful influence, not only to build better athletes but literate ones, too. Standing in the lobbies of American libraries, you would think fathers were an endangered species. Consistently, whether I am in Hawaii, Louisiana, Georgia, Alaska, or Massachusetts, men make up less than 7 percent of my parent audiences. Educators tell me that this is the same figure for male turnout at PTA meetings.

But there is never a shortage of males in our remedial reading classes, where boys make up more than 70 percent of the enrollment. In *American* remedial classes, that is. Boys *don't* constitute 70 percent of the remedial students in Israel and Japan—boys and girls are in equal numbers there. And in England, Nigeria, India, and Germany, the girls outnumber the boys.[3]

So the old genetic argument of boys developing slower than girls doesn't always fly—unless they're making little boys differently in Nigeria and Israel than they are in the United States. What *is* different is the culture. Many American boys are sentenced to remedial classes by fathers who convince their child that the most important things in life are the things we throw and catch. "The important things in *my* life, son, are the things you see me get excited about—the Broncos and the Browns, the Celtics and the Lakers, the Red Sox and the Mets. You don't see me get excited about *Charlotte's Web,* do you?"

Somehow we have to change that pattern among fathers and sons. It is not only possible, it is *preferable* for fathers to be both athletically and intellectually involved in their children's lives. A father can play catch in the backyard after dinner and, on the same night, read to the child for fifteen minutes. He can take him to the basketball game on Friday night and to the library on Tuesday night.

The sports world, in fact, is analogous to the world of reading. Consider the role of fathering in major league baseball. The structure of this sport with its slow, nonviolent nature allows for an intimacy between fathers and sons that has resulted in the highest father-son ratio in professional sports—forty-seven second-generation major-leaguers, by one count. Thus the odds against Ken Griffey's son making it to the majors were only 500 to 1, as opposed to a boy whose father did not play in the majors—25,000 to 1.[4]

The reason the odds favored Ken, Jr. is that he hung around with a major leaguer, played catch with him in the backyard, went to spring training with him, even sat in the dugout with him.

Now compare the odds against a boy or girl whose main role model is seldom if ever seen or heard reading versus the odds against the child who hangs around with a reading parent, a parent who curls up in bed with child and book, who takes the child to the library, who is seen reading a daily newspaper—even sharing parts of it with the child. Who stands the best chance of becoming a lifetime reader? And that is the objective here: lifetime readers, not schooltime readers.

In the long run, the only thing of lasting value you can give a child is your time and the memories of the time you shared together.

Mary Van Dyke, a teacher in Goleta, California, understands that. "My father died thirty-seven years ago when I was sixteen," she explained to me. "My dearest and clearest memories of him are when he read to me from *The Book House* every evening. I remember each detail—the chair, the lamp, how I felt next to him, the way his eyes peered through his bifocals, the bit of saliva at the corner of his mouth, and, most of all, his voice. Fifty years later I still can hear exactly how he sounded. . . . For those few minutes he was all mine, that voice was all for me."

The teacher who wrings her hands in frustration over the parents who won't do the job—that teacher needs to be reminded that *to-morrow's* parents are sitting in her classroom. Plant the joy of reading in that student today and there's a good chance he'll do likewise with his children twenty years down the road.

The analogy with planting reminds me of a Massachusetts family and the adage "Anyone can count the seeds in a single apple, but only God can count the apples in a single seed." The mother in this family told me of the unexpected fruit born from her family's reading and the part that positive reading role models play in the lives of children:

"About a year ago my husband began reading *My Side of the Mountain* to our two sons, ages 10 and 8. He read each evening at 6:00 P.M. The boys are friendly with an older boy in the neighborhood, Scott, age twelve, who happened by on the first evening of reading. He wanted them to come over to his house to play with his new Atari cartridges, but when he saw my husband reading aloud he was disgusted and said he'd wait outside or at home. He actually looked embarrassed, witnessing his friends sitting on their father's lap being read to!

"He was really into stoicism and independence at that time; nevertheless, with a brownie in hand I was able to persuade him to wait for the boys inside our house, in the same room where the disgraceful 'babying' was taking place. I could never do justice with words to the change in his facial expression while waiting. It went from disgust, to puzzlement, to interest, to total involvement. From then on, each evening at 6:00 P.M., Scott would 'happen' to stop by for the boys, and each night with less and less effort he was coaxed into waiting while Sam Gribley's story unfolded.

"I had never seen Scott with library books before, but the following week I saw him by chance at the bus stop—with a copy of *My Side of the Mountain*. Since then his mother tells me he's read it five times."

During fourteen years of reading aloud, my children and I sat in a one-room schoolhouse with Carol Ryrie Brink's *Caddie Woodlawn*, chased monsters with Maurice Sendak and Mercer Mayer, and sweated it out in Mr. McGregor's garden with Peter Rabbit. As they grew older, we mourned the death of a father in *A Day No Pigs Would Die* with Robert Newton Peck, roamed the backwoods of the Ozarks with Wilson Rawls in *Where the Red Fern Grows*, and groped down the dark subway passages of New York City with Felice Holman in *Slake's Limbo*. We laughed, cried, shook with fright, and shivered with delight. And, best of all, we did it together.

I can promise you—as will anyone who reads aloud—once you begin this daily experience, it will become one of the best parts of your day and the children's, too. A mother in Louisiana wrote to me: "It saddens me to think of what I missed—and my parents missed—in my childhood. What opportunities to share that reading would have given us! But now that I've discovered it with my own children, I'm going to make up for lost time. All those books I never met as a child, I'm meeting now—and loving it as much as the children."

More than half a century ago there was a poor Quaker woman who took in a foundling child and began reading Dickens to him every night. Surely she could not have dreamed that the words and stories would have such an enormous impact. The boy, James Michener, would write his first book at age thirty-nine and his thirty-fourth at age eighty-one. In between there would be best-sellers translated into fifty-two languages, selling more than 60 million copies, and enjoyed by countless millions of readers.

A Note on Pronouns

In the interests of smooth reading, I have generally avoided using "he or she" and instead I usually refer to the child as "he" and to the teacher as "she." This does reflect the numbers: a greater percentage of boys than girls have reading problems, and by far the larger proportion of elementary-school teachers is female. But of course this book is aimed at *all* adults—parents, teachers, loving neighbors—for the benefit of *all* children.

You may have tangible wealth untold:
Caskets of jewels and coffers of gold.
Richer than I you can never be—
I had a Mother who read to me.

—"The Reading Mother" by Strickland Gillilan,
from *Best Loved Poems of the American People*

The
New Read-Aloud Handbook

1. Why Read Aloud?

Perhaps it is only in childhood that books have any deep influence on our lives . . . in childhood all books are books of divination, telling us about the future, and like the fortune-teller who sees a long journey in the cards or death by water, they influence the future. I suppose that is why books excited us so much. What do we ever get nowadays from reading to equal the excitement and the revelation of those first fourteen years?

—Graham Greene, from
The Lost Childhood and Other Essays

As the most important discipline in education, reading generates more than 1,200 research projects annually. Inundated with data, the National Academy of Education and the National Institute of Education created a Commission on Reading in 1983 to separate the wheat from the chaff, to boil it down to what works, what might work, and what doesn't work.

The Commission, composed of outstanding men and women in the fields of reading, learning, and child development, spent two years pouring through two decades' worth of reading research and practice and issued its report in 1985—*Becoming a Nation of Readers*. Among its primary findings, one simple declaration rang loud and clear: "The single most important activity for building the knowledge required for eventual success in reading is *reading aloud* to children."[1]

The Commission found conclusive evidence to support its use not only in the home but also in the classroom: "It is a practice that should continue throughout the grades."[2]

Parents said, "I thought the kids were supposed to read to *us*, not us to *them*." Young teachers (who had never been read to) were equally confused: "Throughout the grades? To fifth-graders who already know how to read? Isn't that a waste of time?"

With today's flashy textbooks, coupled with computerized teaching and learning machines, what is it that makes the centuries-old practice of "reading aloud" so important?

Answered simply, the initial reasons are the same reasons you talk to a child: to reassure, to entertain, to inform or explain, to arouse curiosity, and to inspire—and to do it all personally, not impersonally with a machine. All those experiences create or strengthen a positive attitude about reading, and attitude is the foundation stone upon which you build appetites. A secondary reason, and of great importance in an age of rising illiteracy, is the established fact that regular reading aloud strengthens children's reading, writing, and speaking skills—and thus the entire civilizing process.

How does it accomplish all that? By improving children's *listening* comprehension. Let us take, for example, the word "enormous." If a child has never heard the word "enormous," he'll never say the word. And if he's neither heard it nor said it, imagine the difficulty when it's time to read it and write it. *Listening* comprehension must come before *reading* comprehension. The listening vocabulary is the reservoir of words that feeds the reading vocabulary pool.

One of the early and primary abilities of children is imitation.[3] They imitate much of what they see and hear, and it is this ability that allows a fifteen-month-old child to say his first words. By age two, the average child expands his vocabulary to include nearly three hundred words. That figure is more than tripled again in the next year, at the end of which the child already understands two-thirds to three-quarters of the words he will use in future daily life.[4] Once he learns to talk, he will average as many as ten new words a day—

not one of which is on a flash card.[5] Much of that pace is determined, however, by the amount and richness of the language he hears.

Most young parents are unaware of their role as prime models for language; they think children are somehow programmed to speak the language automatically. Most, however, express surprise at how quickly the child imitates what he sees on television—especially the commercials. No matter how often children see a particular commercial, the same fascination returns to their eyes each time.

Even before these repeated showings plant a desire for a particular product within the child, they succeed in anchoring the language of the commercial in the child's memory bank. Just listen to the number of jingles for McDonald's, Coke, and Pepsi recited by preschoolers.

Such deep-rooted success is carefully calculated by advertising agencies on Madison Avenue paying upwards of $50,000 a minute to ensure that your child is enraptured by the commercial. That enchantment is based upon an unofficial but guiding formula devised in the 1950s:

1. Send your message to the child when he or she is still at a receptive age. Don't wait until he's seventeen to try to sell him chocolate breakfast cereal. Get him when he's five or six years old.

2. Make sure the message has enough action and sparkle in it to catch and hold the child's attention. Avoid dull moments.

3. Make the message brief enough to whet the child's appetite, to make him want to see and hear it again and again. It should be finished before the child becomes bored.

As parents and educators, we would do well to learn from Madison Avenue. Indeed, it is this formula that underpins some of the success of reading aloud. Readers-aloud adapt it to sell a product called READING:

1. You read to children while they are still young enough to want to imitate what they are seeing and hearing.

2. You make sure the readings are interesting and exciting enough to hold their interest while you are building up their imaginations.

3. You keep the initial readings short enough to fit their attention spans and gradually lengthen both.

Just as Madison Avenue's triumph is well-documented, so too is reading aloud's. When children have been read to, they enter school with larger vocabularies, longer attention spans, greater understanding of books and print, and consequently have the fewest difficulties in learning to read.[6]

If reading aloud is so successful and so good for children, why is it not more prevalent? Two things have conspired to make reading aloud one of the best-kept secrets in education: the vast number of distractions within the American home, and the "test and measurement" syndrome in the classroom. Each feeds the other and exacerbates the problem. Students who spend most of their time watching television at home don't read much. These nonreaders do poorly in school, thus prompting a heavier dose of skill and drill—both of which must be constantly measured for efficiency and effectiveness. This daily exercise further disenchants the student, driving him to more TV viewing and less reading.

Let's look at the distractions in the home environment:

- Ninety-eight percent of the homes in America have a television set (the average home contains 2.3 sets[7]) and that set is on for an average of seven hours and one minute a day.[8]
- The nation's three-year-olds are watching as much TV as the nation's ten-year-olds—thirty hours a week. Add to that the number of hours spent watching videos and the average kindergarten graduate has already spent nearly 6,000 hours watching television—more time than it takes to obtain a bachelor's degree.[9]
- A Gallup poll in 1988 showed that 78 percent of families owned a VCR, and it is projected that by 1990 all TV homes will own one.[10] Already there are more than 75,000 video rental locations in the U.S. Add to that the 8,000 libraries now circulating videos, and you have a figure nearly five times greater than the number of all our public libraries (17,000).[11]
- Fifty-nine percent of teenagers own their own television sets and 33 percent own a VCR.[12]

Competing with an influence like that is no small sales task for anything—never mind reading. But it can be done. You, all by yourself, can instill a desire for books and reading in an entire family or class. If a plastic box in your living room can turn on your child to chocolate breakfast cereal or talking teddy bears, then you should be able to do ten times as much—because you are a sensitive, intelligent, and loving human being. (They've yet to invent the television or VCR that can hug a child.)

Selling the joys of reading is made more arduous by the fact that many children (overwhelmingly those who have not been read to) have already experienced difficulty in learning to read. Few tasks present us with as monumental a challenge as reading—and few tasks are as far-reaching in their consequences. In describing his own childhood agonies with the printed word, Nobel Prize–winner John Steinbeck once wrote, "Some people there are who, being grown, forget the horrible task of learning to read. It is perhaps the greatest single effort that the human mind undertakes, and he must do it as a child."[13]

Nonetheless, thousands of seven-year-olds learn to read daily. For many children, though, it is with enough pain to keep them from pursuing their newfound talent beyond fourth-grade level, as opposed to those who learn to read without bruises. And there is the catch.

The 1983 *Nation at Risk* report and the subsequent three hundred education reports resulted in numerous reforms aimed at improving basic skills and the level of excellence among U.S. students. At this early stage, children's reading scores are now inching upward (instead of the downward spiral of the 1970s). The book industry figures support this trend with steady gains in sales over the last eight years, including a 50 percent increase in the children's market since 1982.[14]

New tests show we are not a nation of illiterates, much as alarmists would like us to believe so. Modern teaching methods and materials have produced results far superior to those of 1940 (when the school dropout rate was 76 percent) to the point where we can say unequivocally that the average American student *can* read. And 95 percent of twenty-one- to twenty-five-year-olds can perform routine tasks using printed information (one paragraph of simple sentences).[15] Unfortunately (or fortunately, depending on how you look at it) we do not live in a world that makes only simple demands on our minds.

It is a world that grows increasingly complex by the hour. Seventy percent of the reading material in a cross section of jobs nationally is written on a ninth-grade level.[16] Typical is a recent report showing a national shortage of 30,000 properly trained auto mechanics: "Automobile repair has changed from a vocation in which even high-school dropouts could excel to one that demands a two-year college degree in electronics or its equivalent just to get by."[17]

A curriculum consisting largely of programmed drill and skill has produced self-defeating results: students who know how to read but choose *not* to read.

What happens to a society dependent upon print to transmit knowledge from one generation to the next—from plumber to plumber, from technician to technician—if succeeding generations choose not to read? Consider these findings in the youth culture (keeping in mind that many of them are related to reading):

- After years of decline, the school dropout rate has climbed to 28.5 percent[18] (Japan's is 5 percent, the Soviet Union's 2 percent), and one out of every twelve students is absent each school day (one out of six in city schools).[19] Sixty percent of the dropouts are functionally illiterate.[20]
- Fifty-four percent of the seventh-graders and 36 percent of the eleventh-graders cannot explain the meaning of a three-paragraph passage.[21]
- One year away from graduation, 75 percent of the eleventh-graders cannot adequately write a letter to their principal offering reasons for changing a school rule, and most fourth-, seventh-, and eleventh-grade students are termed writing failures while claiming that "writing is not necessary in order to obtain a job."[22]
- Sixteen percent of the eleventh-graders are unable to comprehend a tabloid newspaper, 60 percent cannot understand writing on the level of *The New York Times,* and 80 percent of the twenty-one-year-olds cannot read a college textbook.[23]
- In a test of 8,000 seventeen-year-olds (those still in school), the majority failed a history and literature survey exam—unable to tell (approximately) when the first atomic bomb was dropped, the dates of the Civil War (within half a decade), or

identify the Magna Carta. (More than half the students admitted they do not read for pleasure even once a week.)[24]
- Reading apathy does not begin in high school. In its 1986 evaluation of third- and fourth-grade students, the National Assessment of Educational Progress (the nation's report card) found 90 percent of the students had not read a book or story recently.[25]

Simply put, American children and young adults (who will be tomorrow's parents, teachers, electorate, and consumers) do minimal reading. They don't know very much about yesterday and today unless they've seen it on television. This is *not* called illiteracy (an inability to read on a fourth-grade level); it is called *ignorance* (an unawareness of knowledge) and it is showing throughout the culture:

- In its first recruiting effort in a decade, the New York Telephone Company found that 84 percent of the 22,880 applicants failed the entry-level examination in the first half of 1987.[26]
- Thirty percent of the nation's largest companies (and many of its smaller ones) are collectively paying $25 billion a year teaching remedial math and reading to entry-level employees.[27]
- The federal government spends $100 million annually and state governments an additional $200 million in assisting illiterate adults.
- In the nation's prisons, 60 percent of the inmates are illiterate and 85 percent of juvenile offenders have reading problems.[28]
- In the book industry, 80 percent of the books published are financial failures.[29] One of the world's wealthiest, most educated countries, the U.S. ranks only twenty-fourth in per-capita book buying.[30]
- Forty-four percent of U.S. adults do not read a book in the course of a year—with young adults showing the largest decline,[31] leaving 10 percent of the population to read 80 percent of the books and become powerful through that information.[32]
- Half the population no longer reads a daily newspaper, depending entirely on television for daily information. Among the top twenty nations for per capita newspaper circulation,

the U.S. places nineteenth—behind nearly all the modern industrial powers.[33]

- Sixty-eight percent of U.S. adults report television viewing as their greatest pleasure—outweighing even friends and vacations.[34]

Defenders of the status quo will point to the high influx of illiterate immigrants over the last twenty years as a cause of the illiteracy rates—an increase in the number of adults who never had the benefit of our educational system. That argument loses much of its strength when you consider the reading appetites of those who can read and are graduates of our system: the best-selling weekly magazine on U.S. newsstands is *TV Guide;* in second place is the periodical that declared in 1983 that John Kennedy, Marilyn Monroe, and Grace Kelly were still alive—*The National Enquirer. TV Guide* and *The National Enquirer* are read not by illiterate immigrants but by graduates of our homes and classrooms.

Obviously, if we are spending large amounts of money and time in successfully teaching children to read but they in turn are choosing *not* to read, we must conclude that something is wrong. In concentrating almost exclusively on teaching the child *how* to read, we have forgotten to teach him to *want* to read. And there is the key: desire. It is the prime ingredient in nearly all success stories—in the arts, business, education, or athletics. Somehow we've lost touch with the teaching precept: What you make a child love and desire is more important than what you make him learn. And that's the reason you've never heard of Remedial Driver Education classes in American high schools. Students *want* to learn to drive.

Contrary to popular opinion, desire is not something we are born with. Winners aren't born, they're made; hundreds of coaches take teams with losing reputations, instill desire in them, and motivate them to championships. Desire weighs heavily in reading because, like throwing a baseball or playing the piano, it is an accrued skill; that is, the more you practice (read), the better you get at it; and the better you get at it, the more you like it; and the more you like it, the more you do it. But the practice comes first, and that won't occur without desire—which must be planted by parents and teachers who work at it.[35]

How does one begin to instill in children a desire to read? Follow the lead of the number-one salesman in the world, who opens a new store every seventeen hours: Ronald McDonald. How did McDonald's insure the appetite for its product throughout the world? By advertising over and over, week after week, singing new praises, extolling new tastes. American business learned long ago that nothing sells in this culture without advertising—to the point where the average adult is bombarded by nearly 5,000 audio and visual commercial messages a day.

Since we know advertising works, how does this sound as a reading promotion: "Boys and girls, open your books to page fifty-two and answer questions one through twenty." Not exactly a turn-on, is it?

Reading aloud is the best advertisement because it *works*. It allows a child to sample the delights of reading and conditions him to believe that reading is a pleasureful experience, not a painful or boring one. The first mistake most parents make is not giving the commercial often enough before the child starts school. In essence, they don't advertise. They should have begun with short commercials in the very first year of his life, introducing him at an impressionable age to the joys and discoveries of books.

Usually, a child's first real encounter with reading occurs in school when the child goes into business for himself—sound by sound, syllable by syllable, word by word—learning how to read. The danger here is that with nothing to compare it to, the child begins to think *this* is what reading is all about: skill sheets, workbooks, flash cards, and test scores. And those are not motivators. Have you ever heard of a parent who walked into a child's room late at night and found the child in bed, under the covers, with a flashlight—and a workbook? Of course not.

Children cannot fall in love with drill and skill because they are lifeless. But not pointless. They serve the same purpose—when used in moderation—as spring training in the baseball season. Every spring for a century we've taken these grown men to Florida and drilled them in the mechanics of baseball skills. But no one believes for a second that spring training is what inspires people to become baseball players or fans. You know what does it? Being taken to *real* games, the taste of hot dogs, seventh-inning stretches, watching your older brother rush for the box scores in the sports page, and playing catch in the yard.

The same thing is true with reading. You become a reader because you saw and heard someone you admired enjoying the experience, someone led you to the world of books even before you could read, let you taste the magic of stories, took you to the library, and allowed you to stay up later at night to read in bed.

An essential ingredient is the other person involved in reading—the mother, father, brother, teacher. We are social creatures and reading is a social experience. Without *others* there would be no need for language, be it speaking, writing, or reading. As linguists point out, you can't teach a child to speak by locking him in a room filled with tape recordings. He needs to interact with *others* in order to find meaning.

So too with reading. Skill sheets, workbooks, basal readers, flash cards are not enough. To convey meaning you need someone sharing the meaning and flavor of real stories with the student. Imagine how few baseball fans we'd have left if all we had was spring training: no real games, no pennant drive, no World Series, just spring practice games. What has killed reading in American classrooms? A whole year's worth of spring training, year after year.

The Chicago public schools learned that lesson the hard way. Beginning in 1981, they instituted a reading workbook program (Mastery Learning) that broke reading instruction into a series of separate skills which had to be mastered before progressing to the next. What set Chicago apart from the 1,500 other U.S. school systems using the program was a lack of real books—Chicago focused on the workbook exclusively, never applying the skills to meaningful situations. Five years and $8 million later, with the acknowledgment that 60 percent of its graduates could not read at the twelfth-grade level and half of those were reading at or below junior high level, the city conceded its error. Henceforth, real books would come first, workbooks second.[36]

The resounding approval of reading aloud by reports like *Becoming a Nation of Readers* is convincing a growing number of classroom teachers and administrators of its importance, people who previously considered it to be a waste of valuable instructional time. States like California and Michigan now acknowledge its fundamental legitimacy in the curriculum. And though 50 percent of fourth-grade teachers estimate they regularly read aloud,[37] my experiences over the years with thousands of parents and teachers across America lead me to believe these survey respondents greatly overestimate the frequency of their reading. My estimate—supported also by librarians' observations—would be that only 20 percent of the parents and 30 percent of the teachers regularly read aloud to children.

The current mania for testing doesn't help. In Bibbs County, Georgia, a kindergarten teacher was recently cited by her supervisor in her yearly evaluation for wasting valuable instructional time by reading to her students. This was the same year (1988) Georgia gave 102,000 children a ninety-minute multiple-choice exam to see if they were ready for first grade. In all likelihood that kindergarten teacher is now teaching the test instead of teaching her kindergartners to love reading by reading to them. Unless a supervisor or teacher is convinced that reading aloud helps children pass tests, too, they'll frown on its use.

The discouraging message sent to young readers-to-be by the daily paper chase of worksheets is described by Nigel Hall in his book, *The Emergence of Literacy*. An experienced early primary teacher, discussing with her class why people read and write, told them she kept a book beside her bed. "Why do I do that?" she asked them. After a pause for thought one child answered, "So you can practice." When she told them that she didn't have to practice, there was general disbelief until one child produced a book with what appeared to the child to contain very difficult writing. "Go on, read that then," he said. And for several days thereafter her students continued to bring in apparently difficult print items to test her.[38] It would seem that buried in the 1,000 worksheets[39] assigned annually to each elementary student is this sad message: You've got a lifetime of practice and boredom ahead of you, kid!

The ironic part of it all is that nearly all children begin school with the expectation they'll learn to read and that it will be fun. Any kindergarten teacher will tell you this. And by fourth grade the great expectations are over and disillusionment sets in. Richard Anderson, who chaired the Commission on Reading, and a team of colleagues investigated how literate fifth-grade students spend their free time outside school. Results: Ninety percent of them devoted less than 1 percent of that time to reading and 33 percent of the time to watching television.[40] We are creating *school*time readers instead of *life*time readers.

In other words, by the time the student reaches fourth grade—when all the separate reading skills he's acquired are supposed to coalesce so he can use them to begin *learning* from books—he's lost interest, *especially* if he's one of those children coming from homes where there are few books, magazines, or newspapers.[41] Exercises like this one in a second-grade workbook can't help:

> Say the word in each shape. If you hear a vowel sound that you hear in *hard,* color the shape green. If you hear a vowel sound that you hear in *corn,* color the shape blue. If you hear a vowel sound that you hear in *first,* color the shape orange.[42]

The "reading is work" mentality that children associate with books is supported in the findings of Richard Allington of the State University of New York.[43] Allington observed that remedial-reading classes spent a remarkably small amount of time reading in context without interruption. In fact, the average student read only forty-three consecutive words before being interrupted for questions or corrections. The poorest readers received the heaviest doses of skills instruction and consequently spent the least amount of time on the very objective—READING.

If students are not read to, if day after day the only reading they hear is the drone of fellow members in the "turtle" reading group, they are certain to finish the year sounding like a "turtle." We need to balance the scales and let children know through reading aloud that there is more to reading than worksheets—and we must do it before they close the door on reading for the rest of their lives. The child who is unaware of the riches of literature certainly can have no desire for them.

Mrs. Anne Hallahan of Springfield, Massachusetts, offers an example of that axiom. Assigned at mid-year to teach a sixth-grade class of remedial students, Mrs. Hallahan shocked her new students by reading to them on her first day in class. The book was *Where the Red Fern Grows.*

A hardened, street-wise, proud group (mostly boys), they were insulted when she began reading to them. "How come you're reading to us? You think we're babies or something?" they wanted to know. After explaining that she didn't think anything of the kind but only wanted to share a favorite story with them, she continued reading *Where the Red Fern Grows*. Each day she opened the class with the next portion of the story and each day she was greeted with groans. "Not again today! How come nobody else ever made us listen like this?"

Mrs. Hallahan admitted to me later, "I almost lost heart." But she persevered, and after a few weeks the tone of the class's morning remarks began to change. "You're going to read to us today, aren't you?" Or, "Don't forget the book, Mrs. Hallahan."

"I knew I had a winner," she confesses, "when on Friday, just when we were nearing the end of the book, one of the slowest boys in the class went home after school, got a library card, took out *Where the Red Fern Grows,* finished it himself, and came to school on Monday and told everyone how it ended.

"I didn't care about that. All I cared about was that I'd found the right key to open the lock on that boy's mind."

If the boy's parents had taken the time to introduce him to the book, the same task would have been accomplished. And if they had done it early enough, it's very probable he wouldn't have been in a remedial-reading class in the first place.

Amid all the workbook pages and academic jargon, we daily overlook the very purpose of literature: to provide meaning in our lives. That, of course, is the purpose of all education. Child psychologist Bruno Bettelheim says that the finding of this meaning is the greatest need and most difficult achievement for any human being at any age. Who am I? Why am I here? What can I be?[44]

In his widely acclaimed work *The Uses of Enchantment*, Bettelheim writes that the two factors most responsible for giving the child this belief that he can make a significant contribution to life are parents/teachers and literature.

Literature is considered such an important medium because— more than television, more than film, more than art or overhead projectors—literature brings us closest to the human heart. And of the two forms of literature (fiction and nonfiction), the one that brings us closest and presents the meaning of life most clearly to the child is fiction. That is the reason nearly all the recommendations for read-alouds at the back of this book are fiction.

What is it about fiction that brings it so close to the human heart? Three-time Pulitzer Prize–winning novelist and poet Robert Penn Warren declares that we read fiction because:

- We like it.
- There is conflict in it—and conflict is at the center of life.
- Its conflict wakes us up from the tedium of everyday life.
- It allows us to vent our emotions with tears, laughter, love, and hate.
- We hope its story will give us a clue to our own life story.
- It releases us from life's pressures by allowing us to escape into other people's lives.[45]

Amid the push to excellence, with its measurement and accountability, it is easy to lose sight of a key ingredient in reading a book—the pleasure it brings us, something too many boil down to a dirty word: FUN.

Noticeably absent from Robert Penn Warren's list of reasons for reading were book reports, vocabulary tests, and right/wrong answers. (Indeed, teachers report their biggest turn-offs to reading as children were book reports and reading groups.[46]) Books are meant to be savored and enjoyed, and those who use them exclusively to cross-examine children should, in the words of Alfred North Whitehead, "be prosecuted for soul-murder." In compiling the eight-year report that experts described as "probably the most comprehensive study ever made of American schools" (*A Place Called School*), John Goodlad found laughter and overt displays of feeling to be rarities. Our classrooms, noted Goodlad, are "emotionally flat."[47]

Reading achievement and fun do not have to be mutually exclusive; indeed they work best together. Principal Thomas P. O'Neill, Jr. (pictured on page 86), and his faculty at Boston's Lewenberg Middle School have proven that. Once the pride of Boston's junior high schools during the 1950s and early 1960s, Lewenberg subsequently suffered the ravages of urban decay and by 1984, with the lowest academic record and Boston teachers calling it "loony bin" instead of Lewenberg, the school was earmarked for closing. But first, Boston officials would give it one last chance.

The reins were handed to O'Neill (no relation to the former Speaker of the House), an upbeat, first-year principal and former high school English teacher whose experience there had taught him to "sell" reading's pleasures and importance.

The first thing he did was abolish the school's intercom system ("As a teacher I'd always sworn someday I'd rip the thing off the wall. Now I could do it legally") and then set about establishing structure, routine, and discipline. "That's the easy part. What happens *after* is the important part—READING. It's the key element in the curriculum. IBM can teach our graduates to work the machine, but *we* have to teach them to read the manual." In O'Neill's first year sustained silent reading (SSR—see Chapter 8) was instituted for the nearly four hundred pupils and faculty for the last ten minutes of the day—during which everyone in the school read for pleasure. Each teacher was assigned a room—much to the consternation of some who felt those last ten minutes could be better used to clean up the shop or gym. "Prove to me on paper," O'Neill challenged them, "that you are busier than I am, and I'll give you the ten minutes to clean." He had no takers.

Within a year, his critics had become supporters and the school was relishing the quiet time that ended the day. The books that had been started during SSR were often still being read by students filing out to buses—in stark contrast to former dismissal scenes that bordered on chaos.

Next he added a "reading dragon" to the school corridors, enthusiastically constructed by learning-disability students, with each notch on the tail noting a book read by a student or teacher.

The next challenge was to ensure that each sixth-, seventh-, and eighth-grade student not only saw an adult reading each day, but also *heard* one. Faculty members were assigned a classroom and the school day began with ten minutes of reading aloud—to complement the silent ending. Soon reading aloud began to inspire awareness and new titles sprouted during SSR. In effect, the faculty was doing what the great art schools have always done: providing "life" models from which to draw.

O'Neill's philosophy of "doing simple things well" had some

happy spinoffs. In his first year, he discovered a portrait of Solomon Lewenberg stored in the school basement and began a search for information about this Boston activist after whom the school was named in 1929. He turned up Stephen Lewenberg, Honeywell Corporation's labor counsel in nearby Newton and the grandson of Solomon. After several ceremonial visits, Lewenberg had seen enough to recognize commitment and asked to be included in a more substantive way. He was promptly assigned to a sixth-grade class, to which he reads *Paul Harvey's "The Rest of the Story"* (see Treasury) every Friday morning at seven-fifty on his way to work. When his corporate travels take him out of town, he reads on alternate days but seldom misses a week.

It's nice that they're all enjoying themselves, you say, but how about the reading scores? In the first year, Lewenberg's scores were up; the second year, not only did the scores climb but so too did student enrollment in response to the school's new reputation. By 1988, Lewenberg's 570 students had the highest reading scores in the city of Boston, there was a fifteen-page waiting list of children who wanted to attend, and O'Neill was pictured by *Time* as a viable alternative to force in its cover story on Joe Clark, the bull-horn-and-bat–toting principal from Paterson, New Jersey.[48]

Lewenberg's success is no accident. When you consider the broad areas stimulated by reading aloud, one can only wonder why it is not done in all classrooms. It exposes the student to:

- A positive reading role model
- New information
- The pleasures of reading
- Rich vocabulary
- Good grammar
- A broader variety of books than he'd choose on his own
- Richly textured lives outside his own experience
- The English language spoken in a manner distinctly different from that in television sitcoms or on MTV.

At the same time, the child's imagination is stimulated, attention span stretched, listening comprehension improved, emotional development nurtured, the reading-writing connection established, and, where they exist, negative attitudes reshaped to positive. Outside of all that, reading aloud doesn't do much.

Every coach and every teacher will tell you how important attitude is. Indeed, when 101 reading teachers listed their nine most important instructional priorities, improving attitudes toward reading was rated second only to comprehension. But when those same teachers assessed their instructional day, they found attitude was next to last with only 8.6 percent of their time devoted to it. What was mentioned most often to develop positive attitude? Skill proficiency.[49]

University of Connecticut doctoral candidate Maryellen S. Cosgrove, a devoted reader-aloud to her elementary classes and family, was dismayed by a personal survey that showed few intermediate teachers read aloud to classes. Therefore, her dissertation research focused on these questions: Compared with children who are *not* read to, what impact would regular reading aloud have on intermediate students' attitudes about books and reading? Would it inspire them to read more on their own? Would it help reading scores?

Singling out six diverse Connecticut communities, Cosgrove hired six independent teacher/readers who would visit the schools and read for twenty minutes to a cross section of 212 fourth- and sixth-grade students (in six separate classes), three times a week for twelve weeks. Six control groups (not read to) were established in each community.

To reduce any feelings of coercion and encourage a sense of choice, the readers-aloud brought three different selections (fiction, nonfiction, poetry) from which the students could elect to be read to. After the first novel, fiction became the popular choice, with poetry and nonfiction finishing in that order, and the readers completed an average of five full-length novels during the twelve weeks.

Cosgrove's findings[50] not only showed statistically significant improvements in reading attitudes, independent reading, and comprehension skills among the six classes, but also showed ancillary effects among the teachers in the host classrooms. One host teacher, initially a skeptic, declared that in twenty years of teaching she'd never before seen sixth-grade students voluntarily reading when their seatwork was completed. (She now regularly invites guest readers to her class.) Among the overwhelmingly positive responses of students were two students who initiated read-aloud projects of their own. One now tapes books for a blind grandparent; another became a volunteer reader for the school's first-graders. Parent response was positive enough for an inner-city parent to call Cosgrove long distance one evening to find the names of other books by author Thomas Rockwell because her child was so taken with readings from his book *How to Eat Fried Worms*.

To create a nation in which 90 percent of the children can read and willingly choose to do so is not inconceivable. Invariably, children buy what the culture sells. Imagine what our culture would be like if Americans sold ideas, words, and books with the same creativity we use to sell designer jeans, shampoo, and rock stars. Why, we might end up with people whose attention span for the printed word is longer than the time it takes to read a T-shirt.

2. When to Begin Read-Aloud

Children who are not spoken to by live and responsive adults will not learn to speak properly. Children who are not answered will stop asking questions. They will become incurious. And children who are not told stories and who are not read to will have few reasons for wanting to learn to read.

—Gail E. Haley,
1971 Caldecott Medal acceptance speech

"How old must the child be before you start reading to him?" That is the question I am most often asked by parents. The next is: "When is the child too old to be read to?"

In answer to the first question, I ask one of my own. "When did you start *talking* to your child? Did you wait until he was six months old?"

"We started talking to him the day he was born," parents respond proudly.

"And what language did your child speak the day he was born? English? Japanese? Italian?" They're about to say English when a puzzled look comes over their faces as they realize the child didn't speak *any* language yet.

"Wonderful!" I say. "There you were holding that newborn infant in your arms, whispering, 'We love you, Kevin. Daddy and I think you are the most beautiful baby in the world, do you know that, honey?' You were speaking multisyllable words and complex sentences in a foreign language to a child who didn't understand one word you were saying! You never thought twice about doing it. But most people can't imagine *reading* to that same child. And that's silly. If a child is old enough to talk to, he's old enough to be read to. It's the same English language."

Obviously, from birth to six months of age we are concerned less with "understanding" than with "conditioning" the child to your voice and to the sight of books. Dr. T. Berry Brazelton, chief of the child development unit of Boston Children's Hospital Medical Center, says that new parents' most critical task during these early stages is learning how to calm the child, how to bring it under control, so he or she can begin to look around and listen when you pass on information.[1] Much the same task confronts the classroom teacher as she faces a new class each September.

We have long known the human voice is one of the most powerful tools a parent has for calming a child. And what many previously suspected now has been established in new research indicating that the voice's influence starts even earlier than birth. University of North Carolina psychologist Anthony DeCasper and colleagues explored the effects of reading to fetal children with these results: "Pursuing the idea that infants might be able to recognize something they had heard prenatally, DeCasper asked pregnant women to read a children's story aloud twice a day for approximately six weeks prior to their delivery date. When the babies were born their sucking patterns indicated they preferred the familiar story over another children's book they never heard before.

"The babies' perceptual reactions to the stories have been influenced by earlier exposure," DeCasper explains. "That constitutes learning in a very general way."

DeCasper performed a similar experiment with fetuses during the two and one-half months before birth and found the child's heartbeat increased with the new story, decreased with the familiar one.[2] This clearly establishes that the child becomes familiar with certain sounds while *in utero* and begins associating those tones with comfort and security. The baby is being conditioned—his first class in learning.

Granted, it's hard enough to get parents to read to their children *after* they're born, never mind *before*—but at least we know an early start neither hurts nor wastes time. Be it pre- or postnatally, the earlier you begin, the sooner the child will come to recognize the reading voice as an unthreatening sound, one associated with warmth and attention. And he will gravitate naturally to it.

Dorothy Butler demonstrates this thesis in *Cushla and Her Books,* where the parents began reading aloud to Cushla Yeoman when she was four months of age.[3] By nine months the child was able to respond to the sight of certain books and convey to her parents that these were her favorites. By age five she had taught herself to read.

What makes Cushla's story so dramatic is the fact that she was born with chromosome damage which caused deformities of the spleen, kidney, and mouth cavity. It also produced muscle spasms—which prevented her from sleeping for more than two hours a night or holding anything in her hand until she was three years old—and hazy vision beyond her fingertips.

Until she was three, the doctors diagnosed Cushla as "mentally and physically retarded" and recommended that she be institutionalized. Her parents, after seeing her early responses to books, refused; instead, they put her on a dose of fourteen read-aloud books a day. By age five, Cushla was found by psychologists to be well above average in intelligence and a socially well-adjusted child.

If such attention and reading aloud could accomplish so much with Cushla, think how much can be achieved with children who have none or few of Cushla's handicaps.

Consider a more normal situation, that of Martha Donley and her daughter, Greta, in Centerville, Ohio. She explains:

"I began reading to Greta when she was a newborn (she is now eighteen months). The sound of my voice had a calming effect on her as we spent many long nights together, with me reading from the Bible, *The World Treasury of Children's Literature* (by Clifton Fadiman), or one of the many children's books I'd bought her.

"By the time she was six months old her favorite toy was a

small vinyl book, *God's Blessings A to Z* (now out of print). She would lie on her back studying the book for ten to fifteen minutes at a time, carefully turning the pages.

"When she was about eleven months, she showed a definite opinion about what she wanted to read. She would stand at her 'book box' (a magazine rack we consigned to her a month earlier) and throw books on the floor until she found the one she wanted. It was about this time I started taking her to the library every week for new books. We now begin each week by going to the library.

"At the library, Greta delights in running through the stacks, pulling down books which catch her fancy, and I follow to put them all back properly while glancing through them to see if they are suitable to take home. There have been times when she gets hold of a book which I feel is over her head, and yet she won't let go. So we take it home and, to my surprise, some have proven to be favorites.

"The effect of reading to her is obvious. Greta started speaking at eleven months and by the time she was one year old, she was speaking twenty-five to thirty words; at fifteen months she was saying two-word sentences. She can recognize many different animals (at fourteen months she was saying 'buffalo' and 'giraffe') and never confuses them, whereas her two-year-old friend (who is not read to) calls all animals 'doggie.' At fifteen months she took a keen interest in letters, pointing them out wherever she saw them, and now at eighteen months she knows almost all the letters of the alphabet.

"All this is the result of reading to her. I might add, it has nothing to do with trying to push her to read as an infant—an idea that appalls me. Greta's learning has come at *her* pace, not ours. If she is interested in umbrellas, I find a book with an umbrella in it. If she is interested in letters, we get an alphabet book. Conversely, when she saw something in a book that caught her interest, I would try to show her real examples. One week it was oranges, so we ate an orange; another week it was helicopters—so we watched the beginning of a 'M.A.S.H.' episode so she could see the helicopter.

"I do not know how we could get along without the library. Many days the first words out of this eighteen-month-old's mouth are 'Books—read.' And the last words of the day are a plea for one more book."

As Greta moves toward new heights in her imitative powers, she's imitating both the sounds and actions of her parents (and older siblings, if she had them). These role models are her first "super-heroes" and as such, she is most likely to imitate their doing the things they seem to enjoy the most.

Greta is a perfect example of the "advantaged" child. What about her unfortunate opposite? Martin Deutsch's study, "The Disadvan-taged Child and the Learning Process," demonstrates what happens when the role models do not stimulate the child.[4] In homes where conversation, questions, and reading are not encouraged, the child eventually enters school markedly short of the basic tools he will need to accomplish his tasks. He will ask fewer questions, use shorter sentences, and have both a smaller vocabulary and a shorter attention span than his advantaged classmates.

The crime in such situations is pointed out by the Albany (New York) Area Reading Council in the little brochure it gives to new parents. It begins: "All babies are born equal. . . . Not one can . . . speak, count, read, or write at birth. . . . But by the time they go to kindergarten, they are *not equal!*"[5] The difference, of course, is between the parents who "raise" their children, as opposed to parents who "watch" them grow up.

Let me state that an early interest in a child's intellectual growth is both important and admirable. But you can expect negative con-sequences if this interest takes the form of an obsession with teaching your child to read, says Dr. Brazelton, who, along with hospital work, research, and writing, has been a practicing pediatrician in Cambridge, Massachusetts, for thirty years.

"I've had children in my practice," Brazelton explained to Na-tional Public Radio's John Merrow, "who were reading from a dic-tionary at the age of three and one-half or four, and had learned to read and type successfully by the age of four. But those kids went through a very tough time later on. They went through first grade successfully, but second grade they really bombed out on. And I have a feeling that they'd been pushed so hard from outside to learn to read early, that the cost of it didn't show up until later."

Testimony to the importance of an *unforced* learning schedule in these formative years comes from all corners of the fields of psychology and education—including one that dates back nearly three thousand years: "Avoid compulsion and let early education be a manner of amusement. Young children learn by games; compulsory education cannot remain in the soul," was the advice offered by Plato ⸱ to parents.

None of these experts are saying that "early reading" is intrinsically bad; rather, they feel the early reader should arrive at that station naturally, on his own, without a structured time each day when the mother or father sits down with him and teaches him letters, sounds, and syllables. That is the way Scout learned in Harper Lee's *To Kill a Mockingbird*—by sitting on the lap of a parent and listening, listening as the parent's finger moves over the pages, until gradually, in the child's own good time, a connection is made between the sound of a certain word and the appearance of certain letters on the page.

The mother of a dyslexic child recently wrote to tell me of her experiences after seeing the write-up about *The Read-Aloud Handbook* in a 1983 "Dear Abby" column. The book provoked her and her husband to begin reading to their son and to curtail the amount of television viewing in the home, though they were unaware of his learning disability at the time. When his dyslexia problems surfaced some years later, the child's teachers noted that his comprehension skills were at the top of the class in spite of the reading handicap, and he was the only child in the room to share with the teacher those books he and his mother read. The parents' reading ensured that his first experiences with books would be less painful, that he had the necessary listening comprehension to handle classroom work, and that he had an incentive to overcome his handicap.

A good example of how listening comprehension feeds reading comprehension can be found in the most commonly used word in the English language. Do you know the word we use more often in everyday conversation than any other word? T-H-E. I always ask my audiences if there is anyone present who thinks this little three-letter word is a difficult word to understand, and out of three hundred people I'll get about five who raise their hands—amid snickers from the rest.

I then ask those who didn't raise their hands to pretend I am a Russian exchange student living in your home. It's also important to know there is no equivalent word in Russian for "the," as we use it. Indeed, many languages don't have it. Korean doesn't have it either.

Now, as the Russian exchange student, I've been living in your home and listening to you and your family for three weeks when one day I come to you and say, "Don't understand word you use over and over. What means word 'the'?"

How would you begin to explain the meaning of the word to this person? When no one volunteers to explain it, everyone laughs embarrassedly. Explaining this simple word turns out to be extremely complex. Nevertheless, we do know how to *use* it. And we knew it before we ever showed up for kindergarten.

How did you learn it? One morning when you were three years old your mother took you into the kitchen, sat you down at the table with a little workbook, and said, "Sharon, 'the' is a definite article. It comes before nouns. Now take your crayon and underline all the definite articles on the page." Do you remember that day?

Of course not, because that's not how you learned the word. You learned the meaning in a relaxed, unstructured way—by *hearing* it first, hearing it used by important people in your life (parents, brothers, and sisters) and used in a meaningful way: "the" cookie, "the" bath, "the" potty. That's how you learned this complicated word.

A prime factor in the success of reading aloud to very young children is that most often it is done one-on-one, by far the most effective teaching/bonding arrangement. In studying methods to reverse verbal shortcomings among disadvantaged children, Harvard psychologist Jerome Kagan found intensified one-to-one attention to be especially effective.[6] His studies indicated the advantages of reading to children and of listening attentively to their responses to the reading, but they also point to the desirability of reading to your children separately, if possible. I recognize this approach poses a problem for working mothers and fathers with more than one child. But somewhere in that seven-day week there must be time for your child to discover the specialness of you, one-on-one—even if it is only once or twice a week.

Again and again I am asked by parents, "I have an eleven-year-old, an eight-year-old, and a four-year-old. What one book can I read that will hold all their attentions?" Do they all wear the same size clothes, ride the same size bike, or have the same size friends? When you read a book at the level of the four-year-old, you are insulting the listening level of the eleven-year-old. Consistently reading one book to that divergent a group sounds more like a shortcut for the parents instead of a pleasure for the listeners.

One-on-one time between adult and child—be it reading or talking or playing—is essential to teaching the *concept* of books or puppies or flowers or water. Once the concept of something has been learned, then the foundation has been laid for the next accomplishment: attention span. Without a concept of what is happening and why, a child cannot and will not attend to something for any appreciable amount of time.

Here, for example, are two concepts entirely within the grasp of a three-year-old: the telephone can be used to receive calls as well as make calls; books contain stories that give me pleasure if I listen and watch.

A nursery school teacher told me recently of her experiences on the first day of school with these two concepts. All morning the three-year-olds in her new class used the toy telephone to make pretend calls to their mothers for reassurances that they would be picked up and brought home. They dialed make-believe numbers, often talked for extended periods of time, and used telephone etiquette.

Understanding the concept of the telephone, these children were able to use and enjoy it for a considerable length of time. Their telephone attention span was excellent.

Let's compare that with story time in the same class. Thirty seconds after the story began, several of the children stood up and moved away from the circle, obviously bored. More children quickly joined them. Within two minutes, half the children had abandoned the story.

The difference between the attention spans for each of these two activities is based on the *concept* that each child brought to the activity. Where a child had little or no experience with books, it was impossible for him to have a concept of them and the pleasure they afford.

No experience means no concept; no concept means no attention span.[7]

Short attention spans among three-year-olds are not unusual but when they continue into the early primary grades, there is cause for alarm. With parents averaging about eleven minutes a day of one-on-one time with a child, it's little wonder I receive letters like this, from a speech and language clinician in a Massachusetts school system:

> My language development program is focused on reading aloud to my students. The impetus for this began when, much to my dismay, my caseload of language-delayed kids was rising by leaps and bounds. Before coming to this city, I had worked extensively with culturally deprived and abused children; their language delays were understandable. But why, in this middle-class to upper-middle-class community, was there a rising number of primary children who lacked vocabulary development, memory skills, processing abilities? They often seemed to lack motivation, had limited imaginations and attention spans, and found it difficult to follow directions. In addition, only a handful were diagnosed as learning disabled.
>
> As I became more familiar with the children and their family situations, several possible causes appeared. Many of them have been in child care from infancy and/or early childhood. Many presently go to a child care situation after school. Many parents admitted they had little time or energy to read to them. Nor did they have the patience to answer (or find out together) the unending questions of a curious three- or four-year-old. Television served as a babysitter and pacifier.
>
> Some parents were quick to point out the children were read to in child care and had good experiential learning activities in their centers. But somehow, without the cozy, one-on-one giving of a parent or primary care-giver, the "group" input had lost meaningfulness for many of the children.

Far from being an indictment of child care, those words echo the cries of early childhood educators themselves: We cannot replace parents. Don't ask that of us!

You may be ready to ask: "What else do I need to do? Surely reading stories isn't the whole thing, is it?"

It is as simple or complicated as you wish it to be. For a moment, let's look at the exceptional children who always fascinate parents and teachers—the ones who arrive at kindergarten already knowing how to read. During the last twenty-five years two major studies[8] have been done on these "early readers," the majority of whom were never formally taught to read at home.

The research on these children, as well as that done on pupils who respond to initial classroom instruction without difficulty, indicates four aspects of the home environment of nearly every "early reader":

1. The child is read to on a regular basis. This is the factor most often cited among early readers. In Dolores Durkin's comprehensive 1966 study of early readers, every one of the seventy-nine children had been read to regularly. Additionally, the parents were avid readers and led by example. The reading aloud included not only books but package labels, street and truck signs, billboards, et cetera.

2. A wide variety of printed material—books, magazines, newspapers, comics—is available in the home.

3. Paper and pencil are readily available for the child. Durkin explained, "Almost without exception, the starting point of curiosity about written language was an interest in scribbling and drawing. From this developed an interest in copying objects and letters of the alphabet."

4. The people in the child's home stimulate the child's interest in reading and writing by answering endless questions, praising the child's efforts at reading and writing, taking the child to the library frequently, buying books, writing stories that the child dictates, and displaying his paperwork in a prominent place in the home.

I want to emphasize that these four factors were present in the home of nearly *every* child who was an early reader. None of these involved much more than interest on the part of the parent.

But beyond simple materials, the program requires time: time to read to the child, time to post his drawings on the refrigerator door, time to answer questions, time to point out signs along the highway.

As simple as this appears, poor families are either unaware of it or unbelieving. (Some may be too lazy to care, but I cannot believe they constitute a significant number.) A campaign to alert parents to these factors should be the challenge for educators, clergy, pediatricians, and politicians.

Several years ago I began asking adults (ones I knew to be lifetime readers), "What did you have in your home as a child that helped you become a reader?" They nearly always mentioned being read to, but beyond that the responses form what I call the Three B's, a kind of reading kit that nearly all parents can buy.

The first B is BOOKS: Ownership of a book, with the child's name inscribed inside, a book he doesn't have to return to the library or even share with siblings. I still have the first book I ever bought, the first I ever won, and one of the first I ever received as a gift.

The second B is BOOKRACK (or magazine rack)—placed where it can be used most often. Have you ever stopped to think that there is probably more reading done in the bathrooms of the U.S. than all the libraries and classrooms combined? That's where the bookrack comes in—stocked with books, magazines, and newspapers for impulse reading. Always keep a book or magazine on the kitchen table. With more and more children eating at least one daily meal alone, this is a prime spot for recreational reading. Children don't like eating alone and staring at their food any more than adults do. If there's a book on the table, they'll read it.

And the third B is BED LAMP: Does your child have a bed lamp or reading light in his room? If he doesn't and you wish to raise a reader, the first order of business is to find a shopping mall and buy one. Install it and say to your child: "Katy, we think you're old enough now to stay up later at night and read in bed like Mom and Dad. So we bought this little lamp and we're going to leave it on an extra fifteen minutes [or longer, depending on the age of the child] if you want to read in bed. On the other hand, if you don't want to read—that's okay, too. We'll just turn off the light the same old time." The latter is seldom the case, though.

Parents who worry about the impact such reading in bed will have on children's eyesight can relax. Ophthalmologists assure me such reading has no impact on children's present or future vision. What it affects, however, is children's attitudes about reading—which makes it the most important "night school" your child will ever attend. I wish every parent had the attitude of Christine Ballenger, who once asked me to inscribe a book to her children in this way: "For Heather and Kelly—who haven't gotten to sleep on time in years."

A common mistake among parents (and teachers) who read aloud to children in their early years is to stop once the child learns to read. "He's in the top fourth-grade reading group—why should I read to him? Isn't that why we're sending him to school, so he'll learn to read by himself?" There are many mistaken assumptions in that question.

The listening level of most children is well above their reading level until about eighth grade, when they converge (except among remedial students). This is what allows children reading on a fourth-grade level to understand prime-time television shows—most of which are written on a seventh-grade reading level. The child reading on a fourth-grade level is also entirely capable of *hearing* books written on a sixth-grade level—stories far more exciting, enriching, and challenging than anything he could read on his own. And it is *those* stories that will raise his own reading level. The last thing you want a fourth-grader to think is: What he's reading in fourth grade is as good as books are ever going to get.

A Texas teacher told me this story on herself, with permission to use it as an example of how we often underestimate children's abilities. Remembering with great fondness the book that had been read to her when she was in second grade, she thought she'd like to try it with her own second-grade class. At the local library she found that old favorite, *The Secret Garden,* by Frances Hodgson Burnett.

That evening, in preparation for reading it to her students, she began reading to herself. By the bottom of the second page, she was growing somewhat concerned. "Oh, my," she thought, "I didn't remember the words in this book being so hard: 'Mem Sahib . . . tyrannical . . . stammered . . . governess . . . veranda . . .' My second graders will *never* understand them." So she began underlining.

She arrived at school early the next day and began putting those "hard" words on the board. In fact, she filled the entire board. Before she read to the class, she went over the meaning and pronunciation of each word. During the reading, whenever she came to one of them, she would point to the word on the board. They got through two whole chapters of *The Secret Garden*—that year.

Finally, the light dawned: "The teacher didn't put any words on the board for *us*," she thought two years later. "We figured out what the words meant by the way they were used in the sentence and in the story." That year she didn't put *any* words on the board and they got all the way through the book—all two-hundred-plus pages. And when she'd read the last page, her class exclaimed, "That's the best book we ever read!" Those second-graders thought *they'd* read the book, which is the first step to achievement. If you don't *think* you can read it, you *won't* read it.

Even more important than building vocabularies, when you read to school-age children you are also building emotional bridges between parent and child.

I recall the teacher in New Hampshire who told me the story of Beth, and I wonder if busy parents would have understood about Beth. "I've been a first-grade teacher for seventeen years," the teacher said, "and I have never had a child who didn't *want* to learn to read. That is, until this year.

"This year I had Beth as a student. The more I worked with her the more convinced I became that Beth didn't *want* to learn to read. Then I began to suspect that she already knew how to read but wouldn't admit it for some reason."

When the teacher talked to Beth's mother, she found the mother had similar suspicions. The following day the teacher took her student aside and said, "Beth, I think you've been fooling us. Do you know that? I think you already know how to read but for some reason you don't *want* to read. Is that true, Beth?"

Beth nodded.

"Will you tell me why?" asked the teacher.

"No," Beth replied.

At this point, the teacher asked a question that allowed Beth an escape route. "Do you think you could *ever* tell me why?"

The child thought for a moment and said, "Tomorrow."

The next morning Beth looked up at her teacher and whispered, "After lunch."

When they were sequestered in a room by themselves after lunch, Beth confided to the teacher that she was the oldest of four children. "The only time all day when I have my mother all to myself is when she reads to me at bedtime," she explained. She was afraid that if she admitted to being able to read by herself, then that was what she would be doing each night: reading alone. Beth felt her mother would go off to read to her sisters and brother and leave her without that intimate sharing time each night. As soon as the parent and teacher were able to convince Beth that her mother would continue their bedtime reading ritual, Beth became one of the best readers in the class.

Fortunately for Beth, her mother never bought into the idea that the shorter the book, the better it was. But many parents do. In keeping with the concept of instant parenting, more than 100,000 people have bought the book *One-Minute Bedtime Stories,* and thousands more bought its six sequels. If the idea is to make it as short as possible, why not just say, "Night-night!" and turn off the light? Think of all the time you'd save for your favorite TV shows.

"When do you start reading aloud to classroom children?" asks the teacher. On the very first day of school—whether you are teaching nursery school or kindergarten or seventh grade. And the way you hold that book, the warmth you extract from it, the laughter, the interest, and the emotion—all will tell your class something about you and how you feel about books, and the special place books and reading are going to hold in your class this year. The fifth-grade student who until now has associated books only with remedial classes or workbooks is going to experience a special treat on that first day. He's going to be introduced to a whole new concept of books and reading. He's going to be conditioned to the idea that books mean pleasure as well as work.

A fellow teacher suggested to Deborah Murphy that "when introducing a book to your class, you caress and hold it in your hands as you would a well-loved and precious treasure. While holding the book in this way, tell the children how you feel about the story, any personal experiences you might have had with it." But Murphy, a third- and fourth-grade teacher in a Connecticut inner-city magnet school, is a self-described "no-time-to-waste" teacher, and she doubted the effectiveness of such an approach.

But she gave it a try. She had a favorite book—*Tal, His Marvelous Adventures with Noom-zor-noom*—long out of print and now treasured by her. "With great skepticism," Murphy said, "I introduced *Tal* in this way—speaking about it and touching it as I would a well-respected old friend. And as the weeks passed I saw the children begin to reflect this feeling in the way they would carry the book to me at reading time and in the way they would turn the pages."

And then one day there was a fire drill, and as Deborah Murphy herded the class out the door, reminding them not to think of it as a drill but as a real fire and that nothing mattered except getting out of the school quickly, she saw a boy detour past her desk to save the copy of *Tal*. "I realized then," she concedes, "my friend *Tal* was treasured not only by me."

Some principals and teachers will concede the cognitive benefits of reading aloud but are put off by the "entertainment" involved. So what? Some of the best teachers I ever had were the most entertaining.

Consider, if you will, the definition of a teacher by Nathan Pusey while president of Harvard. "The close observer soon discovers that the teacher's task is not to implant facts but to place the subject to be learned in front of the learner and, through sympathy, emotion, imagination, and patience, to awaken in the learner the restless drive for answers and insights which enlarge the personal life and give it meaning." He could not have described the functions of reading aloud in the classroom more perfectly if he'd wanted to.

Here is a perfect example of "awakening" the reader's mind— even before he can read. During an eight-week period, researchers observed a kindergarten class that had a good classroom library and whose teacher read aloud daily. The library's books consisted of three kinds: *very* familiar (read repeatedly by the teacher); familiar (read once); and unfamiliar (unread).[9]

In monitoring the book selections of the kindergartners during their free time, it was found they chose the *very* familiar books three times as often and familiar books twice as often as the unfamiliar.

In addition, these nonreaders more often imitated the teacher and tried to "read" the *very* familiar and familiar books instead of just browsing, as they did with the unfamiliar. In reading aloud, the kindergarten teacher had shown the way and why of reading, and in so doing inspired her students to try this magic called reading.

U.S. children have shown an identical response to public television's award-winning series "Reading Rainbow." In the year before it was read aloud on the PBS show, *Digging Up Dinosaurs,* by Aliki, sold only 2,000 copies. After the show it sold 25,000. (To obtain a list of the more than two hundred titles featured on "Reading Rainbow," send a self-addressed, stamped envelope (9″ x 12″) with first-class postage to: Reading Rainbow, GPN, P.O. Box 80669, Lincoln, NE 68501.)

Unbeknownst to most readers-aloud, they can actually accomplish some good by occasionally making a mistake. "Until I was in about third grade," a teacher confided to me, "I was petrified to read in front of my classmates. I wasn't a poor reader but I was extremely shy. With each passing year, I grew more fearful of making mistakes in front of my peers and teacher.

"And then in third grade," she continued, "I had a teacher who read to us daily from big thick books with lots of words and few pictures. To my astonishment, she made mistakes in her reading. She'd occasionally stumble over a word here and there, lose her place once in a while, even mispronounce a word. To my further amazement, she would recover without embarrassment and continue on. It was as though she were saying to each of us, 'Hey, no big deal! *Everybody* makes mistakes.' And that marked the end of my reading terrors and the beginning of my reading passion."

The benefits that come from reading aloud help the entire curriculum, especially since reading *is* the curriculum. The principal ingredient of all learning and teaching is language. Not only is it the tool with which we communicate the lesson; it is also the product the student hands back to us in math or science or history class.

In that light, the classroom teacher who reads aloud helps the class to become better listeners and develop greater verbal skills. The more they hear other people's words, the greater becomes their desire to share their own through conversation and writing. The principal in Connecticut who interrupted a fourth-grade teacher's daily read-aloud ("You're wasting time. Get busy," he said) obviously didn't recognize a language arts class when he saw one. There are four language arts: they begin with the art of listening and proceed to the art of speaking, the art of writing, and the art of reading. The teacher, incidentally, told me it was futile to argue the point but she did have her day in the sun two weeks later when the principal had to be out of town all day for a convention. "Do you know what we did all day?" she asked me. "We read *Stone Fox* [by John Reynolds Gardiner]. We cried about it, we talked about it, then we wrote and drew about it. And it was the best day we had all year."

A common mistake is to relegate reading aloud to just the reading or language arts classes. When children love books, it ripples through every part of the curriculum—an aspect not always understood by those who have never taught reading. I am frequently called upon to address a school system's entire faculty—including math, science, art, music, and physical education teachers. My first task is to convince those teachers outside the reading faculty that reading *is* the curriculum and therefore *every* teacher's business. (At this point, the reading teachers nod agreement but the rest of the faculty is unconvinced.)

Take, for example, vocabulary, spelling, and writing skills— three areas in which English and reading teachers come under constant attack. "Sure," says the history teacher, "I'd love to give more essay questions on exams. But those damn English teachers haven't taught these kids how to write." And the science teacher adds, "Their spelling is even worse, and most have the vocabulary of a squirrel." (Everyone is now agreeing—even the English teachers acknowledge that such disparagement takes place.)

How do we improve vocabulary, spelling, and writing? By reading, reading, reading. Vocabulary and spelling words are not learned best by looking them up in the dictionary. You learn the meanings and spellings in the same way teachers learn the names of new students each September: by meeting them again and again, making the connection between the face and the name. The more often you encounter a student, the quicker and better you learn his name. Nearly everyone spells by memory, not by rules. When in doubt, you write the word out several different ways and choose the one that looks correct. The more a child meets words and sees how they are used in sentences and paragraphs, the better he will know, understand, and spell words. Conversely, the less you read, the fewer words you meet and the less certain you are of meaning.[10]

Anyone who knows anything about writing will tell you that nothing improves writing like writing. By the same token, I don't know a single writer who isn't also a reader. It's the same with baseball players—the good ones sit and watch an incredible number of innings, observing how others play the game. Among other things, reading is sometimes a spectator sport; you're watching how the all-stars play the game of writing, how they aim words to catch meaning.

Of all the qualities a teacher might possess, the most contagious is enthusiasm. Are you enthusiastic about books? Do your students ever see you with something other than a textbook in your hand? Have you shared with your class a book you stayed awake reading until two o'clock in the morning? Have you read a magazine article or newspaper column to your students about something that really interested you? Have you let your guard down and showed your enthusiasm lately? And, I might add, if you're not enthusiastic about reading you are in the wrong profession.

In *Becoming a Nation of Readers,* the Commission on Reading stated: "There is no substitute for a teacher who reads children good stories. It whets the appetite of children for reading, and provides a model of skillful oral reading. It is a practice that should continue throughout the grades."[11]

If you want your science or history class to be alive, wrap the facts and figures, the dates and battles, in flesh-and-blood novels. Read *My Side of the Mountain,* by Jean George, or *Path of the Pale Horse,* by Paul Fleischman, to your science class. Open your history class with five minutes from *My Brother Sam Is Dead,* by James and Christopher Collier. Art teacher Donalyn Schofield in New Braintree, Massachusetts, used the quiet time during which her students were doing a stitching project to read aloud *The Hobbit,* by J. R. R. Tolkien.

Secondary students being read to? Certainly. It's the role-modeling and sales pitch for the joy of reading that counts here. When my daughter returned from England after a summer studying at Cambridge University, she told me the professors read aloud to literature classes all the time. A year later, I met a Kansas teacher returning from her second straight summer at Oxford University where she'd been read to regularly. I figure that if it's good enough for Oxford and Cambridge, it's good enough for any junior or senior high school in America.

"But," says a teacher, "these are just stories. I've got a curriculum to cover. I don't have time for *stories!*" Far from suggesting the curriculum be abandoned, I say it should be enriched and brought to life by story. It should be reassuring to know that many of the best teachers—Aesop, Socrates, Confucius, Jesus—used stories to teach their lesson. The Bible has survived the centuries as much for the stories as for its curriculum.

Out of desperation many of today's educators are rediscovering what those teachers knew twenty centuries ago. Story does not exist to teach reading skills. Story is the vehicle we use even when we sleep to make sense out of our lives in a world that often defies logic.

And because the literature of story reaches beyond the dispassionate corners of the intellect, it can also educate the heart—a curriculum very much on the mind of the nation's business leaders and educators these days. With moral or ethical crises constantly on the nation's front pages and television newscasts, many leading business schools have not only grown weary of seeing their alumni in handcuffs on the five o'clock news, they're also trying to correct the situation.

Educators who find "stories" to be a waste of valuable instructional time would do well to pay attention to the likes of the Harvard Business School and Brandeis University.[12] Harvard's first effort was to invite the eminent child psychiatrist Robert Coles to teach a course in ethics at the B School.[13] Coles's course syllabus consisted of nothing but literature—stories and novels that grabbed the young business student where it hurts: the heart. Vicariously through literature, Coles's students explored the gradual slope that leads to compromising one's principles, values, and morality. Quoting William Carlos Williams, Coles states his purpose: ". . . to bring the reader up close, so close that his empathy puts him in the shoes of the characters. You hope when he closes the book his own character is influenced." The Harvard Business School has since launched a $30-million ethics program. Brandeis has been using literature for similar purposes in its business seminars.

If all we're doing in school is teaching students how to answer the calls they'll get someday on their beepers, then the curriculum is worthless. The most important calls will not come on beepers; instead they will be the daily calls for justice, courage, compassion, and integrity. You won't find them addressed in a math book but they abound in literature.

Almost like clockwork, after every speech I give on reading aloud, a worried parent approaches me and asks, "When is it too late? Is there a time when children are too old to be read to?" It is never too late, they are never too old—but it is never going to be as beneficial or as easy as it is when they are two years old or six years old.

Because she has a captive audience, the classroom teacher holds a distinct advantage over the parent who suddenly wants to begin reading to a thirteen-year-old. Regardless of how well-intentioned the parent may be, reading aloud to an adolescent at home can be difficult. During this period of social and emotional development, teenagers' out-of-school time is largely spent coping with body changes, sex drives, vocational anxieties, and the need to form an identity apart from that of their families. These kinds of concerns and their attendant schedules don't leave much time for Mom's and Dad's reading aloud.

But the situation is not hopeless. When the child is in early adolescence, from twelve to fourteen, try sharing a small part of a book, a page or two, when you see he is at loose ends. This only has to be several times a week. Mention that you want to share something with him that you've read; downplay any motivational or educational aspects connected with the reading.

The older the child, the more difficult he is to corral. Here, as in early adolescence, you must pick your spots for reading aloud. Don't suggest that your daughter listen to a story when she's sitting down to watch her favorite television show or waiting for her boyfriend to call. Along with timing, consider the length of what you read. Keep it short—unless you see an interest for more.

Dorothy Mulligan, former director of editorial services for the

National School Volunteer Program in Alexandria, Virginia, confirms that there is no age limit to reading aloud. This is how she picked her spots for read-aloud:

"One summer our twenty-two-year-old son had his four wisdom teeth pulled. A week later, after the stitches came out, one socket began to bleed. Late that night, the oral surgeon had to put in more stitches. Despite painkillers, Greg was miserable during the night. Nothing would calm him. And then I recalled what I had done for the kids whenever they were sick at night.

"First, I tried some of Greg's favorite authors—Mark Twain, Ray Bradbury, et cetera—but I couldn't find a section with enough action to still his moans. A light bulb appeared in a balloon above my head; I reached for a *Reader's Digest*.

"Greg immediately quieted to listen to an article about how the music was selected to go into the space capsules. He is a violinist and one of the selections for the capsule was his favorite string quartet. Then I read about the kidnapping of a young girl, and then two more articles. By now he was lying quietly and told me he wanted to go to sleep."

The desire to read is not born in a child. It is planted—by parents and teachers.

Novelist and short-story writer Roald Dahl offers an example of this in an essay, "Lucky Break," from his book *The Wonderful Story of Henry Sugar*.

Dahl was tucked away in English boarding schools from age eight to eighteen, and his academic childhood was a disaster. "Those were days of horror," he writes, "of fierce discipline, of no talking in the dormitories, no running in the corridors, no untidiness of any sort, no this or that or the other, just rules, rules and still more rules that had to be obeyed. And the fear of the dreaded cane hung over us like the fear of death all the time." His teachers described him on his report cards as "incapable" and "of limited ideas." He hated school and school obviously hated him.

At last there came a ray of hope. One Saturday morning the boys were marched to the assembly hall. The masters departed for the local pubs and in walked Mrs. O'Connor, a neighborhood woman hired to "babysit" the boys for two and a half hours. Instead of babysitting, Mrs. O'Connor chose to read, talk about, and bring to life the whole of English literature. Her enthusiasm and love of books were so contagious and spellbinding that she became the highlight of the school week for Roald Dahl. As the weeks slipped by, she kindled his imagination and inspired a deep love of books. Within a year he'd become an insatiable reader, and Dahl credits Mrs. O'Connor with turning him into a reader, and thus a writer. Today, more than fifty years later, I know of no author who so captivates children, who so excites their imaginations, as Roald Dahl. His *James and the Giant Peach* is the finest read-aloud I have ever known.

How many minds and imaginations have remained unstirred because there was no Mrs. O'Connor? That child in your home or classroom—the one who never seems to be listening, who never completes his work on time, who appears to be forever looking out the window as though waiting for someone—is waiting for someone like Mrs. O'Connor. How long are you going to keep him waiting?

3. The Stages of Read-Aloud

Few children learn to love books by themselves. Someone has to lure them into the wonderful world of the written word; someone has to show them the way.

—Orville Prescott, from
A Father Reads to His Children

Staring at the thousands of books in the children's section of the local library, a parent is filled with the same panic that faces the beginning artist with an empty canvas: Where to begin?

I suggest that you first consider the child's age and maturity; then make your selections accordingly. Let's start with the infant level and work our way upward.

Until a child is six months old, I don't think it matters a great deal what you read, as long as you are reading. What is important up to this stage is that the child becomes accustomed to the rhythmic sound of your reading voice and associates it with a peaceful, secure time of day. Mother Goose, of course, is always appropriate, but my neighbor read aloud Kipling when she was nursing her daughter, who eventually went to Princeton. Did Kipling have anything to do with her going to an Ivy League college? Nothing, compared to her mother's reading to her.

The stumbling block in all this is the awkwardness of reading to a child who doesn't appear to understand what you are doing. Fortunately, the research of recent years gives us a far different view of the child from that of the unaware infant our parents knew and the dubious reader-aloud need only consider a few recent discoveries:

- One-day-old babies can be calmed with tape recordings of their own cries and within days are able to distinguish their own cries from those of peers and older babies.[1]
- Twelve-day-old babies can imitate an adult sticking out a tongue.[2]
- Ten-week-olds, with strings attached to slide projectors that change with movement of the wrist, will watch the changing slides attentively for an average of fourteen minutes.[3]

Coupling these findings with the fetal research reported in Chapter 2 should ease any awkwardness you might have about reading to infants. While many of these infant abilities are in place at birth, like flowers out of water they will wilt and be lost if not cared for over the next two years.

Between six and ten months, the child's sight and hearing are attuned enough for him to recognize not just familiar voices but familiar faces and objects as well. During this period when children begin to respond to voices, there are bursts in cell growth within the speech centers of infant brains. Another burst occurs between twelve and eighteen months when they truly discover that words have meaning. The network of nerves that allows this growth, scientists report, is very much affected by how much exercise it is given. Like muscle massage, the more you talk to children during these critical times, the greater the natural language growth.[4] In fact, a child's brain growth increases with such intensity to meet the challenge of these new words and experiences that between ages four and ten his brain metabolism (brain's heartbeat) is twice that of an adult's. That's the reason children between those ages are able to learn foreign languages and musical instruments so easily—and need naps so often.[5]

With this in mind, your book selections for the next year should be ones that stimulate his sight and hearing—colorful pictures and exciting sounds upon which the child can focus easily. One of the reasons for Mother Goose's success is that she echoes the first sound a child falls in love with—the rhythmic, rhyming "beat-beat-beat" of a mother's heart.

"But," you ask, "where's the plot? The meaning?" At this stage, Mother Goose isn't there for the plot. She's there to take all those sounds and syllables, those endings and blendings, to mix them in with the rhythm and rhyme of language, to be fed to a child who already takes delight in rocking back and forth in his crib repeating a single syllable over and over: "Ba, ba, ba, ba, ba . . ."

Since Mother Goose so wisely populated her rhymes with people as well as animals, the child's visual world is also expanded—particularly with many of the exciting recent editions. My favorite Mother Goose is the one edited by Watty Piper and illustrated by the Hildebrandt brothers. The pictures, large and brightly painted, are perfect for young children. Other outstanding nursery rhyme collections can be found with the *Mother Goose* entry in the picture book section of the Treasury.

Have you ever noticed how many of the Mother Goose rhymes can be applied to a child's everyday activities? "Hush-a-Bye Baby" (sleeping and waking); "Deedle, Deedle, Dumpling" (going to bed); "One, Two, Buckle My Shoe" (getting dressed); "Pat-a-Cake" (eating); "Little Jack Horner" (eating); "London Bridge" (falling down); "Jack and Jill" (falling down); "Little Bo Peep" (losing toys); "Humpty Dumpty" (falling down); "What Can the Matter Be?" (crying); "Rub-a-Dub-Dub" (bathing).

Many parents find that singing or reciting these rhymes during the appropriate activity further reinforces both rhyme and activity in the child's mind. Long-playing records and tapes of these rhymes are available at your library and local bookstore.

Also keep in mind the physical bonding that occurs during the time you are holding the child and reading. To make sure you never convey the message that the book is more important than the child, maintain skin-to-skin contact as often as possible, patting, touching, and hugging while you read.[6] Linked with the normal parent-infant dialogue, this reinforces a feeling of being well-loved.

Recent interest in early learning has spurred investigations on how infants and their parents react in read-aloud situations, though any reading parent can tell you a child's interest/response relationship with books is one of peaks and valleys. But if you are a *new* parent, the valleys can be discouraging. So here is a forecast so you'll not be discouraged or think your child is hopeless.

- At four months of age, since he has limited mobility, a child has little or no choice but to listen and observe, thus making a passive, noncombative audience for the parent, who is probably thinking, "This is easy!"
- Your arms should encircle the child in such a way as to suggest support and bonding, but not imprisonment.
- By six months, however, the child is more interested in grabbing the book to suck on it than listening (which he's also doing). Bypass the problem by giving him a teething toy or other distraction.
- At eight months, he may prefer turning pages to steady listening. Allow him ample opportunity to explore this activity but don't give up the book entirely.
- At twelve months, the child's involvement grows to turning pages for you, pointing to objects you name on the page, even making noises for animals on cue.
- By fifteen months and the onset of walking, his restlessness blossoms fully, and your reading times must be chosen so as not to frustrate his immediate interests.

In nearly all these studies,[7] attention spans during infant reading time averaged only *three minutes* in length, though several daily readings often brought the total as high as thirty minutes a day. There are some one-year-olds who will listen to stories for that long in one sitting but be assured they are more the exception than the rule.

As babies mature, good parent readers profit from earlier experiences. They don't force the reading times, they direct attention by pointing to something on the page, and they learn to vary their

voices between whispers and excited tones. And they learn that attention spans are not built overnight—they are built minute by minute, page by page, day by day.

And once the child begins to respond to the sight of books and
your voice, it is important to begin a book dialogue, *talking* the book
instead of just *reading* it, with questions like "Isn't this a wonderful
book, Jennifer?" or "Would you like a puppy like that someday?"
Even though the baby cannot initially respond, your pausing in the
appropriate places for answers creates a kind of oral road map the
child will soon follow on his own when he starts to talk.[8]

Talking the book requires your reading the pages to yourself
ahead of time, or, in the case below which has a minimum of print,
observing the pictures, then having what amounts to a conversation
with the child. Here, beside the words from Eric Hill's *Spot's First
Walk,* is a transcript of the dialogue between a mother and her twenty-
three-month-old:[9]

Book/Text	Mother/Child
What have you found?	CHILD: What's the dog doing? MOM: He's digging in the dirt looking for his bone. Look what he found there. C: Oh. M: *What have you found,* Spot? C: A doggy bone. M: Yes, he's found a doggy bone. He's having fun outside. C: Yeah. M: What is he doing with his feet? C: What's he doing with his feet, Mom? M: He's digging. C: He's digging.
Now for a drink.	M: Look what he's doing next. He's getting a drink. *Now for a drink* of water.

Don't fall in.

C: There's a fish.
M: There's a fish saying, *"Don't fall in, don't fall in."*

Notice how the mother gently works in the actual words of the book (her italics), something she conveys by a different voice inflection. The give-and-take on the part of reader and child not only builds language skills; it also holds the child's attention to the book. Moreover, it tallies with the Chinese adage: *Tell* me and I forget. *Show* me and I remember. *Involve* me and I understand. The more the child is involved in the reading process, the more he will understand.

Children less than eighteen months often find it difficult to understand complicated illustrations that adults recognize instantly. Book illustrations consisting of many little figures running here and there may be charming to adults but they are incomprehensible to young children. An adult can recognize instantly a three-dimensional rabbit when it is reduced to one dimension on a page, but a fourteen-month-old child is just beginning this complicated process. To help the child in this task, the picture books you choose now should be uncomplicated—a single image to a page and preferably in color. Plot, if there is any, is secondary to the image. Among the very best for this purpose are those by Dutch author-artist Dick Bruna.

Internationally recognized, the Bruna books are masterpieces of simplicity: simple black outlines, solid colors of red, yellow, blue, and green against plain backgrounds. His subjects are simple enough to border on caricature. Bruna packs language, story, emotion, and color into twelve pages. After *Mother Goose,* among your first books should be one of the more than fifty little Dick Bruna books (see Index to Treasury).

During the toddler stage, an important parental role is serving as a kind of welcoming committee for the child, welcoming him to your world. Just think of yourself as the host of a huge party. Your child is the guest of honor. Naturally, you want to introduce him to all the invited guests in order to make him feel at home.

You do this by helping him learn the names of all the objects that surround him, the things that move, the things that make noises, the things that shine. Picture books are perfect teaching vehicles at this stage. Point to the various items illustrated in the book, call them by name, ask the child to say the name with you, praise him enthusiastically for his efforts. Picture books like *The First Words Picture Book* and *The Early Words Picture Book,* by Bill Gillham, are excellent teaching vehicles.

The very best picture book at this stage may be the one you cannot buy in a store or borrow from the library. It is one you make with photographs taken in your home and of your family. Making sure the images are not smaller than four inches, label each with easy-to-read letters, place the picture on cardboard, and cover it entirely with a piece of self-sealing clear plastic. Metal rings through punch holes will hold it all together as a most durable and personalized "book." The materials can be purchased cheaply wherever office supplies are sold.

Once the child is calm in the presence of books and more inclined to listen than to rip, must reading is Dorothy Kunhardt's *Pat the Bunny,* a little book that enables the toddler to interact with the story, using his senses to smell the flowers (perfumed), feel the beard (sandpaper), lift the cloth, pat the bunny (cotton), and see his reflection (mirror). *Pat the Bunny* is never thrown out by a family; it is worn out. Another favorite is Eric Hill's series beginning with *Where's Spot,* with sturdy movable flaps that hide surprise images. Busy babies are most interested in busy books like these.

Since familiarity is important in developing a lasting relationship with books, it's a good idea to purchase your own copies of these "working" infant books. Not only will this be a good beginning in building your child's personal library (see Chapter 6), but libraries find it difficult to keep this kind of book in circulation because the flaps are so easily damaged. Affluent families might keep in mind that is is better to have a limited number of familiar books than numerous titles. Children under two years of age tend to be confused by a different book every day.

Many publishers are now marketing "baby board books," durable volumes printed in nontoxic inks on heavy, laminated pages that are easy for little fingers to turn and can be quickly wiped clean (see Helen Oxenbury's books in the Index to Treasury). Place the board books in the high chair, the playpen, and the crib. Let your child see books at least as often as he sees toys and television.

Families accustomed to treasuring every book are sometimes afraid to leave a book in the hands of a baby. Dorothy White, in *Books Before Five,* described those early books as the ones "fated to suffer every indignity that a child's physically expressed affection could devise—a book not only looked at, but licked, sat on, slept on, and at last torn to shreds." The quandary was settled when White and her husband wisely decided "that the enjoyment of personal ownership was a fact of life more worth knowing than how to look after this or that. How can one learn to hold, before one has learnt to have?" she asked.[10] The gentle and affectionate way the *parent* treats the book is far more important.

Frequently the child who is read to regularly can be seen toddling along with his favorite book, looking for someone to read to him. There are two important elements here. One is to keep in mind that as much as anything else, the child is looking for attention; he wants his body cuddled as much as his mind. The other factor is the idea of a "favorite" book. He has already developed literary tastes, and between now and when he is six, he'll have many favorites, books he asks for often, nightly, for months on end. The more frequently you read and the greater the variety of titles, the broader will be the child's appetite. But too frequently, any kind of favoritism by the child for a particular title will irritate parents who are tired of reading the same book.

These rereadings of the familiar coincide with the way children learn. Like their parents, they are most comfortable with the familiar, and when they are relaxed, they're better able to absorb. The repetition improves their vocabulary, sequencing, and memory skills. Research shows that preschoolers often ask as many questions (and sometimes the *same* questions) after a dozen readings of the same book because they're learning language in increments—not all at once. Each reading often brings an inch or two of new meaning to the story.

Those of us who have seen a movie more than once fully realize how many subtleties escaped us the first time. Even more so with children and books. And often, because they are learning a very complex language at the adult's speaking pace, there are misunderstandings that can only be sorted out by repeated readings. Allerton Kilborne, a history teacher at St. Bernard's School in New York

City, told me how, as a child, he used to ask his grandmother "to read the book about the man who got sick," and then hand her Clement Moore's "The Night Before Christmas." The family couldn't figure out why he called it that until one day his grandmother came to this stanza:

When out on the lawn there arose such a clatter,
I sprang from my bed to see what was the matter.
Away to the window I flew like a flash,
Tore open the shutters and *threw up* the sash.

Because visual literacy comes before print literacy—if you've never *seen* a puppy, when you come to the word *p-u-p-p-y* in print you're not going to understand it—two-thirds of the questions and comments from young children are about the illustrations in the book.[11] The stationary nature of pictures in these favorite books gives them a distinct advantage, allowing a child to "study" the page, unlike film or television where the images move too fast.

In addition, child psychologist Bruno Bettelheim believes the "favorite" book fills a personal need of the child. Some fear or concern is being allayed by the book, a kind of paper security blanket. The child finds nightly courage or comfort in its characters or setting. Don't try and reveal this secret to the child; allow him those important self-discoveries. And Bettelheim offers this hope to weary parents: When a child has gotten all he can from the book or when the problems that directed him to it have been outgrown, he'll be ready to move on to something else.[12]

For as long as possible, your read-aloud efforts should be balanced by the outside experiences you bring to the child. It is not enough to simply read to the child—except in extreme cases like Cushla Yeoman's. The visual literacy I noted earlier applies to life experience as well.

"Reading begins with the first recorded experience," says Phyllis Halloran, national reading consultant and former first-grade teacher. "It is that experience, together with all the others to follow, that allows the child to react and respond to ideas in a book."

Pictures in a book of a flower, a plane, or a puppy hold little attraction for a child who has never seen a flower or a plane or puppy.

They are, instead, obstacles to overcome on the page. But having played and romped with a puppy, having picked flowers, "the child now has an experience bank from which he can draw interpretations and appreciations," Halloran explains.

The term "culturally deprived" refers to this very void in children's lives—children like the three-year-olds living in the shadow of the St. Louis airport who didn't know there were *people* in those planes flying over their homes until their head-start program took a class trip to the airport. Imagine the difference that made in their understanding of the word "plane."

This is also borne out in the lower reading scores of disadvantaged junior high students after the summer when the gap between themselves and their more advantaged peers widens dramatically— even when the poor student attends summer school. Why? Studies attribute the gap to the varied experiences of the traveling advantaged student, as opposed to those students who remained at home over the vacation.[13]

As the child's concept of books begins to evolve, I recommend you begin an important but subtle reading lesson: labeling the book. Point out the title of the story each time you read it, and begin to use words like author, pages, pictures, cover, front, and back of the book. Disregard that old third-grade rule about using your finger when you read. Let your finger do the walking and the talking by lightly running under the text as you read. All these efforts gradually teach the child about the meaning of those black squiggly lines on the page, that reading begins in the front, at the top, and moves left to right. These are essential steps in the act of reading, steps we adults take for granted because they're second nature to us now. But they are not second nature to a child. Given these subtle learning advantages now, he'll have an easier time later on.

As children at this stage are reassured by familiar books, they are also bolstered by certain routines in their lives that offer predictability. Therefore, while allowing for impromptu readings, try to establish a schedule for reading—a time when the child will have few other distractions, a time he can count on, a time as predictable as lunchtime and bathtime.

The time of day my family usually chose was bedtime—both

in the afternoon before naps and in the evening. These are the times when the child looks for security, appreciates the physical closeness, and is tired enough to stay in one place. It is an appropriate time to introduce him to "bedtime" books like *Goodnight Moon,* by Margaret Wise Brown (for toddlers), and *No Jumping on the Bed,* by Tedd Arnold (for older children). Many other books associated with bedtime are listed under these titles in the Treasury of Read-Alouds at the back of this book.

The physical growth of the child also means his moods are changing and his needs are growing. To accommodate those needs he develops a vocabulary that is "near-genius"[14] in scope. A two-year-old will use his basic vocabulary to speak a total of 20,000 words a day, as opposed to a fifteen-year-old who uses his to speak 23,000.[15] As the principal architect in your child's building years, your reading material should keep pace with this little "talking machine."

Because of this high-level curiosity, many children enjoy non-fiction books as much as fiction at this point. As the "label-the-environment" stage moves into high gear, think of all the things that fascinate children: holes, cars, snow, birds, bugs, stars, trucks, dogs, rain, planes, cats, storms, babies, Mommies and Daddies. Beginning around age two, they are interested in everything and have a built-in need to have names for those things. I have only a lukewarm feeling for "Sesame Street" as a TV program, but *The Sesame Street Word Book* is excellent in scope, clarity, and concepts. *The Baby's Catalogue,* by Janet and Allan Ahlberg, is also good.

For nearly every subject of interest to a child, there is a corresponding book. For example, when last I looked there were more than fifty-one different books—fiction and nonfiction—published on the subject of snow. Watch the response of a child or class to your reading *Katy and the Big Snow,* by Virginia Lee Burton, as the first snowflakes fall outside your window.

When you see that your child has developed a fascination for a particular subject, check your neighborhood library for a book on it. The subject listing in the card catalogue will show what the library has on its shelves, and a handy reference guide in all libraries, *Subject Guide to Children's Books in Print,* will show what is available outside the library as well. This volume can be especially helpful with sixth-, seventh-, and eighth-grade students who frequently develop strong appetites for one particular subject and are willing to devour any book about it.

A lesser-known but extremely useful resource found in many libraries is *The Bookfinder,* a two-volume listing of tens of thousands of children's titles under 450 developmental, behavioral, and psychological headings—topics such as adoption, belonging, courage, death, divorce, teachers, and siblings. For example, when the goldfish dies, there is a story to help the child's heart to heal. Another excellent guide to nonfiction children's books is *Eyeopeners!,* by Beverly Kobrin.

During the period between two and five years of age, your child's desire to imitate his parents will extend to reading books. In some cases, by the time the child is four he can recite a book verbatim, page by page. I use "recite" and not "read" because in the majority of cases the child has only memorized what you've been reading to him. He'll boast that he is reading—and that's fine. Reward and encourage his effort by telling him how glad you are to see him enjoying himself with a book, but *don't* convey the impression that you like him more because he reads. His self-worth is not predicated upon a performance. If he were handicapped, wouldn't you love him just as much?

If he keeps on reciting, his approximations gradually come closer to the text and eventually he'll be reading naturally. Two kinds of books are especially helpful in building the confidence, imagination, and vocabulary of prereaders: wordless books and predictable books.

Thirty thousand years ago, in a step toward writing, our ancestors used cave drawings to tell stories—and wordless books follow that tradition. These books convey a story without using words; pictures (interpreted orally by the reader) tell the whole story. Children quickly realize the pictures must be followed in sequence for the story to make sense (sequencing skill) and the story is "told" (verbal skills) instead of read. Once the adult has blazed a reading trail through the book, it's relatively easy for the child to pick it up and talk the book to himself or others using the pictures as story clues.

Children with limited English skills (and illiterate or semi-literate parents) find these books immediately accessible and thus gain reading confidence. Writing teachers often ask their students to write the missing text. An increasingly popular genre in recent years, there are now more than one hundred wordless books in print, running from simple (like *Moonlight,* by Jan Ormerod) to complex (*The Silver Pony,* by Lynd Ward, 176 pages).[16] (See Wordless Books listing at the beginning of the Picture Book section of the Treasury.) Educators who work with the children of illiterate and semi-literate adults should make such books available to these parents, many of whom desperately wish they could read to their children. Wordless books offer that opportunity in a vicarious sort of way—they can "talk" the book by looking at the pictures and interpreting the pages.

Though the "predictable book" has been around for ages in folk tale and song, only recently have educators discovered how helpful it is in building readers. Because the story line contains phrases that are repeated over and over ("Then I'll huff and I'll puff and I'll . . ."), the child can easily predict what's coming—and often joins in on the reading (which enhances comprehension). For example, in Barbara Seulling's *The Teeny Tiny Woman,* the words "teeny tiny" are repeated fifty times throughout the book's thirteen sentences. In addition, predictable books often contain a cumulative sequence as in *Henny Penny:* "So Henny Penny, Chicken Licken, Turkey Lurkey, and Foxy Loxy went to see the king."

These books allow children to put the oral language they already own to immediate use, thus experiencing at least partial success with "memorized reading." It is of critical importance that the child's early experiences with print be successful ones—even if the "success" is only in his own mind.

In classes that have predictable books in the classroom library, beginning readers attempt to read these books twice as often as others during free reading time—largely because they are less intimidating.[17] The same would apply to home libraries as well. The key is: Someone must expose them to the book's pattern through read-aloud. (See Predictable Books in Picture Book section in the Treasury.)

Predictable, wordless, and controlled-vocabulary books (like Dr. Seuss's *Cat in the Hat*) build the beginning reader's self-confidence, but beyond a certain point they have limited value as vocabulary builders. Indeed, a continued diet of controlled-vocabulary books is an insult to your child's growing listening vocabulary.

Therefore, don't limit your read-alouds to that genre. After you've familiarized the child with the book, let him read it by himself (that's what it's for) and you introduce him to others, especially books with richer vocabulary and more complex stories.

On the subject of Dr. Seuss, keep in mind that his controlled-vocabulary books are only a small portion of the staggering number he has written. The very best ones—like *If I Ran the Zoo*—have a story filled with what Seuss calls his "logical nonsense"; that is, children find the sights and sounds logical while adults find them nonsensical. The rich vocabulary, verbal gymnastics, and humor permeating these books keep children intrigued and delighted. What more do you want for pleasureful reading?

Even before the child is ready for kindergarten, he can pride himself on having a sense of humor—especially if it has been cultivated with some simple joke and riddle books you've read to him. Start with the books listed with *Bennett Cerf's Book of Animal Riddles* in the Treasury. For beginning readers, put them in handy places like the kitchen table, his bedside, or in the bathroom and he'll be reading them, then memorizing and trying them out on family members. Nothing builds self-confidence and esteem like a well-told and well-received joke.[18]

The joke book can be an effective tool for all ages. Reading consultant Bill Halloran suggests that every teacher begin the day with a joke. "All over the country teachers are starting out the day with 'Take out your books.' Why can't they ease into the day with an elephant joke?"

You can also cultivate children's senses of humor with picture books and novels. Keep in mind, however, that what strikes *you* as funny may be quite serious to a five-year-old. I immediately think of *Ira Sleeps Over,* by Bernard Waber, the story of a child's indecision about bringing his teddy bear to his first sleep-over. In reading it thousands of times to adults and children, I have always found that the older the audience is, the funnier the book is. You read *Ira Sleeps Over* to a kindergarten class and nobody laughs! To them, it's hard-core seriousness. And that's part of literature's greatness—its meaning grows as we do. Read *The Little House,* by Virginia Lee Burton, as a second-grader and again as an adult and you've got two distinct books.

Shared laughter makes everybody feel better. Try these funny picture books: *The Stupids Step Out,* by Harry Allard; *Amelia Bedelia,* by Peggy Parish; *Thomas' Snowsuit,* by Robert Munsch; *I'm Telling You Now,* by Judy Delton; and *The Cut-Ups Cut Loose,* by James Marshall. And here are four hilarious novels: *Freckle Juice,* by Judy Blume; *Mr. Popper's Penguins,* by Robert Lawson; *The Best Christmas Pageant Ever,* by Barbara Robinson; and *Skinnybones,* by Barbara Park.

Before most parents realize it, a growing child is ready, in his own mind at least, to go out and challenge the world. In the last two thousand years, nothing has filled this exploratory need as well as the fairy tale.

I know what you may be thinking. "Fairy tales? Is he kidding? Why, those things are positively frightening. Nobody tells those to children any more. Children see enough violence on television— they don't need kids pushing witches into ovens, and evil spells and poisoned apples."

Stop for a minute and remind yourself how long the fairy tale has been with us—in every nation and in every civilization. Surely there must be something important here, an insight so important as to transcend time and mountains and cultures to arrive in the twentieth century still intact. There are, for example, nearly four hundred different versions of *Cinderella* from hundreds of cultures. Nevertheless, they all tell the same story—a truly universal story.

What characterizes the fairy tale—sets it apart from the rest of children's literature—is the fact that it speaks to the very heart and soul of the child. It admits to the child what so many parents and teachers spend hours trying to cover up or avoid. The fairy tale confirms what the child has been thinking all along—that it is a cold, cruel world out there and it's waiting to eat him alive.

Now, if that were all the fairy tale said, it would have died out long ago. But it goes one step further. It addresses itself to the child's sense of courage and adventure. The tale advises the child: Take your courage in hand and go out to meet that world head on. According to Bruno Bettelheim, the fairy tale offers this promise: If you have courage and if you persist, you can overcome any obstacle, conquer any foe. And best of all, you can achieve your heart's desire.

By recognizing the child's daily fears, by appealing to his courage and confidence, and by offering him hope, the fairy tale presents the child with a means by which he can understand his world and himself. And those who would deodorize the tales, eliminating the references to dragons or conflict, impose a fearsome lie upon the child. J. R. R. Tolkien wisely cautioned, "It does not pay to leave a dragon out of your calculations if you live near him." Judging from the daily averages, our land is filled with dragons. On a typical American day, someone is robbed every eighty-seven seconds, someone is raped every eight minutes, someone is murdered every twenty-seven minutes, and at the Los Angeles Olympics, security guards outnumbered the athletes 18,000 to 10,000. To send a child into that world unprepared is a crime.

The core of the nursery tale, G. K. Chesterton wrote, is ethics: Happiness and peace in life are conditional upon meeting certain requirements. There is no charge card for true happiness; it must be earned—a message that is also central to the Book of Genesis. And we must expose future generations to the credentials of heroes and heroines so they can distinguish them from impostors. Is this commercial selling me empty promises or magic beans? If the candidate poses for pictures in front of a school, does that automatically make him a friend of education or is it the "emperor's new clothes" syndrome? And when the handsome soldier in the green uniform declares the sky is falling—do I believe him on the basis of his medals or is he really "the boy who cried wolf"?

If there is one flaw in the fairy tale, it is that most popular tales are top-heavy with heroes and short on heroines. For balance, readers-aloud will want to try Ethel Johnston Phelps's two collections: *The Maid of the North* and *Tatterhood and Other Tales*. These are traditional tales about nontraditional, courageous, resourceful, and witty heroines from a variety of ethnic cultures. You might also try coupling Trina Schart Hyman's excellent version of *Sleeping Beauty* with Jane Yolen's *Sleeping Ugly*. *The Ordinary Princess,* by M. M. Kaye, and *Once upon a Test: Three Light Tales of Love,* by Vivian Vande Velde, both take a tongue-in-cheek look at the stereotyping in fairy tales.

The last four years have seen a wave of outstanding fairy tale anthologies, from the simpler tales found in Anne Rockwell's *Three Bears and 15 Other Stories* to the more complex included in *Favorite*

Folktales from Around the World by Jane Yolen. (See Anthologies section of the Treasury.) They are excellent for the bedside and to keep in the car in case of emergencies (a long wait in the doctor's office and you forgot to bring a book). But until seven years of age, children generally won't gravitate on their own to heavy books like anthologies. Therefore, in the picture book section of the Treasury (under *Household Stories of the Brothers Grimm* and *Hans Andersen's Fairy Tales*) I have listed dozens of books containing outstanding *individual* tales.

With preschoolers, a good way to start is with the simple fairy tales as interpreted by artist Paul Galdone (see the listing of his books under *The Three Little Pigs* in the Treasury).

From here you can progress gradually in length and complexity as the child's maturity and imagination demand. While I don't recommend *Hansel and Gretel* for three- and four-year-olds, I most heartily recommend it for children of five and older who wonder to themselves: How long could I survive alone out there if nobody loved me? Or my parents died? Books that water down the essence of the tales do an injustice to the book and insult the naturally curious mind.

The very best in contemporary children's books borrow the strong flavor of adventure and mystery from fairy tales. Maurice Sendak's *Where the Wild Things Are,* one of the most popular children's books of our time, deals with a child's rage at his parent and his subsequent triumphs in the land of monsters. Ludwig Bemelmans allows his heroine in *Madeline* to enter numerous predicaments, always to emerge devilishly triumphant. In William Steig's *Sylvester and the Magic Pebble* the hero is turned into a stone (talk about predicaments and a cruel world!), but finally emerges triumphant through his own persistence and the unfailing love of his parents.

Even when you go beyond the picture book, some of the best writers for children often follow the lead of the fairy tale. Natalie Babbitt confronts a ten-year-old girl in *Tuck Everlasting* with a kidnapping, a jailbreak, a murder, and a life-or-death decision. No life-leached pap here! And no adult or child can read this book without coming to terms with some of life's basic issues.

It is this internal struggle to find out how we feel or who we are that is so central to the idea of reading. More than helping them to read better, more than exposing them to good writing, more than developing their imagination, when we read aloud to children we are helping them to find themselves and to discover some meaning in the scheme of things. When Robert Penn Warren wrote, "We turn to fiction for some slight hint about the story in the life we live," he meant children as much as adults. All the best qualities of great adult fiction can be found in great children's literature, but particularly in the fairy tale. When Professor Richard Abrahamson of the University of Houston studied the "Children's Choices for 1979," a list of favorite books chosen by children across the United States, he found most children preferred books with "episodic plots involving confrontation with a problem and characters who have opposing points of view. . . ."[19]

Because of the variety involved, fairy tales offer us an excellent opportunity to introduce children to comparative literature. Read Paul Galdone's traditional version of *The Three Little Pigs* and then Tony Ross's *The Three Pigs,* in which the pigs build their own homes because the bank refused to loan them the money ("We're not a *piggy bank!*" says the bank manager). *Jim and the Beanstalk,* by Raymond Briggs, continues the story of *Jack and the Beanstalk* (also by Paul Galdone), this time with the son of the original giant. And Janet and Allen Ahlberg give us two wonderful fairy tale parodies in *The Jolly Postman* (the pages of which form envelopes containing letters, postcards, and junk mail from famous fairy tale characters), and *Jeremiah in the Dark Woods* (who, in seeking the missing tarts, meets three bears, seven dwarfs, a frog prince, some sleeping beauties, et cetera).

Used holistically, children's picture books can and should be incorporated throughout the curriculum. "Hawaiian children often have a narrow perspective of the world," explained a kindergarten consultant there. "They think there are only two places: Hawaii and the mainland (which includes everything else)." To give her children a sense of geography, she incorporated a large world map into her literature program, on which students place stickers when she reads *The Red Balloon* (France), *Curious George* (Africa), *The Story of Ferdinand* (Spain), and *The Five Chinese Brothers* (China). This is such a commonsense idea, it should be used by all parents and teachers— especially after a 1988 Gallup survey of 10,000 people in nine countries showed U.S. young adults finishing sixth—far worse than their counterparts in 1947—with 20 percent unable to locate their own country on a world map.[20]

"Critical thinking" is another curriculum area under heavy scrutiny these days and read-aloud can assist here, too, if you ask the right questions (not the paper-and-pencil kind). Simple warm-up questions can be used with preschoolers: "What do you think this book will be about?" (holding up the cover of the book for them to see). "This book is written and drawn by Robert McCloskey. Have we read anything else by him?" At an important part, stop and inquire, "What do you think is going to happen next?" These are nonthreatening questions, soliciting children's opinions but also nurturing their memory and predictive skills. And by involving them in the reading, you enhance understanding.

Educators report that the most important critical thinking skill is recognizing the essence of a problem. So, as a problem begins to be defined in the book, stop and ask, "What's the problem here?" "What do you think is wrong?" "What would *you* do in this situation?"

With novels, you can begin by asking, "Let's see—where did we leave off yesterday?" or "What's happened so far?" and thus strengthen memory and sequencing skills. With books that have unnamed chapters, let children take turns naming the chapters at the end of the day's reading. Reading aloud can accomplish many of the same things you do with paper and pencil—depending on how much pleasure you incorporate into (or draw from) the experience. One note about asking questions: Studies reveal most teachers wait only one second or less for answers. But further research showed if they expanded that to three to five seconds before and after the answer, student responses grew more frequent and more logical, and complex thinking skills improved significantly.[21] In other words, slow down!

Teachers and parents often ask me, "When do you stop the picture books and start with the 'big' books—the novels?" Although I understand their impatience to get on with the business of growing up, I wince whenever I hear them phrase it that way.

First of all, there is no such time as "a time to stop the picture books." I know nursery school teachers who read Judith Viorst's *Alexander and the Terrible, Horrible, No Good, Very Bad Day* to their classes and I know a high school English teacher who reads it to his sophomores twice a year—once in September and, by popular demand, again in June.

Shouldn't those fifteen-year-olds have outgrown a picture book like *Alexander and the Terrible, Horrible, No Good, Very Bad Day*? Not by my standards. I read a picture book (*Ira Sleeps Over*) to every adult group I address and no one ever objects; in fact, it may be the best part of my entire presentation. A good story is a good story. Beautiful and stirring pictures can move fifteen-year-olds as well as five-year-olds. A picture book should be on the reading list of every class in every grade through twelve years of school.

I might also add that most U.S. high school students were not read to regularly in primary grades and have done little or no reading on their own. In spite of this shallow foundation, we insist on rushing them into the classics during high school. ("Why, if they don't read *The Red Badge of Courage* now, they'll *never* read it!" exclaims the faculty member, who sounds like he thinks they're all going to die on prom night. My counter questions: *Why* will they never read it? Were classics forced on them too soon?) In any case, let's *also* let them hear what they missed in primary years—*The Pied Piper of Hamelin* (retold in a lovely new edition by Barbara Bartos-Hoppner) and *Sleeping Beauty* and *The Story of Ferdinand* (Munro Leaf's little book that pushed *Gone With the Wind* out of the number-one spot on the best-seller list half a century ago). The fact is that many of our students are at the doorstep of parenthood. In New York City alone, there are 12,000 kindergarten children with teenage mothers; nationwide, *every day* forty teenage girls give birth to their *third* child.[22] If they and their friends are ignorant of childhood's stories, how can they share them with their children?

Do teachers think their eighth-grade classes wouldn't sit still for a picture book? That they'd be insulted? Not if you picked the right book and matched it with the right moment and the right attitude on the part of the reader. Try reading *The Shrinking of Treehorn*, by Florence Parry Heide, to teenagers. I can almost guarantee there will be someone at your desk at the end of the class asking, "What was the name of that book again?"

Writing in *The Journal of Reading*, William Coughlin, Jr., director of English education at the University of Lowell (Massachusetts), explained the difficulties he encountered in trying to teach literary form (plot, setting, character) to secondary-school students.[23] The complexity and subtlety of the text he was using, Herman Melville's *Moby Dick,* appeared to overwhelm the class. Coughlin began to wonder if the mistake was in trying to teach a simple idea with a complex book. Why not introduce the concepts of plot and point of view through a simple book and then apply them to a complex work?

Coughlin chose to work with Leo Lionni's *Frederick,* a picture book he describes as "a story of less than six hundred words, but the beautifully structured craftsmanship with which its elements of form interrelated exhibited perfectly what I wanted my students to see when they read." The response by his class was immediate and the results positive. In the same article, coauthor Brendan Desilets explained how picture books are used in a similar manner at Bedford (Massachusetts) High School. Both authors agree that "to ignore children's literature in the high school classroom is to overlook a valuable resource for teaching advanced reading skills."

Elementary school teachers who only have the opportunity to read to a group of slow, medium, and fast students should remember that, while those students may read and write on different levels, they usually listen on the same level. "Read-aloud time is often the one time then *everyone* is equal," teacher/librarian Jan Lieberman reminds us. With that in mind, your initial read-aloud choices should be aimed at the majority—and guided by their mental, social, and emotional level. As you progress through the year, you increase the caliber and complexity of the stories.

One of the first criteria for lengthening the read-aloud session beyond picture books is the attention span of the child or class. It is no secret among teachers that children's attention spans appear to be growing shorter each year. And in this battle, because of our primal need to find out what happens next, read-aloud is a particularly effective tool. Just keep in mind that endurance in readers—like runners—is not built overnight; start slowly and build.

If I had a primary class (or child) that had never been read to (like the ones who spent all of kindergarten filling in blanks and circling letters), I'd start the school year with the repetition of *Tikki Tikki Tembo,* by Arlene Mosel; the poignancy of *The Biggest Bear,* by Lynd Ward; the mystery of *The Island of the Skog,* by Steven

Kellogg; the humor of *Foolish Rabbit's Big Mistake,* by Rafe Martin, and the suspense of Paul Zelinsky's retelling of *Rumpelstiltskin.* The following week would be called "A Walk in the Woods," focusing on children's adventures in the woods—starting with Trina Schart Hyman's *Little Red Riding Hood* and followed by books chosen from the eight titles listed with it in the Treasury.

Moving to books with more words, I'd schedule "Bill Peet Week." In anticipation of the event, I would have written to his publisher (Houghton Mifflin, Promotions Dept., 2 Park St., Boston, MA 02108) and ordered (for $2) the Bill Peet poster and six-page autobiography. Author weeks are greatly enhanced with such promotional material. Then I would choose a week's worth of reading from his thirty-seven books (enough to have a Bill Peet *month*). On the day I read *Kermit the Hermit* (a stingy hermit crab), I'd introduce it with "Hector the Collector" from Shel Silverstein's poetry collection, *Where the Sidewalk Ends.* From then on, I'd begin or end the reading with a poem—not necessarily connected to the reading—and gradually sprinkle poetry throughout the day: waiting for the bell in the morning, between classes, et cetera.

I'd culminate Bill Peet Week (or month) by introducing *Bill Peet: An Autobiography,* his extraordinary 190-page book that explores the roots of his life and books—with pictures on every page. Then I'd move on to something a little more complex—like Carol and Donald Carrick's eight-book series (listed with *Sleep Out* in the Treasury) that follows a child's maturing and heartwarming struggles with sleeping out, the death of his dog, and being lost on a class trip. Eight books, eight days, all linked by the common thread of one family and their concern for one another.

From here it's an easy jump to "chapter books"—either long picture books or short novels of sixty to one hundred pages. These are books that don't have to end with Monday and can be stretched into the afternoon or into Tuesday and Wednesday. ("Boys and girls, that's the end of Chapter 1; tomorrow we'll have Chapter 2." "Teacher, what do you mean, 'Chapter'?" "Jonathan, it's like a miniseries." "Oooooh!" the child exclaims with understanding.)

Even preschoolers can enjoy "chapter" books. Given the opportunity, they'll respond enthusiastically to picture books divided into chapters, like *Andy and the Lion,* by James Dougherty; *The*

Foundling Fox, by Irina Korschunow; *Grandaddy's Place,* by Helen Griffith; *Emily's Own Elephant,* by Philippa Pearce; Barbara Brenner's *Wagon Wheels;* and *The Josefina Story Quilt,* by Eleanor Coerr.

Sometimes you'll encounter a picture book that may be too long for one sitting. Solve the problem by dividing it into chapters yourself. That works especially well with Rumer Godden's classic Christmas book, *The Story of Holly and Ivy* (you've got to love a book that opens on Christmas Eve in an orphanage). Excellent starter short novels are *The Courage of Sarah Noble,* by Alice Dalgliesh, and William McCleery's *Wolf Story.* And don't miss *The Iron Giant,* by Ted Hughes (a terrific science fiction tale for primary grades) and *Lafcadio, the Lion Who Shot Back,* a slapstick novel by the always popular Shel Silverstein.

I am firmly convinced that some of the blame for children's short attention spans must be placed on the shoulders of parents and teachers who continually underestimate these capacities. "That story would be too long. They'd never sit still that long," says the teacher, forgetting the fact that the children sit still for three hours of television every day. They have no trouble enjoying and understanding the movie *Star Wars* and they'll have no difficulty appreciating lengthy books—if they are exciting and meaningful.

Shortly after speaking in Southfield, Michigan, I received this letter from Jan Clark, a kindergarten teacher there: "When you recommended we read longer stories to kindergartners—even *Charlotte's Web*—I wasn't sure my students could sit still for a book with only a few illustrations. Twenty-two chapters seemed endless. But I decided to give it a try.

"Well, it has been a delightful experience. My kids can't wait to hear the next chapter. They get upset if our schedule doesn't allow enough time for more than a few pages. One sunny day they even voted for story time instead of playing outdoors on the playground."

Charlotte's Web (written on a fourth-grade reading level but easily understood by six-year-olds) is 184 pages of prose by one of the great essayists of this century and is unequivocally the novel most frequently read by American schoolchildren. The challenge it offers adults is this: Childhood reading doesn't have to stop with *Charlotte's Web.* Teachers and parents need to familiarize themselves with life beyond *Charlotte* if they expect children's reading appetites to grow.

If kindergarten children handle it with ease, then it is well below the *listening* level of fourth grade. It would be a good idea if faculties did a little coordinating so children are not dosed with *Charlotte* every year for the first four grades.

The difference between short novels and full-length novels (I've arbitrarily chosen one hundred pages as a demarcation point) is sometimes found in the amount of description, the shorter ones having much less detail, the longer ones requiring more imagination on the part of the listener/reader. Children whose imaginations have been atrophying in front of a television for years are not initially comfortable with long descriptive passages. But the more you read to these children, the less trouble they have in constructing mental images. Indeed, research shows us that listening to stories stimulates the imagination significantly more than television or film.[24]

In approaching longer books, consider the fact that all books are not meant to be read aloud. Some books aren't even worth reading to yourself, never mind boring a family or class with them. Still others are written in a style intended for reading silently. And then there are those whose literary style coincides perfectly with the oral tradition. The great Canadian adult novelist Robertson Davies alluded to this in the preface to a volume of his speeches in which he asked readers to remember they were reading *speeches*—not essays: "What is meant to be heard is necessarily more direct in expression, and perhaps more boldly coloured, than what is meant for the reader."[25] This is a fact missed by most speakers, preachers, and professors who write their speeches as if the audience were going to read them instead of listen to them.

Look at this one-sentence example of Edgar Allan Poe's prose that makes for distinguished silent reading but horrendous reading aloud: "It was this deficiency, I considered, while running over in thought the perfect keeping of the character of the premises with the accredited character of the people, and while speculating upon the possible influence which the one, in the long lapse of centuries, might have exercised upon the other—it was this deficiency, perhaps, of collateral issue, and the consequent undeviating transmission, from sire to son, of the patrimony with the name, which had, at length, so identified the two as to merge the original title of the estate in the quaint and equivocal appellation of the 'House of Usher'—an appellation which seemed to include, in the minds of the peasantry who used it, both the family and the family mansion."[26] Enough said?

How will you know if children are ready for a full-length novel? Does the child ask you each night to keep reading? What kinds of questions does he ask about the stories you read? Are the descriptions or characters confusing for him?

The first novel I read to Jamie would be my first choice a thousand times over, for almost any child or class—*James and the Giant Peach*. I know a kindergarten teacher who ends her year with this book and I know a sixth-grade teacher who has started her September class with it for twenty years. Any book that can hold the attention and lift the imaginations of six-year-olds as well as eleven-year-olds has to have magic in it. And *James and the Giant Peach* has that.

Once a child or class has reached the novel stage, it is increasingly important for the adult to preview the book before reading it aloud. The length of such books allows them to treat subject matter that can be very sensitive, far more so than a picture book could. As the reader, you should first familiarize yourself with the subject and the author's approach. Ask yourself as you read it through, "Can my child or class handle not only the vocabulary and the complexity of this story, but its emotions as well? Is there anything here that will do more harm than good to my child or class? Anything that might embarrass someone?"

Along with enabling you to avoid this kind of damaging situation, reading the book ahead of time will enable you to read it the second time to the class or child with more confidence, accenting important passages, leaving out dull ones (I mark these lightly in pencil in the margins), and providing sound effects to dramatize the story line (I'm always ready to knock on a table or wall where the story calls for a "knock at the door").

A publisher once remarked that toy companies are not the only one who must be careful about producing objects with sharp edges for children. Some stories have sharp edges that can hurt or confuse unformed minds and that must not be ignored.

When Jamie was in first grade, I picked out a book by Elliott Arnold called *Brave Jimmy Stone*. It is a dramatic and touching story that describes a boy and his father on a hunting trip. They are two days away from civilization when the father falls and breaks a leg and the boy has to travel through a blizzard to get help. It was a short novel, just the right pace for Jamie, and the vocabulary was well within his grasp.

Mistakenly I considered only the intellectual level of the story and ignored the emotional level. It wasn't until Jamie woke up crying for the second straight night that I realized that I had forgotten about the emotional side of the story. Jamie had thought that because this was happening to Jimmy Stone and his father, it probably would happen to Jamie Trelease and his father, also. He was too young to deal with the realistic emotional drama of the scenes and became blind to the difference between fact and fiction. *Brave Jimmy Stone* is worth reading. It is a beautiful book. The mistake was mine in reading it too soon. I should have waited until Jamie was in third grade.

Which brings me to the subject of censorship. Though I'm a strong First Amendment advocate, I confess to "censoring" everything I read—newspapers, books, billboards, junk mail, what I read to myself and what I read aloud. Another word for it would be "editing." If I'm bored with something I'm reading for pleasure, I usually skip over it, as most people do. (Incidentally, Charles Dickens, whose publisher paid him by the word, edited out the extra adjectives and adverbs when he read his works aloud.) If there is something in the text that will detract from the book's impact or disturb the class or child, skip it or change it. *You're* running the program, not the person who wrote the book, who has no idea what the problems are in your classroom or home. I am not suggesting, as one author friend feared, that you rewrite the book to the tastes of the reader. Reason is called for, not revisionism. The business of plodding along word-for-word, never missing a line, said Clifton Fadiman, is "chronic reverence," something that may be good manners, but also a "confounded waste of time."

If you edit calmly you can save for classroom consumption many books that ordinarily might have to be scrapped. A teacher in South Hadley, Massachusetts, confirmed this approach in reading Lois Duncan's *Killing Mr. Griffin* to her eighth-grade remedial-reading class. Her students were thirteen-year-olds reading on a third-grade level. The story of four teenagers who decide to kidnap and frighten their overstrict English teacher is controversial enough, but the occasional four-letter words if read aloud could put the teacher in hot water. Nevertheless, she knew the story was worth saving. In reading it to her class she skipped or changed the swear words and read on. The resulting class attention and enthusiasm were sky-high. By the middle of the book, half the class wanted to find a copy in the school library in order to read it for themselves.

"I choose to read one chapter a day, no more. That way," the teacher explains, "if a child is absent, he doesn't miss too much of the story. I also do the reading at the beginning of the class. As a result, I never have to call for order. They are 'shush-ing' each other as they walk in the door. There is perfect order at the sound of the bell and seldom is there a late arrival."

But more important, they became involved in the story. They immediately recognized the peer pressures that fertilized the kidnapping scheme. They took sides and began to form judgments about the characters, putting themselves in their places. These eighth-grade remedial students had become emotionally, intellectually, and socially involved in the story.

"For me," the teacher enthuses, "that is a dream come true."

One question arising from a book like *Killing Mr. Griffin* is: Won't remedial students reading on a third-grade level miss much of the story's meaning?

Fader and McNeil answer this question in their book *Hooked on Books*. Dr. Daniel Fader writes of his experiences in turning reluctant readers into willing readers, particularly at the W. J. Maxey Boys' Training School in Michigan. Many of the delinquent boys at the school were semi-literate, but that didn't stop them from reading books that interested them. Fader points to the boy who wanted to read Nathaniel Hawthorne's *The Scarlet Letter*. When the boy was cautioned that the book might be too difficult, he replied. "Ain't this the one about a whore?" When he was told that, indeed, that description came fairly close to the mark, he proceeded to read it. "If it was a book about a whore, it was a book for him," Fader wrote.

The author convincingly points out that his experiences at Maxey show that children definitely can read and understand without knowing every word in the book:

Semi-literate readers do not need semi-literate books. The simplistic language of much of the life-leached literature inflicted upon the average schoolchild is not justifiable from any standpoint. Bright, average, dull—however one classified the child—he is immeasurably better off with books that are too difficult for him than books that are too simple. . . . Reading is a peculiarly personal interaction between a reader and a book—but *in no case* does this interaction demand an understanding of every word by the reader. The threshold . . . even in many complex books, can be pleasurably crossed by many simple readers.[27]

By citing Dr. Fader's argument here I am not suggesting that every book you read aloud be over the head of your audience. A child hears a story on at least three different levels: intellectual, emotional, and social. In the Maxey and South Hadley incidents, while the students were on a third-grade level, their emotional and social levels were often those of their own age or older.

Many of the guidelines suggested for reading to younger students also apply to older ones. Just because they are older doesn't mean they have longer attention spans or that they've been read to previously. Tailor your initial readings to the class situation, win their confidence, and then broaden the scope and introduce them to times and places other than their own.

Humor can be an especially good ice-breaker with adolescents. I recall the August day my neighbor Ellie Fernands asked me, "Which book do you think I ought to start off the year reading aloud?" (She was returning to junior high teaching after a fourteen-year hiatus to raise her own children.) We settled on *Be a Perfect Person in Just Three Days!,* by Stephen Manes, a funny short novel about early adolescence.

At the end of that first week of school she confided, "I don't know what I would have done without *Perfect Person* those first few days. I was so nervous that they wouldn't like me and I guess they were nervous that I wouldn't like them. Our shared laughter was the ice-breaker, and it won their confidence." Since then, she notes, reading aloud has become the best part of the day.

Where time constraints make a novel impossible, or for a change of pace, read a poem from *Where the Sidewalk Ends,* then try reading from Jane Yolen's *Favorite Folktales from Around the World* or Louis Untermeyer's *The World's Great Stories,* or a selection from *Paul Harvey's "The Rest of the Story."* The latter book (like its two sequels) contains nearly one hundred historic and contemporary true stories originally read aloud on Harvey's national radio program of the same name. Written by his son, Paul Aurandt, the stories are only four minutes in length and each is highlighted by an O. Henry ending. These readings also can serve as corrective exercises for short attention spans.

In choosing novels at elementary and secondary levels, avoid falling into the old book-report trap of "thicker is better." There are thousands of children every day who report to the media center and tell the librarian: "My teacher said this book doesn't count for a book report—it's gotta be at least 125 pages." And that's how you kill a reader! There is no connection between thickness and quality.

Like the elementary teachers who can't seem to get beyond *Charlotte's Web,* secondary teachers need to broaden their spectrum beyond *Lord of the Flies* and *A Separate Peace,* neither of which were written for teenagers in the first place.[28] There are masterfully crafted short novels (novellas) ideal for reading on the secondary level. I'll match Janni Howker's *Isaac Campion* against almost any eighty-four-page book (and most of the others, too) on your high school curriculum list. The thinness (fifty-three small pages) of *The Friendship,* by Mildred Taylor, belies the breadth of its power. If I had only forty-five minutes to teach the meaning of the civil rights struggle, I'd read this book aloud. Too often high schools force-feed "old adult" literature to students and ignore great "young adult" literature like *Goodnight, Mr. Tom,* by Michelle Magorian.

Read-aloud selections don't even have to be books. In your leisure reading, if you find a magazine article your class would enjoy, read it to them. Reading aloud a newspaper column may turn a student into a daily newspaper reader. You'll know you're on the right track when a student stops you between classes and asks, "Did you read Bob Greene's column last night? Wasn't it great?" (There are several collections of Greene's newspaper and magazine columns, *American Beat* and *Cheeseburgers,* that make wonderful reading aloud with adolescents and older children. As with everything you read aloud at this stage, though, be selective—a few of them may not be appropriate for classroom consumption.) And if you are looking for a fast-moving novel that will grab even the most reluctant audience, try Avi's *Wolf Rider!* It's the fastest two hundred pages I've read in years.

All that stoic posturing on the part of adolescents might even make you believe they aren't listening—but they are. A few years ago a newspaper reporter named Jim Haynes from Greenville, Pennsylvania, was interviewing me and the subject of influential teachers came up. He recalled his seventh-grade teacher in Ann Arbor, Michigan, Carol Bryer, who did *not* read to the class. But she and her English professor husband used to read to each other and she'd begin each class by reporting on the previous night's readings. Years later he still remembers that H. P. Lovecraft was among their favorite choices to scare each other. "By the end of the seventh grade," Haynes said, "I'd decided that when I looked for a wife, I'd look for someone I could love *and* read with. And that's exactly what I did." Could a seventh-grade English teacher have made a better impression?

An aspect of American secondary schools that deeply troubles educators is the image of a factory assembly line, each student being just a number in the register. It's a worrisome, even dangerous, image when perceived by students. The relaxed tone of reading aloud certainly lessens that impersonal image, especially when it is done by people like Cindy Gipson at Norfolk Junior High in Nebraska. She reads aloud to her regular English classes and to an additional group rotated into her room from a study hall each day. "The first day, I round them up from the main study, tell them I'm going to read aloud to them, watch the ninth-graders roll their eyes, the seventh-graders chew their lips, and the eighth-graders measure the distance to the door and contemplate the likelihood of making it there undetected, and then I make them listen for twenty minutes. The second day, returning is entirely voluntary; if they want to just fade back to study hall, that's fine, but so far the return rate has been between 75 percent and 99 percent."

From that day until the book is finished, the routine is twenty minutes of study hall and equal time for read-aloud. At the end of the book, she brings in another bunch of eye-rollers and lip-chewers and begins again. "The departing class, however, is angry they have to rotate out and wait awhile before they can come back. They frown, argue, whine, and cajole to get me to start another book and not tell the next group," she explains.

Cindy also recalls the day she sealed the happy fate of read-aloud with one particular study hall class. She was reading *The Dog Days of Arthur Cane,* by T. Ernesto Bethancourt, to the class when she came to a line about a character who is always after good-looking girls. "I can't remember their exact word now," she says, "but a reference was made about his 'something-ing' girls and I saw it just as I got to it, changed it quickly to 'chasing' girls just because whatever the author said sounded chauvinistic to me, and I went right on reading—congratulating myself at doing it with only the slightest hitch in my speaking rhythm.

"But then I heard a funny giggle and, without stopping my reading, I glanced up quickly to find three or four ninth-grade boys laughing soundlessly. I hadn't been as smooth as I thought and they were busy replacing 'chasing' with all kinds of other participles, no doubt much worse than the only slightly bothersome one I had changed. Well, my color changed (I'm told) from red to pale to crimson, the entire room joined in until we were all (me, too) nearly in convulsions, with tears running down our faces. But, boy, I never stopped reading! No, sir, I didn't miss a lick. I giggled and squealed and even blew my nose through two or three more pages to a background of near howling. I never looked up again either, until blissfully, the bell rang and I escaped to do hall duty with mascara puddles around my eyes." Teachers like Cindy Gipson and her partner Shirley Burkhardt create *lifetime* readers, not just *schooltime* readers. And they make schools feel less like factories.

A parent can use read-aloud to challenge a child's mind and take care of his emotional needs in other ways. But classroom teachers are limited in the ways they can reach and touch children. Each day millions of children arrive in American classrooms in search of something more than reading and math skills. They come to school looking for a light in the darkness of their lives, a Good Samaritan who will stop and bandage a bruised heart or ego. Most of us can still remember the massive rescue effort in 1987 to free the one-year-old Texas girl who had fallen into an abandoned well. What we need to recognize is that tens of thousands of schoolchildren have fallen into emotional wells and are waiting to be rescued. We fail to reach them with the daily curriculum often enough for one thousand teenagers to attempt suicide every day, and one succeeds every ninety minutes.

Katherine Paterson spoke eloquently about the healing salve of books when she accepted the 1979 National Book Award for *The Great Gilly Hopkins,* a book that offers hope and affection to those thousands of children who have found themselves rated "disposable"—foster children.

Mrs. Paterson told her Carnegie Hall audience, "A teacher had read aloud *The Great Gilly Hopkins* to her class and Eddie, another foster child, hearing in the story of Gilly his own story, did something that apparently flabbergasted everyone who knew him. He fell in love with a book. Can you imagine how that made me feel? He was a twelve-year-old who knew far better than I what my story was about, and he did me the honor of claiming it for himself. It seemed to me that anyone who liked a book as much as Eddie did should have a copy of his own, so I sent him one. On Saturday I got this letter:

Dear Mrs. Paterson:
  Thank you for the book, *The Great Gilly Hopkins.* I love the book. I'm on page 16.
  Your friend always,
  Eddie Young[29]

If "lobster" were an important subject in the curriculum, we would have lobster classes for twelve straight years: where to find them, how they live, and, of course, how to catch, prepare, cook, and eat them. But if, after graduating from school, the end result was a lifelong loss of appetite for lobster, there would be a reassessment of the lobster curriculum. And this is precisely what has happened to poetry in the United States—except no one is reassessing the curriculum.

The truth of the matter is that poetry dies for most people on graduation day. The thickest coat of dust in a public library can be found in its poetry section. Is that *because of* or *in spite of* the way we teach it in school? I say the former.

Let me repeat what I noted earlier in this chapter: Children come into the world, thanks to mother's heartbeat, with a natural love of rhythm and rhyme. This stays with them until they are introduced to obscure or archaic poetry, forced to analyze, dissect, and memorize it—all the while being told "this is good for you," as though it were chopped liver. And that is precisely what students begin thinking poetry tastes like. Is the objective to create English professors or poetry readers?

The contrast between child and adult responses to poetry is seen most strikingly in two facts: 1) The best-selling children's book in the last five years is a poetry book that spent more time (186 straight weeks) on the *New York Times* best-seller list than any book in the previous fifty years. 2) The worst-selling department in book-stores is adult poetry: it sells so poorly, many stores no longer even stock it.

That children's poetry book, *A Light in the Attic,* by Shel Sil-verstein, and its predecessor, *Where the Sidewalk Ends,* are so popular with children that librarians insist they are now the most frequently stolen books. For years I've been asking audiences of teachers if they know *Where the Sidewalk Ends* (two million copies in print) and three-quarters of the teachers raise their hands. "Wonderful!" I say. "Now, who has enough copies of this book for every child in your room?" Nobody raises a hand. In the last five years, only one teacher—Laura Amstead, a second/third-grade mentor teacher in Saddleback Valley, California—had enough copies in her room for every child (thirty copies of *Sidewalk* and forty-five copies of *Attic).*

I continue, "Do each of you know the books in your classroom no child would ever consider stealing? The book they groan about every time you tell them to open it?" They nod in recognition. "Do you have enough copies of *those* books for every child in the room?" Reluctantly, they nod agreement. Here we've got a book kids love so much they'll steal it and we haven't got enough copies; but every year we've got twenty-eight copies of a textbook they hate like blazes. Does that make sense?

Shel Silverstein revolutionized the children's book industry, thanks to the healthy push his books received from librarians and teachers. With the publication of *Where the Sidewalk Ends,* poetry suddenly became marketable beyond Mother Goose and a few Dr. Seuss books in rhyming verse. Because children demanded it for birthdays and holidays, parents bought it and then exclaimed. "Hey, this poetry is terrific! Why wasn't poetry like this around when I was a kid?" Some of it *was* around but it was presented in such an unappealing format, it died on the vine.

Following in the wake of Silverstein's success, four major anthologies have been published in the last four years, any one of which exceeds nearly everything done in the previous fifty years (excepting Silverstein's): *The Random House Book of Poetry* and *Read-Aloud Rhymes for the Very Young,* both collected by Jack Prelutsky: *Side by Side: Poems to Read Together,* collected by Lee Bennett Hopkins; and *Sing a Song of Popcorn: Every Child's Book of Poems,* collected by Beatrice Schenk deRegniers. It can be said without exaggeration that we have never been as rich in children's poetry as we are today. Whether parents and educators take advantage of this abundance is another question.

If we wish children to believe poetry is important, the *worst* way to teach it is to develop a two-week poetry block, teach it, and then forget it—because that's what children will do with it. The *best* way is to incorporate meaningful poetry throughout the day. The question of which poems to read has already been answered for you by the anthologists and poets mentioned above, who pored through tens of thousands of children's poems to come up with children's favorites. (See the Poetry section of the Treasury.)

Dr. Bernice Cullinan, New York University professor of childhood and elementary education, in her book *Literature and the Child,* took a hard look at poetry tastes and summed them up this way: "Children's poetry choices remain stable and consistent over the years. Many children today, like those of fifty years ago, prefer humorous poems. Most children do not like sentimental and serious poetry, or poems difficult to understand. Poetry with clear-cut rhyme and rhythm is well liked; poetry that depends on imagery is not."[30]

The rules for retaining or developing a love of poetry within children are: Read it aloud; read it often; keep it simple; keep it joyous or spooky or exciting. Remember, poetry appreciation is like a ball. "It is more caught than taught," explains poet Leland Jacobs. For this purpose, keep an anthology of poetry handy at the bedside or on the teacher's desk.

Using anthologies as resources, you often can link an appropriate poem with a book you are reading aloud, either before or after the story, even later in the day. Examples of possible read-aloud books with their accompanying poems would include: *Call of the Wild* and "The Cremation of Sam McGee"; *The Little House* and "A House Is a House for Me," by Mary Ann Hoberman; *Hang Tough, Paul Mather* and "Casey at the Bat." By familiarizing yourself with the books noted in the Treasury as well as the poetry anthologies that are divided into categories, you will be able to come up with a limitless list of your own to fit your child or class. In fact, when you've got a list, send it to me; maybe we can collect them and do a book.

There was a time when poetry was not only taught but also honored. Poetry recitations (as Donald Hall details in his magnificent Afterword in the centennial edition of "Casey at the Bat") were once a public art in America, and children reciting verse before peers and kin was commonplace. And as recently as the 1950s, poetry regularly appeared on editorial pages of American newspapers. A changing culture and the mistaken idea that memorization stifles creativity eventually eliminated poetry recitations. Teenagers who can easily recite the names of twenty rock groups would be hard-pressed to name four poets. When they are handled correctly, such recitations are as useful as any school drama, spelling bee, or chorus, improving children's vocabulary, grammar, diction, short-term memory, recall, library usage, and self-esteem.

We spend 30 percent of our time speaking and only 16 percent reading and 9 percent writing,[31] so it flies in the face of logic to spend so much time improving children's reading and so little time improving the way children speak. "If George Bernard Shaw's Professor Higgins made the rounds of today's high schools," commented *New York Times* columnist Fred Hechinger recently, "he would have to mass-produce his technique of turning many adolescents into intelligible people."[32] Memorization programs nurture verbal skills, whereas three-word answers in class or filling in blanks is hardly adequate preparation for business communication—even behind the counter at a 7-Eleven. If you read intelligently but talk unintelligently, you are language-deficient. Many critics of memorization are nonetheless advocates of teaching critical thinking. They seem to forget that the mind needs memories in order to think—and that's why memory is so important. Trying to think without memories is like driving a car without gas. The more extensive the memory skills, the greater the thinking skills and recall.

When librarian Lonna McKeon of Blessed Sacrament School in Johnson City, New York, first thought of a poetry recitation in her school (K–3), she wondered what response it would receive. She'd been having monthly poetry choral readings but this would go beyond that: individual competitions by class, each volunteer student reciting a short poem of his choice with winners (four to five from each class) performing before a parent audience at open house.

Student response was immediate. The children's librarian in nearby Binghamton reported her poetry shelf was bare for the first time ever. Scores of parents showed up early for open house recitals (to the faculty's surprise and delight), and, best of all, children fell in love with poetry. Afterwards, parents noted how wonderful it was to see children memorizing poetry and applauding it, too. The humor of the selections also surprised the parents, who could not recall ever studying poetry that was not dry, boring, or incomprehensible.

There were special rewards for the event that went far beyond the awards—ones that were hard to measure—like the "best in the show" accolade going to the shyest girl in second grade.

Penelope Laurans teaches English at Yale University and testifies to the ignorance of poetry in students coming from the preparatory schools as well. "I am surprised at how cut off from poetry, especially the wonderful old chestnuts of American poetry, many of my students are. When introduced to the pleasures of reading and memorizing it, . . . they are amazed at what they have been missing." But she worries that because they have come to it so late in life, it will never be a habit. "They will not have poems in their heads to recite as they travel down highways on long car trips or to comfort them when they are lonely or sad, or unlucky in love." And where did Dr. Laurans discover her poetic roots? Her fifth-grade teacher, Miss Ciaburri at Winslow Grammar School in New Bedford, Massachusetts, who required her students to exercise their memories and thus "introduced us to poetic music and verbal magic."[33]

Far and away the best primer on poetry for the adult who wants to discover the world of children's poetry is *Pass the Poetry, Please,* by Lee Bennett Hopkins. The book offers profiles and interviews on twenty children's poets, suggests classroom poetry activities, and presents poetry in an unthreatening, most accessible fashion. I love it!

The other area commonly overlooked for read-aloud is the comic book, and my first choice would be the incomparable *Tintin.* If you looked closely at Dustin Hoffman while he was reading a bedtime story to his son in *Kramer vs. Kramer,* you would have noticed he was reading *Tintin.* Or if you read the list of favorite read-alouds offered by historian Arthur Schlesinger, Jr., in *The New York Times Book Review,* you would have found Hergé's *Tintin* between *Huckleberry Finn* and the Greek myths.[34]

Begun as a comic strip in Belgium in 1929, *Tintin* now reaches, in comic-book form, thirty countries in twenty-two languages and is sold only in quality bookstores. The subject of this success is a seventeen-year-old reporter (Tintin) who, along with his dog and a cast of colorful and zany characters, travels around the globe in pursuit of mad scientists, spies, and saboteurs.

Two years were spent researching and drawing the seven hundred illustrations in each issue. These pictures vary in size, shape, and perspective, and run as many as fifteen panels to a page. This layout, with its minute detail and run-on dialogue, inhibits the child from understanding the book by merely looking at the pictures, as he can with most comics. To be understood, *Tintin* must be read— and that is the key for parents and teachers who care about reading. Each issue contains 8,000 words. The beautiful part of it is that children are unaware they are reading 8,000 words. They are reading for the fun of it—the important first step toward all other kinds of reading.

I am not recommending comic books as a steady diet for reading aloud but as an introduction to the comic format. Young children must be shown how a comic "works": the sequence of the panels; how to tell when a character is thinking and when he is speaking; the meaning of stars, question marks, and exclamation points. A comic can be viewed as an interesting sequential diagram of con-versation—a language blueprint. Once the blueprint is understood, the child will be ready and willing to follow it on his own without your reading it aloud.

Parents and teachers who provide a wide variety of reading materials for the child need not fear that the child or class will develop a "comic-book mentality." A recent study showed that more top students (nearly 100 percent) in all grades, read comics or comic books than did lower-ranking students.[35]

4. The Dos and Don'ts of Read-Aloud

Writing begins long before the marriage of pencils and paper. It begins with sounds, that is to say with words and simple clusters of words that are taken in by small children until they find themselves living in a world of vocables. If that world is rich and exciting, the transition to handling it in a new medium—writing—is made smoother. The first and conceivably the most important instructor in composition is the teacher, parent, or older sibling who reads aloud to the small child.

—Clifton Fadiman, from *Empty Pages: A Search for Writing
Competence in School and Society*

Dos

- Begin reading to children as soon as possible. The younger you start them, the better.
- Use Mother Goose rhymes and songs to stimulate the infant's language and listening. Simple but boldly colored picture books arouse children's curiosity and visual sense.
- Read as often as you and the child (or class) have time for.
- Try to set aside at least one traditional time each day for a story. In my home, favorite story times are before going to bed and before leaving for school.

- Remember that the art of listening is an acquired one. It must be taught and cultivated gradually—it doesn't happen overnight.
- Picture books can be read easily to a family of children widely separated in age. Novels, however, pose a problem. If there are more than two years between the children, each child would benefit greatly if you read to him or her individually. This requires more effort on the part of the parents but it will reap rewards in direct proportion to the effort expended. You will reinforce the specialness of each child.
- Start with picture books, and build to storybooks and novels.
- Vary the length and subject matter of your readings.
- Follow through with your reading. If you start a book, it is your responsibility to continue it—unless it turns out to be a bad book. Don't leave the child or class hanging for three or four days between chapters and expect their interest to be sustained.
- Occasionally read above the children's intellectual level and challenge their minds.
- Avoid long descriptive passages until the child's imagination and attention span are capable of handling them. There is nothing wrong with shortening or eliminating them. Pre-reading helps to locate such passages and they can then be marked with a pencil in the margin.
- If your chapters are long or if you don't have enough time each day to finish an entire chapter, find a suspenseful spot at which to stop. Leave the audience hanging; they'll be counting the minutes until the next reading.
- Allow your listeners a few minutes to settle down and adjust their feet and minds to the story. If it's a novel, you might begin by asking if anyone remembers what happened when you left off yesterday. Mood is an important factor in listening. An authoritarian "Now stop that and settle down! Sit up straight. Pay attention" is not conducive to a receptive audience.
- If you are reading a picture book, make sure the children can see the pictures easily. In class, with the children in a semicircle around you, seat yourself just slightly above them so that the

children in the back row can see the pictures above the heads of the others.

- In reading a novel, position yourself where both you and the children are comfortable. In the classroom, whether you are sitting on the edge of your desk or standing, your head should be above the heads of your listeners for your voice to carry to the far side of the room. Do not sit at your desk and read or stand in front of brightly lit windows, which strains the eyes of your audience.
- Remember that even sixth-grade students love a good picture book now and then.
- Allow time for class and home discussion after reading a story. Thoughts, hopes, fears, and discoveries are aroused by a book. Allow them to surface and help the child to deal with them through verbal, written, or artistic expression if the child is so inclined. Do not turn discussions into quizzes or insist upon prying story interpretations from the child.
- Remember that reading aloud comes naturally to very few people. To do it successfully and with ease you must practice.
- Use plenty of expression when reading. If possible, change your tone of voice to fit the dialogue.
- Adjust your pace to fit the story. During a suspenseful part, slow down, draw your words out, bring your listeners to the edge of their chairs.
- The most common mistake in reading aloud—whether the reader is a seven-year-old or a forty-year-old—is reading too fast. Read slowly enough for the child to build mental pictures of what he just heard you read. Slow down enough for the children to see the pictures in the book without feeling hurried. Reading quickly allows no time for the reader to use vocal expression.
- Preview the book by reading it to yourself ahead of time. Such advance reading allows you to spot material you may wish to shorten, eliminate, or elaborate on.
- Bring the author to life, as well as his book. Consult *Something About the Author* at the library, and read the information on your book's dust jacket. Either before or during the reading, tell your audience something about the author. Let them know

that books are written by people, not by machines. You also can accomplish this by encouraging individual children (not the class collectively—authors hate assembly-line mail) to write and share feelings about the book with the author. *Something About the Author* will provide an address, or you can write care of the publisher. It is important to enclose a self-addressed, stamped envelope *just in case* the author has time to respond. The child should understand from the start that his letter's purpose is not to receive a response.

• Add a third dimension to the book whenever possible. For example: have a bowl of blueberries ready to be eaten during or after the reading of Robert McCloskey's *Blueberries for Sal;* bring a harmonica and a lemon to class before reading McCloskey's *Lentil;* buy a plastic cowboy and Indian for when you read *The Indian in the Cupboard,* by Lynn Reid Banks.

• When children are old enough to distinguish between library books and their own, start reading with a pencil in hand. When you and the child encounter a passage worth remembering, put a small mark—maybe a star—in the margin. Readers should interact with books and one way is to acknowledge beautiful writing.

• Reluctant readers or unusually active children frequently find it difficult to just sit and listen. Paper, crayons, and pencils allow them to keep their hands busy while listening.

• Follow the suggestion of Dr. Caroline Bauer and post a reminder sign by your door: "Don't Forget Your *Flood* Book." Analogous to emergency rations in case of natural disasters, these books should be taken along in the car, or even stored like spares in the trunk. A few chapters from "flood" books can be squeezed into traffic jams on the way to the beach or long waits at the dentist's office.

• Fathers should make an extra effort to read to their children. Because 98 percent of primary-school teachers are women, young boys often associate reading with women and schoolwork. And just as unfortunately, too many fathers would rather be seen playing catch in the driveway with their sons than taking them to the library. It is not by chance that most of the students in remedial-reading classes are boys. A father's early involvement with books and reading can do much to elevate books to at least the same status as baseball gloves and hockey sticks in a boy's estimation.

- Regulate the amount of time your children spend in front of the television. Excessive television viewing is habit-forming and damaging to a child's development.
- Arrange for time each day—in the classroom or in the home—for the child to read by himself (even if "read" only means turning pages and looking at the pictures). All your read-aloud motivation goes for naught if the time is not available to put it into practice.
- Lead by example. Make sure your children see you reading for pleasure other than at read-aloud time. Share with them your enthusiasm for whatever you are reading.

Don'ts

- Don't read stories that you don't enjoy yourself. Your dislike will show in the reading, and that defeats your purpose.
- Don't continue reading a book once it is obvious that it was a poor choice. Admit the mistake and choose another. Make sure, however, that you've given the book a fair chance to get rolling; some start slower than others. (You can avoid the problem by prereading the book yourself.)
- If you are a teacher, don't feel you have to tie every book to classwork. Don't confine the broad spectrum of literature to the narrow limits of the curriculum.
- Consider the intellectual, social, and emotional level of your audience in making a read-aloud selection. Challenge them, but don't overwhelm them.
- Don't read above a child's emotional level.
- Don't select a book that many of the children already have heard or seen on television. Once a novel's plot is known, much of their interest is lost. You can, however, read a

book ahead of its appearance on television or at the movies. Afterwards, encourage the children to see the movie. It's a good way for them to see how much more can be portrayed in print than on the screen.

- Don't be fooled by awards. Just because a book won an award doesn't guarantee that it will make a good read-aloud. In most cases, a book award is given for the quality of the writing, not for its read-aloud qualities.
- Don't start a reading if you are not going to have enough time to do it justice. Having to stop after one or two pages only serves to frustrate, rather than stimulate, the child's interest in reading.
- Don't get too comfortable while reading. A reclining position is bound to bring on drowsiness, and a slouching position produces similar effects because the lungs can't easily fill to capacity.
- Don't be unnerved by questions during the reading, particularly from very young children. Answer their questions patiently. Don't put them off. Don't rush your answers. There is no time limit for reading a book but there is a time limit on a child's inquisitiveness. Foster that curiosity with patient answers—then resume your reading.
- Don't impose interpretations of a story upon your audience. A story can be just plain enjoyable, no reason necessary. But encourage conversation about the reading. Only seven minutes out of 150 instructional minutes in the school day are spent on discussions between teacher and student.
- Don't confuse quantity with quality. Reading to your child for ten minutes, given your full attention and enthusiasm, may very well last longer in the child's mind than two hours of solitary television viewing.
- Don't use the book as a threat—"If you don't pick up your room, no story tonight!" As soon as your child or class sees that you've turned the book into a weapon, they'll change their attitude about books from positive to negative.
- Don't try to compete with television. If you say, "Which do you want, a story or TV?" they will usually choose the latter.

That is like saying to a nine-year-old, "Which do you want, vegetables or a donut?" Since *you* are the adult, *you* choose. "The television goes off at eight-thirty in this house. If you want a story before bed, that's fine. If not, that's fine, too. But no television after eight-thirty." But don't let books appear to be responsible for depriving the children of viewing time.

5. Read-Aloud Success Stories

"I have one of [Frank Packard's *Gray Seal*] novels put away in my basement, along with copies of about six Tom Swift books, and all of Edgar Rice Burroughs' *Tarzan* and *John Carter of Mars* books. Not a classic among them. And yet, if I am not part jungle hero, Martian adventurer, cohort of L. Frank Baum and friend to Tom Swift, I am nothing. Shakespeare was to come later, with his friend G. B. Shaw. But my love of them was nothing to the mad love I had for Tantor the elephant or Kala the Ape. Oh, keeper of the Gray Seal, where are you now that we need you?"

—Ray Bradbury

A magazine survey recently showed "word of mouth" to be the most important influence in women's shopping choices—over advertising, sales, and coupons.[1] Human nature is such that when we discover an otherwise unknown medicine, detergent, movie, or recipe, we feel compelled to share it with as many friends as possible. They, in turn, trust the message because it came from a friend. If reading is to survive as a meaningful part of this culture, it will need this same endorsement. Plato addressed this thousands of years ago when he said it is the responsibility of people who carry torches to hand them on. The death of a culture is imminent when the torchbearers stop passing their torches.

Therefore, the pleasure and success you experience with reading aloud must be shared with neighbors, relatives, and coworkers. This chapter addresses the variety of ways I've seen people share that success. And while these exciting parents and educators cannot be cloned, they *can* be imitated.

Since most parents will not have read *The Read-Aloud Handbook* or any other book on children's literature, teachers are their principal resource for information and enthusiasm. Share it by compiling short lists (long lists frighten working parents) that can be given to parents at parent conferences and before school vacations, and used for holiday shopping guides. Research shows us that 58 percent of parents rarely or never receive such tips on how they can be more involved in the learning process.[2]

Teachers compiling lists should be sure to make the distinction between those books read *by* the child and those intended for reading *to* the child, explaining briefly the differences between listening levels and reading levels—something few parents consider until it is brought to their attention. When you have students mesmerized by a book, you can be sure they are talking about it at home, too. Capitalize on that by letting parents know about the books by that author or related books (as I do in the Treasury). Such communications are all the more important as parent-teacher conferences grow rarer with both parents working.

For example, when Jane Boyer, a teacher in Harrisburg, Pennsylvania, experienced a phenomenal response from her twenty-two inner city kindergartners after reading *James and the Giant Peach,* she followed up with an enthusiastic three-page letter to each child's parents, sharing with them the reason why their children may have come home so excited about this book.

I can easily see the day when educators begin to tap present-day technology in order to reach stay-at-home parents—the ones who are anchored to their televisions. They'll be videotaping messages, read-aloud demonstrations, and samples of the child reading or reciting (or acting up), and sending the videos home to the parent.

In Springfield, Pennsylvania, the school district's Community Education Council sponsored a Read-Aloud Week and solicited parent tips on how to foster reading interest in the home. They then collected nearly 150 of these tips in a handy community booklet. (I was surprised by the creative and intelligent responses I found in it.)

Generally speaking, though, parents are very reluctant to pass along unsolicited suggestions to teachers, and this is unfortunate. Good teachers are honored, not threatened, by such well-intentioned suggestions. Conversely, the teacher who responds negatively to parents' ideas is probably a bad teacher, and therefore your involvement is even more necessary to encourage your child during the school years. Three-fourths of my children's elementary teachers did NOT read aloud. Therefore it behooved me to continue reading— and be more involved.

If it becomes apparent that your child's teacher is not reading aloud daily, you might consider either scheduling a conference or writing a note describing the benefits of your home read-aloud program, even listing some of your child's favorite titles. Suggest that a similar program might be a good idea for the classroom, that it develops listening comprehension, vocabulary, and positive attitudes toward the pleasures of reading and not just the skills of reading. And for documentation, obtain a copy of *Becoming a Nation of Readers* from the library and photocopy the title page, the commission members on page iii, and then pages 23 and 51, which state that reading aloud is the best activity, in school or out, to create readers. Emphasize that your note is not intended to interfere with the curriculum but to reinforce it. Unlike parents who are writing notes to teachers requesting permission to take a child out of school for vacations, shopping trips, and sports tournaments, you are writing to add something to learning instead of subtracting from it. Or devote one of the school's monthly PTA meetings to the topic of read-aloud and there you can clarify the need for it. Needless to say, if *Becoming a Nation of Readers* is so important that the California Superintendent of Public Instruction required every superintendent in the state to read it, then you'd better make sure your principal reads it.

I know parents who give their children a day off from school on their birthday (tell me what that tells the child). I would suggest a more positive approach, like the one used at the Waldorf School in Lexington, Massachusetts, where parents are encouraged to purchase a book for the school library on the occasion of their child's birthday. The program, which has brought hundreds of books to the school, is sponsored by the parents and faculty, with the librarian providing a list of recommended titles. Teachers in Dana Point, California, used a similar approach to defuse a classroom-birthday "competition" among parents: "We will no longer accept cupcakes or pizzas for your child's birthday but you *may* donate a book to our school library in his or her name."

Incidentally, a day-care or child-care program requires just as much—if not more—concern on your part. There are almost ten million children enrolled in such programs today—a sizable investment in tomorrow. We cannot afford just to assume that the care and feeding of our children's minds is being done every day. We must insure it with our involvement. Such local centers seldom have their own libraries and your initiative to begin one is critical.

Anything you can do as a parent or educator to heighten public awareness of reading is a plus—be it in large ways like Principal George Holland or small ones like Anne Marie Russo. In Sergeant Bluff, Iowa, Holland and fifty parents planned an "overnight read-in" that took place in the school's multipurpose room and hosted 194 (K–4) children with sleeping bags. Between 7:00 P.M. Friday and 7:00 A.M. Saturday, there was silent reading, storytelling, exercise, a snack, writing time, read-aloud, creative dramatic presentations by high school students, a closed-caption movie, "lights out," breakfast (cooked by parent volunteers), and more reading. The event proved so popular that succeeding ones focused on certain grade levels and were attended by nearly half the school.

When my friend Anne Marie Russo of Holy Cross School in Springfield, Massachusetts, saw how fascinated her kindergartners were with the book *My Teacher Sleeps at School,* by Leatie Weiss, she scheduled a classroom "sleep-over." On the appointed day, students came to school equipped with bathrobes, slippers, teddy bears, toothbrushes, and sleeping bags. Then they went through the usual sleep-over ritual—movie, snacks, a read-aloud book (*Ira Sleeps Over*), prayers, tooth brushing, and sleep before the buses arrived to end the day.

If we can find the wherewithal to work out intricate bus and class schedules to allow our student athletes to compete all over the state, we can also devote the same ingenuity to transporting children's *minds* to far-off places through the world of books—as media specialist Louise Sherman does at Anna Scott School (K–4) in Leonia, New Jersey.

Seeing the one-hour lunch period as ripe with opportunity, Sherman sent notes home to parents advising them that a thirty-minute storytime would be offered to all interested children during lunch. Since then, volunteer readers (parents, teachers, principal, superintendent) read novels four times a week to about one hundred students who listen and eat lunch.

The program covers about ten novels a year, has significantly increased library circulation, and generates enthusiasm like this from the mother of a fourth-grade reluctant reader: "At first he didn't want to be in it. Now he can't wait to find out what's going to happen each day." Two special education teachers were inspired enough to begin a similar project with multiply handicapped students.[3]

Combating students' stereotypic view that all readers are women or teachers, many school systems (and individual teachers) are sponsoring guest-reader programs in which community leaders, parents, and volunteers visit classrooms to read-aloud to students and demonstrate that reading is for everyone, of every age, of every color, and from every walk of life. Here are three of the more comprehensive programs:

- In Anne Arundel County, Maryland (under Coordinator of Reading Dr. Joseph Czarnecki), 27,000 students were read to by 1,400 adults during the year, including Governor Harry Hughes (who read a chapter from *Dicey's Song,* by Maryland resident Cynthia Voight—also a guest reader), and sixty Naval Academy midshipmen (basketball star David Robinson among them). The program has been operating since 1985 and now includes 90 percent of the elementary schools (one of which has 100 guests a year) and four middle schools.
- The Garvey School District (covering Rosemead, Monterey Park, San Gabriel, and South San Gabriel, California) celebrates National Library Week with 265 guests reading to 7,000 (K–8) students. Garvey's student population includes a broad socioeconomic cross section representing Anglo, Latino, and

Asian primary languages. Begun in 1982, the guest-reader program has included celebrities likes singer Helen Reddy and local television anchors, highway patrolmen, paramedics, doctors, dentists, nurses, professors, company presidents, and alumni.

- In my home city, Springfield, Massachusetts, an urban community of 160,000, the 9,300 (K–4) students are read to three times between September and November by 350 guest readers. Because the project has generated so much support from educators and readers since its beginning in 1986, Westvaco Envelope Division, a local business, has contributed $10,000 each year to fund promotion and coordination efforts, and the school system adds another $12,000 so that each of the 1,050 books can be given to the class by their guest reader. A thirty-six-page guide to the program is available by sending a self-addressed, stamped (for eight ounces) 9″ × 12″ envelope to: Springfield Read-Aloud Project, School Volunteers Office, Springfield Public Schools, 195 State Street, Springfield, MA 01103.

Unlike the complexities of district-wide events, guest-reader programs for an individual classroom are comparatively easy. Ann Taylor of West Chester, Pennsylvania, had the mayor, superintendent, reporters, custodian, nurse, social worker, and her husband read to her second-graders. Caution: An important part of volunteer efforts is the preparation of the guest reader and the selection of books to be read. Don't leave it up to the reader! In Ashland, Wisconsin, they are still talking about the reader program where the principal of one elementary school didn't show up at his allotted time and when he did arrive, he passed out skill sheets and read from the Wisconsin Blue Book about the state seal and symbols. How's that for creating lifetime readers!

But many principals are doing sterling work to encourage reading. For example:

- Principal David Ivnik and his faculty chose pages and miles in challenging the 330 students at Maercker School (Gr. 3–5) in Westmont, Illinois, "to read to the moon and back!" That meant they would have to read at least 480,000 pages outside school. Motivated by the two fifteen-minute read-aloud and SSR periods scheduled daily, students finished 1988 with 750,000 pages (2,200 pages per child). In addition, 142 families participated in a family reading program, discipline problems and remedial reading referrals were down in spite of increasing enrollment, and the school's reading scores are all above average, with most at the highest level. Ivnik reads aloud to every class, and the faculty's lunch conversations are often about children's books.

- Boulder Elementary School library (450 students) in Montgomery, Illinois, circulates eighty books a day. The reason can be found in the directive Principal Jerald Tollefson gives to his teachers each fall: "I believe children need to be read to every day and given time to practice whole reading (SSR). These two things should take place every day without fail. Yes, even if it means a basal reading story hasn't been done, vocabulary words not finished, and a workbook page must be skipped." Willing to lead by example, Tollefson spends sixty hours a year reading aloud to his students, beginning the year with daily readings to the fifth grade from *The Cay,* by Theodore Taylor. Completing that, he shifts to the fourth grade and begins another novel with them. In addition, his librarian reads an average of six novels a year to her "lunchtime listeners."
- Long an advocate for students being read to daily at Seth Plaine Elementary (Illinois), Principal Jim Giordano was continually dismayed by the number of incoming kindergartners who had never been read to. "Education will have to start earlier than kindergarten," he reasoned, "and it must begin with new parents." He created the Johnny Appleread Program that gives all new parents in his school district a book on reading aloud, compliments of the PTAs for School District 95, two local bookstores, and the local hospital.

Until recently, maternity ward programs to promote reading among new parents have largely been left to libraries. But now many state and local councils of the International Reading Association are joining that effort. The ultimate model for such efforts can be found in Beginning with Books, a Carnegie Library–affiliated program in Pittsburgh, Pennsylvania, that was begun in 1984 by Drs. Joan Friedberg and Elizabeth Segel. Working through the Well Baby Clinics of Allegheny County, the project gives three children's books (*Goodnight Moon, 500 Words to Grow On,* and *Peter's Chair*) to child and parent, a coupon for *Mother Goose* that can be redeemed at a local library, and information on the importance of reading and the role of the library. In addition, interns visit clinic waiting rooms weekly to share stories with families.[4]

Of course, volunteers for such programs are often hard to come by. Far more available but often overlooked are siblings and peers as readers-aloud—that is, brothers, sisters, babysitters, and older students in the school. After his exhaustive study of American education (*A Place Called School*), John Goodlad commented: "One of the blind spots in American schooling is our almost complete failure to use peer teaching. In British schools you see children helping each other. The teacher has twenty-five assistants, so when a child comes in, a couple of other children take that child over, just as older brothers and sisters in big families do."[5] Indeed, in forty-five of fifty-two studies, students who were tutored by older students outperformed those in comparison groups, with significant improvements in student attitudes.[6]

The reading department in the Pittston Area Schools in Pennsylvania recognized the advantages of peer learning and started the PAC-Readers program in 1983 (PAC-Reader stands for Pittston-Area-Capable-Reader). Fifth- and sixth-grade student volunteers began reading aloud to first- and second-grade classrooms during the preschool breakfast time. After being trained in reading aloud, discussing an appropriate book choice with a teacher, and rehearsing the book (with a teacher or aide), the PAC-Reader introduces himself and his book to the first grade, says a few words about the author, and begins reading aloud.

"The response was unbelievable," explains Principal Ross Scarantino. "We initially thought the sixth-grade boys might feel too sophisticated to go into the lower grades, but were we ever wrong! Boys have been volunteering as often as girls," he notes. Listener reaction has been just as positive. "The appearance of that excited fifth-grader with a book in hand says more to that first-grade beginning reader than the teacher could say in an entire week." The volunteer visits are biweekly, thus allowing adequate preparation time. When I visited the community in 1986, parents told me their first-grade beginning readers could often be heard in their bedrooms, imitating their PAC-Readers: "Good morning," they would say to a teddy bear or sibling, "My name is Bobby Snyder and I'm your PAC-Reader and today I'm going to read . . ."

Parents can use the Pittston idea by encouraging older siblings to read to younger ones when you are busy. Reading aloud should also be included among the tasks of every babysitter. (Make sure you provide the appropriate books.) Why not get your money's worth from the sitter? Watching TV is hardly worth the cost of babysitting today.

The far-flung influence of a dedicated individual is seen in a state-wide project called READ-ALOUD Delaware, founded there by State Representative Kevin W. Free in 1984. A native of New Zealand, Free remembered the achievements of that country's Plunkett Society, a health-maintenance organization working with parents to meet the physical needs of young children, and he wondered if the same principles couldn't be applied to the intellectual needs of the child.

Why not start a kind of Plunkett Society for the minds of young children in the state of Delaware? Representative Free believed that the best start for the mind is to be read to. Within months of conceiving the idea, he founded READ-ALOUD Delaware, a nonprofit corporation to ensure that every preschool child in the state has someone to read to him or her. The program now has a full-time executive director and full-time coordinators in three counties, is funded annually by the state board of education for $111,000, and is supported by numerous Delaware foundation grants.[7]

Every Delaware newborn and parent receives a Mother Goose book (Scott Paper grant), along with a booklet, "Reading Begins with You" (Gannett Foundation), that explains the importance of reading aloud. Recruiting from local libraries, day-care centers, Scout groups, and Red Cross classes, the organization has collected hundreds of volunteers willing to read to children who otherwise might not have a reader within the family. They do this in neighborhood health clinics where a parent and child are waiting for pediatric help, demonstrating the interaction between reader, child, and book—pointing to pictures, turning pages, asking and answering questions.

Concerned with the shameful tide of illiteracy in West Virginia, Mary Kay Bond and thirty community women (mostly mothers like Mary Kay) took heart from Delaware's example and formed READ-ALOUD West Virginia in 1986. With illiteracy woes and state dimensions far surpassing Delaware's, the West Virginia group is not yet state-wide. Nonetheless, they already provide books and material to new families, supply speakers for prenatal classes, PTAs, and civic groups, and send regular guest readers to fifty schools.[8]

Becky Frischkorn is one of those founding mother-members of the West Virginia group, as well as a landscape architect and community activist. These are her reactions to her first guest-reader visit:

"I was assigned to an elementary school in the far reaches of Kanawha County where the unemployment rate is above 80 percent and illiteracy rates top 40 percent. An hour with all the fourth-, fifth-, and sixth-graders, and forty-five minutes with the learning-disabled and first, second, and third grades. 'Just make sure they all fall in love with reading, okay?' Sure!

"So I found myself in a freezing gymnasium with thirty kids, bundled in jackets, staring up at me as if to say, 'What can this foreigner do to put on a show for us? All *we* want is for school to be over.' A tough group. These kids may have fancy television sets in their homes but little chance of a book being found there. So what did I do? I began by warning them that my son had looked at me with scorn that morning when I told him what I was going to read to them. 'Oh, Mum, what if you start crying like you did when you read it to me?' That got their attention.

"So I read them *Stone Fox,* by John Reynolds Gardiner, and their eyes widened with rapt attention, the feigned defiance dropped away, and they were with me all the way to the climax. At which point, I looked up, my eyes brimming, to discover at least ten of the kids and two of the teachers on the edge of tears also. And then, as the children crowded around to thank me for the story, a little girl came up, looked at me pleadingly and asked, 'Can you teach my brother to read?'

" 'Perhaps,' I replied. 'How old is he?'

" 'Twenty-three,' she answered.

"So, after the necessary transfer of information, I found myself with not one but two new projects. Not only am I now a devoted friend and reader at this school, with a mind full of ideas of how we can change the status quo in this community, but I am also a liaison between a literacy volunteer and a very needy twenty-three-year-old. Why, oh, why can't I take on a project and just do it halfway? Why can't I just go to a school, give them an entertaining afternoon, and be done with it? Because the read-aloud idea is the most compelling project imaginable and I am convinced we can change this impoverished state."

There *are* places that thrive on books and the excitement of reading. If yours is not one of those classes, schools, or communities, ask yourself, Why? And then, Why not? I've personally met most of the people I've written about here and please be assured, only one or two of them would I label "genius" and most are not in affluent situations. These are quite average people—until you look at their extraordinary dedication, leadership ability, and willingness to pursue dreams that others label "impossible" before they have even tried.

6. Home and Public Libraries

The library is not a shrine for the worship of books. It is not a temple where literary incense must be burned. . . . A library, to modify the famous metaphor of Socrates, should be the delivery room for the birth of ideas.

—Norman Cousins,
ALA *Bulletin* (October 1954)

Long before children are introduced to their neighborhood public library, books should be a part of their lives. Begin a home library as soon as the child is born. If you can provide shelving in the child's room for such books, all the better. The sooner children become accustomed to the sight of the covers, bindings, and pages of books, the sooner they will begin to develop the concept that books are a part of daily life.

Admittedly, we were late in starting our home library for Elizabeth, our first child. Public library books were heavily relied upon until she was about four years old—the time when her younger brother, Jamie, was born. Since we had begun to see the positive effects of reading aloud to Elizabeth, my wife and I decided at that point to begin the children's home library. We had no idea, of course, that this library would eventually serve not only the children but their parents as well. Within a few years of Jamie's birth, Susan took a teaching degree in elementary education and used the books every day in her classes. It was the reaction of my own children and of those in my wife's classes to these books that first inspired me to write this handbook.

I'd like to make a few suggestions that may prove helpful to those beginning a home library, particularly if you have children under the age of four.

Divide your books into two categories: expensive and inexpensive. The higher-priced or fragile books should be placed up on shelves out of the reach of sticky fingers, dribbles, and errant crayons. While out of reach, they should still be within sight—as a kind of goal. On lower shelves and within easy reach should be the less expensive and, if possible, more durable books. If the replacement price is low enough, you'll have fewer qualms about the child "playing" with the books. This "playing" is an important factor in a child's attachment to books. He must have ample opportunity to feel them, taste them, and see them.

Where space allows (and this goes for school and public libraries as well), have your home library books positioned on the shelf with the cover facing out. Decades ago, paperback publishers discovered the impact covers have on reading selection. When the cover can be seen, it stimulates the child's curiosity, causing him to wonder what is happening in both the picture and the book. Long before he could read and even as a beginning reader, Jamie used to lie in bed in the morning, gaze at the books on his shelf, and daydream "what the book was about."

I was reminded of those days when I received a letter from Dr. Charles Allen Holt. Someone had told me of this young osteopath who preached the doctrine of read-aloud to the undereducated, poor parents he met during his internship at Cardinal Glennon Memorial Hospital for Children in St. Louis. Curious about his background, I wrote and asked if he could spare a minute during his rounds to tell me how he came to be a reader and a proponent of reading aloud.

He told me that during his childhood in Jefferson City, Missouri, his parents read to him all the time, that television viewing was controlled in his home, and that books were available even before he could read. Dr. Holt also explained, "I remember my (school-teacher) mother placing a *World Book Encyclopedia* on the floor in front of me to peruse in my leisure hours. By the time I was in kindergarten, I could find something within one minute in the encyclopedia on any topic you could suggest."

Reading that sentence set off bells in my memory bank as I recalled sitting through long hours of my own childhood in the 1940s with volumes of our encyclopedia in my lap, studying the picture pages from A to Z. (My brothers and I were fascinated with the circulatory system in the anatomy section and the photos from the early stages of World War II.) Knowing now that visual literacy precedes print literacy, it comes as no surprise that while I can't recall any of the print from those volumes, I can close my eyes and see the pictures from those pages vividly. Moreover, they helped me feel comfortable with books, letting me overcome any negative feelings brought on later by workbooks and watered-down texts. And in that formative stage, the stimulation of curiosity by those pictures eventually set the stage for reading and writing.

While an encyclopedia is an excellent family investment, at $500 it is not inexpensive. While you are saving for one, you might consider as a short-term and immediate substitute these four excellent picture-book reference volumes relating to areas about which children of all ages are curious: *Do Animals Dream,* by Joyce Pope; *How the Human Body Works* and *Life Through the Ages,* both by Giovanni Caselli; and *The Kids' Question and Answer Book,* by the editors of *Owl* magazine. At a total cost of approximately fifty dollars, these books will give a child thousands of hours' worth of stimulation, information, and entertainment both before and after he learns to read. (Details on these four books can be found in the Picture Book section of the Treasury.)

As I noted earlier, until about two years of age your child's reading interest is usually better served by a few books that he sees and hears regularly than by dozens and dozens with which he never develops a working familiarity. However, as his attention span and interests grow, that home library should expand as your family allowances permit. "Immediate availability" is a major factor cited in studies of children who learn to read without great difficulty.[1] Harvard's Jeanne Chall points to the lack of a home library as a critical factor in the reading gap between low-income and middle-class children. Her research showed these two groups were on the same reading level in second grade but by fourth grade the gap appeared, largely because the low-income children "do not have enough books on which to practice." (Chall referred to trade books, not textbooks.)[2]

One study found that children in schools with in-class libraries (as opposed to one library serving the entire school) read up to 50 percent more books.[3] Richard Anderson's classroom research prompted him to call for a "virtual book flood," that is, a thoughtfully constructed classroom library of paperback trade books introduced by an interested and motivated teacher—if we sincerely wish to raise a nation of readers.[4] Expensive? Yes, but not as expensive as a nation that doesn't read or write.

A living example of this approach to reading is my friend Kathy Nozzolillo's room at White Street School in Springfield, Massachusetts. Working each year with the bottom fourth-grade reading group, Kathy sees her immediate goal as dismantling the frightening barriers these urban children have erected between themselves and books—to turn books into friends, not enemies.

Kathy reasons that her classroom is like an orchestra—it can't function without a conductor. As such, she reads aloud three times a day (picture books and novels), drawing from the 450 volumes in her classroom library. Reading enthusiasm begins with her and spreads to the students. She knows her books as well as her class and quickly connects the right book with the right child. SSR is offered throughout the day.

Yes, she uses the required basal and skill sheets—but they exist to support real books, not the other way around. Each May she borrows two hundred of my best picture books for her students to read during the last month of school—no basals, no skill sheets. (She could also borrow from the library.) They just talk books, keep journals, and compare authors and illustrators. And by year's end, despite the IQ differences, her "bottom" reading group's scores are as high as those of the school's top group.

What prevents that from happening in all classrooms? Generally speaking, it's not money or equipment, it is ignorance on the part of educators who don't read the research.

Here are some ideas I found helpful in building my home library, especially in those areas most challenging to struggling young parents and teachers: cost, where to buy the books, and which books to buy. (These same ideas also work for librarians and grandparents on tight budgets.)

Twenty years ago, most of the books in my family library were bought secondhand at garage sales, the Salvation Army thrift shop, and used bookstores. As a result, I think my children were nearly ten years old before they realized not all books came with scribble marks and strange names crayoned inside the covers. Given the choice, I guess we all prefer the qualities of a brand-new book—its bright, crisp pages, its clean smell. But struggling young families and teachers don't always have the money. If it's any consolation, barring damage, one reads as well as the other but costs one-tenth as much.

Over the years, we never visited a new city or town without checking the Yellow Pages for secondhand bookstores, goldmines for book-shopping parents and teachers. Indeed, I shopped in the secondhand department of Johnson's Bookstore (in Springfield, Massachusetts) so often that many of the customers, and even some of the employees, thought I worked there. I recall John Updike's analogy in which he compared bookstores to the vacant lots through which he romped and fantasized in his childhood. "Bookstores should feel, I think, like vacant lots—places where the demands on us are our own demands, where the spirit can find exercise in unsupervised play."[5] Libraries, I might add, should fill a similar need.

In justifying the money you spend on books, compare inflation within the book industry with the rise in price for a movie or dinner. Moreover, the day after that movie or dinner, all you have left is the memory. With a book, you have both the memory and the book in hand—which can be enjoyed again and again at no extra cost. And the paperback revolution in publishing provides a further savings for home libraries. Unlike a decade ago when a handful of publishers controlled the children's paperback industry and only the sure-sellers (and relatively few picture books) made it into paperback, today nearly all the hardcover publishers are producing softcover editions at half the cover price of hardcovers. That, in turn, allows bookstores to stock more children's titles and greatly improves the quality of choices.

Most schools today subscribe to one of several young people's paperback book clubs. These clubs offer nearly forty monthly selections at half price. The paperback your child pays $1.50 for in class will cost $3.00 in the bookstore and $9.95 in hardcover. Encourage your child's school to belong to one of these clubs and look over the selection sheets each month. By adding your choices for the family library to the child's selections, you'll be saving a considerable amount as well as showing the child your interest in books.

The question of durability frequently arises in discussing paperbacks. If the book is to be used only as a read-aloud by a teacher or parent, then this is not a problem. But if it is going to be handled by a family of children or circulated through a classroom, its durability becomes important. My own solution, and one which has had considerable testing, is to protect the paperback with clear plastic self-sticking shelf paper, which can be bought in your local supermarket or discount department store.

Measure the cover beforehand to allow an overlap of several inches, cut the laminate, and adhere it to the cover of the paperback in the same manner you use to cover school books. For good measure, cut a pair of two-inch-wide strips for where the cover and pages meet at the spine (front and back). For classroom or home, these procedures lengthen the life of the book, and they also protect the cover from peanut butter and cocoa stains.

Another way for parents, teachers, and school librarians to cut costs is to compile a wish list of books you would like to have. In families, this is given to grandparents or other relatives who prefer to give long-lasting gifts like books but need title suggestions. And schools should make their lists available to parents several times a year through the principal's newsletter, PTA meetings, and open house programs.

Parents who are looking for the best literary bargain available should consider a subscription to *Cricket: The Magazine for Children*. Geared for children between ages three and twelve, *Cricket*'s monthly offering includes more than twenty stories and features from many of today's finest artists and writers, a potpourri of literature: poetry, fiction, nonfiction, humor, fables, mystery, and sports. The price of each issue represents a substantial savings for a family when you consider that many of its features have previously appeared in book form at five times the price of the magazine. If you haven't seen a copy, check the children's department of your local library or bookstore.

Magazines, in fact, are one of your best reading bargains, especially with teenagers, who seem to gravitate to them. (Essayist Fran Lebowitz once wrote that magazines most often lead to books and therefore should be regarded by the prudent as the heavy petting of literature.) I recall the mother who said to me, "I just don't know what to do with my thirteen-year-old. He hates to read."

When I asked what his interests were, she replied, "Sports." But when I suggested a subscription to a sports magazine, she said, "Oh, he already gets *Sports Illustrated*. He reads it cover to cover."

"Excuse me, but I thought you said he hates to read?" I inquired. The woman looked puzzled for a moment and responded, "Well, I didn't think *Sports Illustrated* counted." I quickly explained to her that it did count, that I had read (and saved) every issue of *Sports Illustrated* from the time I was thirteen until I was eighteen and that was where I first encountered Faulkner, Hemingway, and J. P. Marquand. "A literate person," I said, "reads *everything*. It would help, of course, if occasionally *you* read *Sports Illustrated*."

If America reads anything, it is magazines. We publish four hundred new magazines a year, and yet one is hard-pressed to find them in the curriculum. I believe many of the same skills we teach with textbooks could be taught with magazines—perhaps more effectively. For example, there are more than one hundred automobile magazines, three of which have a total circulation of more than two million. Don't tell me those junior and senior high school remedial students wouldn't do their homework if it were assigned in *Car and Driver*. Someone in the high school English department should chase down the April 25, 1988, issue of *Sports Illustrated* and read the cover story profiling the sad history of Muhammad Ali's entourage. I'll bet the languages and sentences are richer, more interesting, and do more to stimulate reading interest than much of what you have in the classroom text. Not only is it riveting in its portrayal of the human condition, it should be required reading for every high school and college athlete in America.

~*What* children read is less important than the fact *that* they read. If we know magazines can reach certain students better than textbooks, capitalize on that approach. In a New York literacy project, forty-two illiterate men who wanted to qualify for an exterminator's license were taught with the exterminating manual instead of a textbook. Not only were there no dropouts; they all learned to read well enough to pass the exam and most opted to continue their reading instruction.

How should you decide which books to buy? This handbook, with its list of read-alouds, should solve at least part of that problem. You'll also find that neighbors, friends, librarians, and teachers who read aloud are eager to share the names of their favorites.

If your child's teacher reads aloud, she probably has a long list of choices she can't possibly get to in the course of the year. At your next parent-teacher conference, ask her for some recommendations. She may even have one she thinks is particularly suitable for your child.

If you are fortunate enough to have a bookstore that specializes in children's books in your community (or a general bookstore that gives more than cursory attention to children), by all means tap them as a resource. Many have free newsletters to keep you abreast of new children's books.

Most libraries have a variety of outstanding and inspiring resource books on children's literature, books like Beverly Kobrin's *Eyeopeners!* and Bernice Cullinan's *Literature and the Child,* two comprehensive collections of specific teaching ideas and activities centered on hundreds of wonderful children's books.

In addition, your neighborhood library subscribes to several journals that regularly review new children's titles, including *The Horn Book, Kirkus Reviews, Booklist,* and *School Library Journal.* These will give you an idea of what's new, good and bad, in children's publishing. For the average parent or classroom teacher subscriber, though, *The Horn Book* is the most practical resource for your money.

Additionally, there are several inexpensive newsletters on children's books:

- Published each fall, winter, and spring, T'N'T (*Tips and Titles of Books for Grades K–6*) is a newsletter for busy parents and teachers, covering more than a hundred books each year. Written by Jan Lieberman, a former elementary teacher who understands children and their reading appetites, each issue covers a cross section of literature—old and new, fiction, nonfiction, and poetry—with creative tips on related activities. Subscribers are free to make copies for faculties and PTA groups at no extra charge. Send three self-addressed, stamped envelopes (legal size) with $1.00 in cash or stamps to: Jan Lieberman, *T'N'T,* Division of Counseling Psychology and Education, Santa Clara University, Santa Clara, CA 95053.
- *The Web* (*Wonderfully Exciting Books*), primarily aimed at teachers, is published quarterly out of the College of Education at Ohio State under the direction of Charlotte Huck and Janet Hickman, two leading authorities on children's literature and education. Subscribers should send a check or money order for $10.00 to: *The Web,* The Ohio State University, Room 200, Ramseyer Hall, 29 West Woodruff, Columbus, OH 43210.
- Largely unknown to parents and teachers but one of my favorite resources for new titles (books and audiocassettes) are the fall and spring Children's Book issues of *Publishers Weekly* magazine, which can be purchased individually without subscription. Each season's titles are listed with plot synopses, along with 150 pages of advertising from the major publishers promoting their top authors. In addition, there's a sneak preview of what's coming next season from each publisher. The issues must be requested separately each spring or fall by sending a check or money order for $5.00 to: Magazine Circulation Department, R. R. Bowker Co., 205 East 42nd Street, New York, NY 10017.
- Several year-end lists of the best of each year's children's books are available. "Children's Books (year)" is published by the Library of Congress and covers preschool through junior high. It is available for $1.00 from the Superintendent of Documents, U.S. Government Printing Office, Washington, D.C. 20402 (Library of Congress Catalog Card Number 65–60015).

- The American Library Association's "Notable Children's Books (year)" is available for fifty cents (and a self-addressed, stamped envelope) from: American Library Association, ALSC, 50 East Huron Street, Chicago, IL 60611.
- The Cooperative Children's Book Center (CCBC) at the University of Wisconsin–Madison is a unique state-funded center for the study of children's and young adult literature. Its "CCBC Choices (year)" lists two hundred of the best in eighteen categories (preschool through young adult) and can be obtained by sending $4.00 to: CCBC Choices, P.O. Box 5288, Madison, WI 53705.
- Two of the most reliable booklists for what students not only *should* read but also *will* read are "Children's Choices" and "Young Adult Choices," compilations of 10,000 students' votes throughout the U.S. These are the books the kids like best from those nominated by educators. To obtain a free single copy of either list, send a self-addressed #10 (4¹/₂″ × 9³/₈″) envelope stamped with first-class postage for two ounces to: IRA, 800 Barksdale Road, P.O. Box 8139, Newark, DE 19714–8139 (separate envelopes for each list).

In your search for which books to buy for your home or classroom library and which books to read aloud to children, look to guidebooks, friends, teachers, librarians, and reviews. But always reserve the final decision for yourself. Only *you* know the level and interests of your children. Only you can appreciate their special needs and capacities.

Occasionally you will make a mistake. The book will be boring or too far above or below the child. The best thing to do in that case is to admit the mistake and go on to another book. But such mistakes will occur less frequently when you take the time to seek the advice of experts in the field.

As important and convenient as a home library is, it cannot replace a public library. The home library should act as an appetizer, stimulating the child's taste for the vast riches offered by the free public library. It is a town's or city's most important cultural and intellectual asset. Nevertheless, in this age of declining literacy and skyrocketing inflation, libraries face increasingly difficult times.

At a library trustees' meeting I attended, the chairman asked the library director, "What can be done to turn things around for library circulations?"

"Well," the director hedged for a moment, "a good Depression might help . . ."

There were chuckles around the table, but the truth of the statement was lost on none of us. It is only in hard times that we appreciate the community services we receive for free. America's free public library systems received unprecedented use during the Depression years when other forms of entertainment or enlightenment were too costly.

Dollar for dollar, the greatest bargain in America today is still the free public library system—yet less than 10 percent of the American people are regular patrons. I can't begin to estimate the number of times I've heard parents (rich and poor) say they'd like to bring their children to the library more often but there just isn't time. And to each of them I reply, "Would you estimate that you've taken your child to the shopping mall ten times more often than to the library or one hundred times more often?" What does this say to your child about your priorities in life? When Cabbage Patch dolls held center stage during the 1983 Christmas shopping season, I couldn't help but wonder whether those same dedicated parents would have driven as far, stood in line as long, or paid as much for a library card as they did for those dolls. It is a terrible indictment of our time and culture that the majority of those parents would *not* have been willing to make the same sacrifices for the library card. Saddest of all is the fact that those children's priorities inevitably will someday reflect those of their parents.

Some libraries are attempting to survive the cultural and economic pressures by shedding old habits in favor of new vigor and aggressive marketing. Sadly, not all libraries are able to do so; there are still some who don't have either the money, the community support, or the staff leadership to initiate such changes.

If, as a parent or teacher, you feel your local library is not adjusting to the times, protect your rights as a taxpayer and become involved. Join with your friends to form a "Friends of the Library" group which can, among other things, lobby local government or the library administration for positive change. In the majority of cases, however, it is not the staff but the community that needs prodding.

Libraries cannot afford to stand by and wring their hands over the decline in reading habits. If they are to survive they must:

1. Shed the image of "Marian the Librarian," who governs the stacks with a rule of silence, in favor of an image that shouts to the community, "Hey! Come on in—look what we've got for free!"

2. Sell the healthful advantages of its services to the community in much the same way we sell the United Way, Catholic Charities, United Jewish Appeal, and the March of Dimes.

3. Become competitive with television.

Here are some specific examples of how this approach works. The common denominator among these libraries is that they don't hide their light under a barrel. They are aggressive and creative in promoting themselves and their products.

Many good libraries live the philosophy that "the early bird catches the worm." In outstanding library systems (large and small) like Orlando, Florida; Harrisburg and Pittsburgh, Pennsylvania; Cuyahoga County, Ohio; and Decatur, Illinois, extraordinary efforts are being made to reach new parents. Using gift books, brochures, parent education programs, and videos, these programs are all aimed at promoting both library usage and community spirit. The best example I've found of this early approach is "Babies & Books: A Joyous Beginning," an outstanding parent/infant guide developed by the Baby Talk division of the Decatur Public Library, under a Title I grant, and the Illinois State Library. Copies are available at cost for $3.00 (prepaid) from: Rolling Prairie Library System, 345 West Eldorado Street, Decatur, IL 62522.

The early intervention trend is also seen in the increasing number of toddler story-hours sponsored by public libraries, including some that schedule them on Friday evenings when fathers can bring the child to the "bedtime" story hour.

The Baltimore County Public Library, worried about the disadvantaged families that never came to the library, created the

"Growing Day-by-Day" program that delivers and collects packages of books and records to the homes of day-care–affiliated parents who often lack transportation to libraries.

Innovative libraries provide registration tables at nursery and elementary schools in the first week of school to distribute library information and register parents and children for cards.

If you want to see what creativity can do to promote a library, check out the Sunday, August 28, 1988, edition of *The New York Times*. There you'll find three full pages promoting the New York Public Library's campaign for National Library Card Month. How could they afford the *Times*'s ad rates? They tied the campaign into Macy's back-to-school ads, allowing the New York department store to photograph its models at the library and offering Library Sweepstakes prizes to cardholders who present their cards in the children's department of Macy's. For those who feel such tactics are too commercial for their tastes, I suggest they count the number of people in their local video store at 7:30 P.M. next Friday and compare it with the number in the library.

The Indianapolis–Marion County Public Library made its Family Read-Aloud Month as commercially appealing as possible. Along with forty-three read-aloud events at their twenty-two libraries, they designed a 12″ × 18″ poster of a cutaway house that included sixteen different places for reading. For every fifteen minutes of family reading, a sticker was placed over one of those places. With the poster filled (four hours' worth of reading), it could be redeemed for a free pizza at any one of the local Noble Roman pizza shops.

Unwilling to knuckle under to the TV/video competition, many libraries are sponsoring "pull-the-plug" campaigns to heighten community awareness of television's pervasive and negative influence (see Chapter 7).

Library systems are beginning to realize what fast-food chains and billboard advertisers learned long ago: If you want business, you go where the people are. And the largest collection of people on any given day in any community in America will invariably be found in the shopping mall. With that in mind, a handful of pioneering libraries have opened branches in shopping malls. One such is the Clackamas County branch in the Town Center Mall in Milwaukie, Oregon. A deal struck by the county commissioners with the initial mall petitioners allows the library to rent space for a token one dollar a year. Nestled among the indoor ice rink and eighty stores, the branch is open seven days a week and has been circulating five hundred books a day since opening in 1982.

"We are not a reference library," explains Clackamas librarian Katharine Jorgensen. "We're set up like a bookstore—no Dewey Decimal System—and our stock in trade is paperbacks. Situated as we are, we've issued new cards to a remarkable number of former patrons who had lost the reading habit—including many tired husbands who come in now to relax and read." The three mall bookstores, instead of viewing the branch as a competitor, recognized it as a valuable partner in the reading business and donated shelving, display racks, and signs. The spinoff effect has been a marked increase in circulation within the two other Clackamas branches.

Reading is one area where the private and public sectors can and should join hands in cooperative ventures. When it is done right, in places like Wyoming County, New York, the results can be spectacular. In that northern New York county, Project Read was initiated in 1978 under the inspired leadership of Mrs. Mardi VanArsdale of Castile, New York, with the cooperation of principals, teachers, public and school librarians, reading specialists, United Way, the Departments of Social Services and Health, and parents.

Project Read's primary aim is to foster parental involvement with children's leisure reading. This is done on a long-term daily basis and can be summed up neatly by the phrase "family reading," that is, parents reading to children as well as parents and children reading to themselves. What has made Project Read so successful over the years is not its concept but its members' indefatigable efforts to market it: story hours in libraries and on local radio stations, booths at all school Open Houses and kindergarten registrations, workshops for parents taking court-mandated parenting courses, two booths staffed by hundreds of volunteers at the week-long County Fair where children's books are both sold and read aloud, along with thousands of school recognition awards to children whose families were involved in the program, and the compilation/distribution of recommended reading lists to guide both parent and child. That is dynamic leadership and promotion.

It is my firm opinion that most school systems are missing the boat in not cooperating more closely with the community library. The best communities are those where the library and schools work together, like Bensenville, Illinois, and Fairport, New York. The unhealthiest communities are those where school and library don't even talk. They need to follow the example of Kent County Library System and its sixteen school districts in the Grand Rapids, Michigan, area. Together they run the First-Grade Roundup, a program that brings all of the county's 4,500 first-graders to the library, registers each for a library card, and has local civic leaders present the card to the student as "their first proof of citizenship." The library feels that card should be as much a rite of passage for seven-year-olds as drivers' licenses are for sixteen-year-olds. In a follow-up study, Kent County found 50 percent of those first-graders were continuing to use their cards a year later. And that tells us that half the parents are doing their homework and the other half are not.

One day somebody at the Minneapolis Public Library stopped to think how much of the gross national product is dependent upon gift-giving. The toy industry markets toys as the perfect gift. Why don't libraries and bookstores market just as creatively? Conceding that many adults don't know the appropriate books for certain age groups, the Minneapolis library—as well as numerous other libraries—publishes pamphlets that list titles and synopses, grouped by age, for both book buying and borrowing.

Books make the perfect gift. Unlike toys, they are difficult to break. They're ready-made and powerful, but with no assembling or batteries needed. Portable and noiseless, they can be enjoyed anywhere, at any time of day, by any age group, and they take up less space than most toys. Unlike clothes, they never go out of style, nor do you have to worry over the child's size. And with the fourth-class book rate, they are cheaper to mail.

Why isn't THE BOOK being promoted the way we promote politicians, seat belts, and the dangers of smoking? What we need is an ongoing public awareness campaign—perhaps under the direction of the Library of Congress Center for the Book and financially supported by the American Booksellers Association, the American Library Association, and the International Reading Association. Their recent joint programs for The Year of the Reader and The Year of the Young Reader were well done but they were one-year efforts.

Reading is supposed to be a lifetime experience, so why not full-time efforts?

In films, when Paul Newman picks up a can of Bud Light, Sylvester Stallone reaches for Wheaties, or E.T. nibbles Reese's Pieces, each of these moves is carefully orchestrated by producers who are paid handsomely for product placements like these. We need a major effort from the book world to coordinate with the networks and Hollywood studios to make books and reading more visible on entertainment screens, just the way the assistant dean of the Harvard School of Public Health convinced the networks and studios in 1988 to coordinate a public service attack on drunk driving through the dialogues on popular shows.

If we can get reports out of Camp David about what movie the President and First Lady saw, why not what they've been reading? This would at least counterbalance statements like that of then-governor Arch Moore of West Virginia who told teachers they could avoid the negative aspects of this world if they didn't read so much.[6]

So far, the best commercial television show[7] on the subject of reading, "Drop Everything and Read," came not from librarians, educators, or booksellers but from Westinghouse Broadcasting's KDKA studios in Pittsburgh, conceived, written, and produced by someone within the *television* industry. *That* is a sad commentary on the ingenuity and energies of the American Booksellers Association, the American Library Association, the Library of Congress, and the International Reading Association—each of whom could have and should have produced a show like it ten years ago.

Two potentially valuable links in the family-reading-library connection are churches and pediatricians. Churches have a proud history of support for family reading. Unfortunately, it is largely *ancient* history, going back to Colonial America when church elders regularly inspected homes and businesses to ensure that children and servants were being taught to read. Since church theology held that only those who read the Bible could be saved, those who denied that opportunity would be held accountable.[8]

In a strange turn of events, today's reading connection with churches seems to be more negative than positive, with churches often focused on the banning of books. Indeed, organized religion could be doing a whole lot more with literacy. Family is still the centerpiece in most congregations, and since few experiences tighten family ties and strengthen the minds of future generations the way reading does, why is the subject addressed so seldom in the nation's pulpits? In much the same way that black churches have stepped in to repair the damage to black family life in the wake of desertions, teenage parenthood, and economic despair, so too can American clergy attempt to repair the ravages of illiteracy and aliteracy. Librarians and educators must work together to provide materials and reminders so that a year doesn't pass without clergy reminding parents of the importance of reading aloud within the family, the ease of obtaining a library card, and the dangers of too many hours in front of the television.

Urban clergy might also remind their parishioners that in the midst of drug abuse and moral decline, the library can be a physical as well as an intellectual haven. In that respect, things haven't changed a great deal since writer Pete Hamill grew up in a working-class section of Brooklyn during the forties, surrounded by mobster hitmen, youth gangs, homeless rummies, deranged vets still fighting old wars, cops on the take, and brawling dock workers. "As a boy," he recalls, "I was afraid of them, a condition that went beyond the normal fears of childhood. But I knew one thing: none of them ever came to the library. So, in one important way, the library was a fortified oasis." Impoverished parishioners should be read parts of Hamill's essay[9] that describes being one of seven children in a poor family: "The library allowed me to borrow the first beautiful things I ever took home. When I was not reading them, I would place them on tables, on the mantelpiece, against a window, just to be able to see them, to turn from dinner and glance at them in the next room. I hated to bring them back, and often borrowed some books three or four times a year, just to have them around."

With the deterioration of the extended American family, pediatricians (along with the churches) are a prime resource for teaching the business of parenting, providing the common sense formerly passed along by grandparents. Almost everyone brings a child to a pediatrician. As new parents, my wife and I didn't see the pediatrician's words as suggestions or even recommendations. As far as we were concerned, his words were carved in stone and handed down from the mountain. In the eyes of new parents, a pediatrician is the closest you can come to God on earth. Imagine, therefore, the impact they could have on a nation's literacy if their message reinforced that of clergy, educator, and librarian: that is, the need for parents to read to their child and control family television-viewing. Pediatricians tell me they are never approached by teachers or librarians to work in concert.

Librarians and educators must make a concerted effort to put the brochures promoting library/reading programs in the hands and waiting rooms of physicians, dentists, and health clinics. If you have to lead them by the hand, then do it. With more and more of these professionals using VCRs to entertain patients and families in their reception areas, they offer yet a new possibility for reaching the American family. Librarians and teachers should be developing videocassettes to be used in these areas, including demonstration cassettes of an adult reading to a child. These would instruct parents on the importance and pleasure of reading aloud while at the same time holding the attention of the patients.

Medical professionals looking for tax write-offs might seriously consider both of these options: improving the quality of children's books in their waiting rooms; and giving each family one new book a year, inscribed by the doctor.

Watching my children eat breakfast one morning some years ago, it occurred to me that if we want to send book messages to the largest number of children in one place at one time, all we have to do is put them on the back of a cereal box. Judging from my classroom discussions with thousands of schoolchildren, I strongly suspect that more children voluntarily read the backs of cereal boxes each day than any other form of print. And what is on these boxes? Advertisements for ballpoint pens, T-shirts, and model trains. That is not very exciting stuff, but at a time when more American children are eating breakfast alone than at any other time in the last hundred years, anything to read is better than staring at what is in the bowl.

What would happen, I wonder, if the back of the cereal box contained an advertisement for libraries? To my way of thinking, the best kind of library advertisement would be a chapter from a children's book; a chapter so funny, so intriguing, or so exciting that it would bring those young breakfast readers to the library door first thing after school. Imagine how the publishers would compete to have their book chosen; imagine how authors would love it. Moms would go out of their way to buy that particular brand—not because it had less sugar, not because it was cheaper, but because it sent their children to the library.

But what about the pens and the T-shirts? Alternate them every month with book chapters, if need be. But I don't think you'd have to. The largest cereal manufacturer in America, controlling 42 percent of the U.S. cereal market, netted $396 million in 1987. I don't believe they need those T-shirts and pens but I *do* think they would love to be known as the cereal company that lured one million kids into libraries so they could finish *Freckle Juice*, by Judy Blume.

Impossible? Not if you make literacy—the ability to read, write, and communicate clearly—the business of *all* America and not just that of teachers and librarians. If all sectors of the community work together to bring the excitement of books into our homes early enough and to develop libraries that are truly "delivery rooms for ideas," then we need not fear an electronic Pied Piper stealing our children's minds and imaginations.

7. Television

I believe television is going to be the test of the modern world, and that in this new opportunity to see beyond the range of our vision we shall discover either a new and unbearable disturbance of the general peace or a saving radiance in the sky. We shall stand or fall by television—of that I am quite sure.

—E. B. White,
from "Removal from Town,"
Harper's (October 1938)

My first job in the business community was selling television sets. I was nine years old and living in Union, New Jersey, when a Philco television store opened at the corner of my street. To the astonishment of the neighborhood kids the store manager immediately told us, "You kids are welcome to come by and watch TV any time you want." Those of us who were used to being thrown out of the five-and-dime store for reading comics were further astounded when he provided us with chairs! The result was a daily late-afternoon and early-evening caucus of ten normally rambunctious children tranquilized into passivity.

It wasn't until years later that my father explained the man's

generosity: We were being used as demonstration models for prospective customers, living testimonials to an electronic Pied Piper
who would solve parenting and babysitting woes the world over.
"Take a look at these kids, folks. Would you believe they've been
here for an hour. Not one peep out of them, not one fight, and no
one's even had to go to the bathroom," the salesman announced.

Since then, television has become the most pervasive and powerful influence on the human family and, at the same time, the major
stumbling block to literacy in America. The A. C. Nielsen Company
reports the average television set ran for four hours, thirty-five minutes each day in 1950; by 1987, the daily total had risen to seven
hours.[1] (Adding daily VCR use to that figure would bring it to seven
hours, thirty minutes.)

But fear not—I am not one of those purists urging you to throw
out your television set. I am a realist who recognizes both the enormous potential *and* the liabilities of the medium. As a teacher, television could be unparalleled. Consider how well it educated the
public during the two great struggles of the last thirty years: civil
rights and Vietnam. Had the network cameras not been in Selma
and Saigon, who knows how long the public might have been forced
to tolerate those conflicts.

The elitists who dismiss television as vacuous must have their
heads buried in the sand. How do they explain the rebel forces engaged in life-and-death struggles throughout the globe who make
the government's television station their first objective, or the op-
position party in Nicaragua that demands its own television channel
as part of the peace process? These instances exemplify television's
potential—its ability to instruct a vast audience for change.

Most Americans, however, use television as entertainment, not
for instruction or information. Informational programming like
news shows has such a small audience that only one such program
turns a profit—"Sixty Minutes"; the rest lose money and are out-
drawn by game shows.

There is nothing wrong, of course, with entertainment. To my
way of thinking, we all need a daily dose of entertainment to break
the routine in our lives. It's like dessert, something to look forward
to. The danger comes when you allow it to become the main course.
And over the last thirty years, entertainment, which is television,

has become the main course in children's and families' intellectual lives. Both children and adults average nearly four hours a day passively letting someone else do all the thinking, speaking, imagining, and exploring. The result has been an unprecedented negative impact on American reading and thinking habits.

I want to suggest a method for dealing with television. This approach was used in my own home and in countless others, and proved to be a reasonable and workable solution to the problem of what to do about television. In order to make it work, however, parents must believe in it, must understand fully why they are using it, and what the consequences are to family and child if it is not used.

It is just as important for teachers to understand because television, as the main preoccupation of adults and children, is the prime teacher. Children spend more time in front of television than in front of parents or teachers. Like it or not, television is the prime competition for every teacher and parent and it is here to stay. The challenge is to make it work *for* us instead of *against* us.

We have to recognize its power fully. I've already stated its potential for good, but what about its negatives? Two decades ago when author Marie Winn called TV the "plug-in drug," it was not without reason. Its psychological control of humans is demanding and extensive. Prison officials at the maximum-security prison in Erie Country, New York, found that the most effective threat against even the most incorrigible inmates was to deny them television privileges. In 1986, the inmates voted unanimously to give up their right to receive packages from outside the prison (the prime source for drugs) in exchange for the option to buy personal televisions for their cells.[2]

Children are even more susceptible to the influence it has over their appetites, attention, and loyalties. It will largely determine what they wear and won't wear, what they eat and won't eat, what they play and won't play, what they read and won't read. If there were a medicine that had as much influence on child behavior, it would be strictly monitored, would it not? Yet only 36 percent of parents set any limits on their children's television viewing.[3]

An important step toward teaching children to cope with television is to put the same controls on your television that you already have on your medicine cabinet.

The first serious alarm was sounded by a small cluster of educators in 1964 when the scores were computed for that year's college admission tests. That year's high-school seniors, born in the late 1940s, were the first generation to be raised on a steady television diet. Their Scholastic Aptitude Test (SAT) scores showed an unprecedented decline from previous years. From an average verbal score of 478 in 1963, U.S. students dropped to a low of 424 in 1981. By 1988 they had risen slightly, to 428.[4]

Naturally there are those in the television industry who claim that these lower standards have nothing to do with their medium. Social scientists, educators, and psychologists respond loudly that there is every connection between the two. Television, they declare, interrupts the largest and most instructive class in childhood: life experience.

Paul Copperman, president of the Institute of Reading Development and author of *The Literacy Hoax,* sees the interruption in these terms: "Consider what a child misses during the 15,000 hours [from birth to age seventeen] he spends in front of the TV screen. He is not working in the garage with his father, or in the garden with his mother. He is not doing homework, or reading, or collecting stamps. He is not cleaning his room, washing the supper dishes, or cutting the lawn. Hs is not listening to a discussion about community politics among his parents and their friends. He is not playing baseball or going fishing, or painting pictures. Exactly what does television offer that is so valuable it can replace thse activities that transform an impulsive, self-absorbed child into a critically thinking adult?"[5]

What it offers is a steady stream of entertainment based on daily social and business values that would qualify most people for prison terms! Parents regularly use television as a babysitter—yet how many would hire a sitter who systematically taught children to solve most of their problems violently, to desire things they didn't need, and to lie and cheat because most of the time you'd never be punished. Farfetched? Read on.

A New York University dean recently spent eight hours with twenty-four public high school students from diverse socioeconomic and ethnic groups; their conversations focused on several shows portraying corrupt businessmen. To the dean's dismay, the student consensus was not only that such practices are the norm in business;

they are also acceptable, even admirable. Asked if they would dump chemicals into a town sewer system in order to save their business, the students' pragmatic response was they would do it as long as they made enough money and it didn't hurt their own relatives.

The dean's conclusions were alarming: The continuous unethical and unpunished behavior of *heroes* from "Dallas," "Knots Landing," and "Dynasty," fed into children's unformed consciences, does not portend good things for tomorrow's society. His *New York Times* recounting[6] of those student discussions should be studied by all concerned educators, parents, and clergy interested in exploring American ethics with classes of children.

Research offers cause for both alarm and hope. In 1980, California's Department of Education administered a standard achievement exam and survey to all the state's sixth- and twelfth-graders (half a million students). When they correlated each child's grade with the number of hours the student spent watching television, the findings were conclusive: The more time in front of TV, the lower the scores; the less time, the higher the scores. The statistics proved true regardless of the child's IQ, social background, or study practices.[7]

Tannis Macbeth Williams of the University of British Columbia came to similar conclusions when she studied three Canadian towns—two with television and one without. Children in the community without television had higher reading scores—until television was introduced to the town. Not surprisingly, the scores then declined. Such research speaks directly to the need for limits on family TV viewing and for children to discover the pleasures of books before the pleasures of television.[8]

The parents who are always asking me, "What about 'Sesame Street'? How about 'Mr. Rogers'?" can take heart from a recent two-year study of 326 five- and seven-year-olds that showed viewing of educational television has a positive effect on children's reading while noninformative shows (situation comedies) have a detrimental effect.[9] A distinction should be made as to the *kinds* of television programs children watch, though even educational programs hurt when they become substitutes for play or socializing or when viewed to excess—more than fourteen hours a week. That same long-term project concluded that the biggest influence on children's reading development and skills was parent attitudes about reading and the availability of books in their homes. On the subject of educational TV, it is my opinion (and shared by many) that "Mr. Rogers," with its civil, value-oriented focus on children through conversation, is the finest programming for children today and proves you can hold their attention without car chases or violent robotics.

"Reading Rainbow," the award-winning PBS series on children's books, shows what can be accomplished when the industry makes up its mind to educate and entertain. Conceived by producer Twila Liggett as a way to encourage reading during summer vacations, the series' sixty shows boast a unique power: Once a book is spotlighted on the show, libraries and bookstores report an immediate positive response among children and their parents. It is not unusual for a book that normally sells 1,200 copies to sell 20,000 after appearing on "Reading Rainbow."

"Reading Rainbow" is the programming exception, rather than the rule. Most of today's programming is a serious impediment to children's growth because of both what it offers and what it does *not* offer:

1. *Television is the direct opposite of reading.* In breaking its programs into eight-minute commercial segments (shorter for shows like "Sesame Street"), it requires and fosters a short attention span. Reading, on the other hand, requires and encourages longer attention spans in children. Good children's books are written to hold children's attention, not interrupt it. Because of the need to hold viewers until the next commercial message, the content of television shows is almost constant action. Reading also offers action but not nearly as much, and reading fills the considerable space between action scenes with subtle character development. Television is relentless; no time is allowed to ponder characters' thoughts or to recall their words because the dialogue and film move too quickly. The need to scrutinize is a critical need among young children and it is constantly ignored by television. Books, however, encourage a critical reaction; the reader moves at his own pace as opposed to that of the director or sponsor. The reader can to stop to ponder the character's next move, the feathers in his hat, or the meaning of a sentence. Having

done so, he can resume where he left off without having missed any part of the story.

The arrival of remote control is only exacerbating the attention span problem: the average family "zaps" once every three minutes, twenty-six seconds, versus those who have no remote (once every five minutes, fifteen seconds); and higher-income families zap three times more often than poorer families.[10]

2. *For young children television is an antisocial experience, while reading is a social experience.* The three-year-old sits passively in front of the screen, oblivious to what is going on around him. Conversation during the program is seldom if ever encouraged by the child or by the parents. On the other hand, the three-year-old with a book must be read to by another person—parent, sibling, or grandparent. The child is a participant as well as a receiver when he engages in discussion during and after the story. This process continues to an even greater degree when the child attends school and compares his own reactions to a story with those of his classmates.

3. *Television deprives the child of his most important learning tool: his questions.* Children learn the most by questioning. For the thirty-three hours a week that the average five-year-old spends in front of the set, he can neither ask a question nor receive an answer.

4. *Television interrupts the child's most important language lesson: family conversation.* Studies show the average kindergarten graduate has already seen nearly 6,000 hours of television and videos before entering first grade, hours in which he engaged in little or no conversation. And with 30 percent of all adults watching TV during dinner and 36 percent of teenagers owning their own sets (and presumably watching alone in their rooms), the description of TV as "the great conversation stopper" has never been more appropriate.

5. *Much of young children's television viewing is mindless watching, requiring little or no thinking.* When two dozen three- to five-year-olds were shown a "Scooby Doo" cartoon, the soundtrack of which had been replaced by the soundtrack from a "Fangface" cartoon, only three of the twenty-four children realized the soundtrack did not match the pictures.[11]

6. *Television presents material in a manner that is the direct opposite of the classroom's.* Television's messages are based almost entirely on moving pictures and our emotional response to them. Conversely,

the classroom relies heavily on reading the printed word, and a critical response to those words, not just on raw emotion. School also requires large amounts of time to be spent on a task. The minutes spent doing things like multiplication tables and spelling are often boring and repetitious when compared with "Family Ties." Whereas the classroom pursues subjects in depth, television treats nearly all areas superficially. The networks' nightly newscasts contain approximately 3,500 words—only slightly more than you find on *half* a newspaper front page; yet more than half the adults in the U.S. now depend entirely on TV for their daily news information.

7. *Television is unable to portray the most intelligent act known to man: thinking.* In 1980 Squire Rushnell, vice-president in charge of ABC's children's programming, said that certain fine children's books cannot be adapted for television. Much of the character development in these books, Rushnell noted, takes place inside the character's head. He said, "You simply can't put thinking on the screen." As a result, a child almost never sees a TV performer thinking through a problem.[12]

8. *Television encourages deceptive thinking.* In *Teaching as a Conserving Activity,* educator Neil Postman points out that it is implicit in every one of television's commercials that there is no problem which cannot be solved by simple artificial means.[13] Whether the problem is anxiety or common diarrhea, nervous tension or the common cold, a simple tablet or spray solves the problem. Seldom is mention ever made of headaches being a sign of more serious illness, nor is the suggestion ever made that elbow grease and hard work are viable alternatives to stains and boredom. Instead of thinking through our problems, television promotes the "easy way." The cumulative effect of such thinking is enormous when you consider that between ages one and seventeeen the average child is exposed to 350,000 commercials (four hundred a week) promoting the idea that solutions to life's problems can be purchased. Moreover, alcohol, the number-one form of drug abuse in America, is promoted as a pleasureful form of recreation with 100,000 beer commercials viewed by children between ages two and eighteen.[14]

9. *Television, by vying for children's time and attention with a constant diet of unchallenging simplistic entertainment, stimulates antischool and antireading feeling among children.* A 1977 study showed that the majority

of the preschool and primary school students examined felt that school and books were a waste of time.[15] Offered the same story on television and in book form, 69 percent of the second-grade students chose television. That figure increased to 86 percent among the third-grade pupils—the grade where national reading skills begin to decline.

10. *Television has a negative effect on children's vital knowledge after age ten, according to the Schramm study of 6,000 schoolchildren.*[16] It does help, the report goes on to say, in building vocabulary for younger children, but this stops by age ten. This finding is supported by the fact that today's kindergartners have the highest reading-readiness scores ever achieved at that level and yet these same students tail off dismally by fourth and fifth grades. Since television scripts consist largely of conversations that contain the same vocabulary words these students already know, few gains are made. Moreover, a study of the scripts from eight programs favored by teenagers showed a sentence averaged only seven words (versus eighteen words in my local newspaper), and 72 percent of the language in the shows consisted of simple sentences or fragments.[17]

11. *Television stifles the imagination.* A study of 192 children from Los Angeles County showed children *hearing* a story elicited greater imaginative responses than did their seeing the same story on film.[18] Consider for a moment this single paragraph from Eric Knight's classic, *Lassie-Come-Home:*

> Yet, if it were almost a miracle, in his heart Joe Carraclough tried to believe in that miracle—that somehow, wonderfully, inexplicably, his dog would be there some day; there, waiting by the school gate. Each day as he came out of school, his eyes would turn to the spot where Lassie had always waited. And each day there was nothing there, and Joe Carraclough would walk home slowly, silently, stolidly as did the people of his country.

If a dozen people were to read or hear those words, they would have a dozen different images of the scene, what the boy looked like, the school, the gate, the lonely road home. As soon as the story is placed on film there is no longer any room for imagination. The director does all your imagining for you.

12. *Television overpowers and desensitizes a child's sense of sympathy for suffering, while books heighten the reader's sense of sympathy.* Extensive research in the past ten years clearly shows that television bombardment of the child with continual acts of violence (18,000 acts viewed between the ages of three and seventeen) makes the child insensitive to violence and its victims—most of whom he is conditioned to believe die cleanly or crawl inconsequently offstage.[19]

Though literature could never be labeled a nonviolent medium, it cannot begin to approach television's extreme. Frank Mankiewicz and Joel Swerdlow noted in *Remote Control: Television and the Manipulation of American Life* that you would have to watch all thirty-seven of Shakespeare's plays in order to see the same number of acts of human violence (fifty-four) that you would see in just three evenings of prime-time television.

Television and sponsors have found the one sure way to hold audience attention (and prevent zapping) while at the same time solving story dilemmas is violence, at the rate of 13.3 incidents per prime-time hour. Nearly half the videos on MTV (Music Television) portray violence of one form or another.[20] In one week in 1986, the University of Pennsylvania's Annenberg School of Communications counted a combined 168 acts of violence during just the "family hour" (8:00–9:00 P.M.) on the three major networks.[21]

The addition of cable television and VCRs has only increased the amount of violence to which children of all ages are exposed. Librarians in Panama City, Florida, told me of the day-care class that visited the children's room one morning in 1987 where the librarian announced excitedly that the day's stories were going to be about "monsters!" This prompted the dozen four-year-olds to cheer, "Ohhhhhh—Freddy Krueger!" referring to the psychotic killer with the razor-clawed gloves from *A Nightmare on Elm Street,* which many of these preschoolers had been allowed to view that week when it was a late-night cable channel selection. This was a far cry from the tame storybook monsters the librarian was going to read about in *There's a Nightmare in My Closet,* by Mercer Mayer, and *Harry and the Terrible Whatzit,* by Harry Gackenbach. One can only wonder what these preschoolers will be ready for in adolescence.

13. *Television is a passive activity and discourages creative play.* The virtual disappearance of neighborhood games like I spy, kick the can,

spud, hopscotch, Johnny-jump-the-pony, stickball, red light, Simon says, flies up, giant steps, and statue attests to that.

Compared to reading, television is still the more passive of the two activities. In reading, educators point out, a child must actively use a variety of skills involving sounds, spelling rules, blendings, as well as constructing mental images of the scene described in the book. Television requires no such mental activity.

14. *Television is psychologically addictive.* In schools and homes where students voluntarily have removed themselves from TV viewing, their subsequent class discussions and journals report the addictive nature of their attachment to television: It draws upon their idle time and there is an urgency to watch it in order to fulfill peer and family pressure. I recall the Oregon elementary school principal and father of five who told me he and his wife had refused to have a television until the children were grown. During all those years, he explained, he read an average of two books a week. Three months before I spoke with him, his wife bought their first television and, he sheepishly confessed, he hadn't read a book since the day it arrived.

15. *Television has been described by former First Lady Betty Ford as "the greatest babysitter of all time," but it also is reported to be the nation's second largest obstacle to family harmony.* In a 1980 survey by the Roper Organization, 4,000 men and women listed money as the most frequent subject of fights between husband and wife. Television and children tied for second, and produced three times as many arguments as did sex.

16. *Television's conception of childhood, rather than being progressive, is regressive—a throwback, in fact, to the Middle Ages.* In *Teaching as a Conserving Activity,* Postman points to Philippe Ariès's research, which shows that until the 1600s children over the age of five were treated and governed as though they were adults.[22] After the seventeenth century, society developed a concept of childhood which insulated children from the shock of instant adulthood until they were mature enough to meet it. "Television," Postman declares, "all by itself, may bring an end to childhood." Present-day TV programming offers its nightly messages on incest, murder, abortion, rape, moral and political corruption, and general physical mayhem to 85 million people—including 5.6 million children between ages two and eleven who are still watching at 10:30 P.M.[23] The afternoon

soap operas offer a similar message to still another young audience. Of the twenty-one children (ages seven to nine) in my wife's second-grade class one year, all but four of them were daily soap opera viewers. The Center for Population Options in Washington, D.C., pointing to a survey of midwestern teenagers who said television was their major source of sexual information, estimates the average viewer will see more than 9,000 instances of "sexually suggestive comments or suggested sexual intercourse," each year.

17. *Television presents a continuous distortion of physical and social realities, thus reinforcing false stereotypes.* Extensive studies by major research firms[24] point out these misrepresentations:

- TV shows are populated by three times as many men as women, and men are usually ten years older than women. (In reality, women outnumber men, 52 percent to 48 percent, with a median age two years older than men's.)
- Children make up only one-tenth of the TV population. (In reality, 27 percent.)
- Only 4 percent of TV characters suffer from obesity. (In reality, 30 percent.)
- Only 6 to 10 percent of TV characters hold blue-collar or service jobs. (In reality, 60 percent.)
- TV characters seldom wear glasses. Fifty percent of the population wears them.
- Two out of every three TV businessmen are portrayed as foolish, greedy, or criminal.
- TV characters seldom wear seat belts, yet never sustain crippling injuries from TV car crashes.
- Murder is 200 percent more prevalent as a TV crime than it is in reality.

Children's television is just as heavily distorted. A study funded by the Ford and Carnegie foundations showed thirty-eight hours of Boston children's programming contained these misleading statistics: Of the 1,145 characters, 3.7 percent were black; 3.1 percent were Spanish-speaking; only 16 percent were women. In reality, the following statistics hold true: blacks—11 percent; Spanish-speaking—6 percent; women—52 percent.

18. Some *books are simple-minded;* most *television is simple-minded.* When Grant Tinker was chairman of NBC, he admitted the industry's philosophy of gearing programs to the lowest possible denominator in the audience and placed the blame squarely on a viewing public that swallows unflinchingly much of the worst programming it is fed. "They are such a disappointment," he said. "I had to watch a pilot of a new program awhile ago and we made the decision: It's a little too good. That's a terrible decision to make."[25] It is also either a scathing indictment of American education or an insult to the intelligence of its alumni.

Bob Keeshan, most often seen and heard in his role as Captain Kangaroo, places the prime responsibility for television's negative influence upon the parent. "Television is the great national babysitter," Keeshan says. "It's not the disease in itself, but a symptom of a greater disease that exists between parent and child. A parent today simply doesn't have time for the child, and the child is a very low priority item, and there's this magic box that flickers pictures all day long, and it's a convenient babysitter. I'm busy, go watch television. . . . The most direct answer to all our problems with television and children is the parent, because if the parent is an effective parent, we're not going to have them."[26]

Keeshan's call for parental control of the television set is more easily said than done, as any parent can tell you who has ever tried it. I know firsthand.

My family's restricted viewing began in 1974, at about the time I'd begun to notice a growing television addiction in my fourth-grader daughter and kindergarten-age son. There had even begun a deterioration of our long-standing read-aloud time each night because, in their words, it "took too much time away from the TV."

One evening while visiting Marty and Joan Wood of Longmeadow, Massachusetts, I noticed that their four teenage children went right to their homework after excusing themselves from the dinner table.

I asked the parents, "Your television broken?"

"No," replied Mary. "Why?"

"Well, it's only six-forty-five and the kids are already doing homework."

Joan explained, "Oh, we don't allow television on school nights."

"That's a noble philosophy—but how in the world do you enforce it?" I asked.

"It is a house *law*," stated Marty. And for the next hour and a half, husband and wife detailed for me the positive changes that had occurred in their family and home since they put that "law" into effect.

That evening was a turning point for my family. After hearing the details of the plan, my wife, Susan, agreed wholeheartedly to back it. "On one condition," she added.

"What's that?" I asked.

"*You* be the one to tell them," she said.

After supper the next night we brought the children into our bedroom, surrounded them with pillows and quilts, and I calmly began, "Jamie . . . Elizabeth . . . Mom and I have decided that there will be no more television on school nights in this house—forever."

Their reaction was predictable: they started to cry. What came as a shock to us was that they cried for four solid months. Every night, despite explanations on our part, they cried. We tried to impress upon them that the rule was not meant as a punishment; we listed all the positive reasons for such a rule. They cried louder.

The peer group pressure was enormous, particularly for Elizabeth. "There's nothing to talk about in school anymore," she sobbed. "All the kids were talking about 'Starsky and Hutch' at lunch today and I didn't even see it."

There was even peer pressure from other parents directed at Susan and me. "But, Jim," they would ask, "not even for an hour after supper?" in a tone that suggested our plan was a new form of child abuse. "And what about all the National Geographic specials? Aren't you going to let the kids watch *those*?" they'd ask.

It should be pointed out that a great many parents use National Geographic specials, Jacques Cousteau specials, and "Sesame Street" as the salve on their consciences. I can count on one hand the number of children I know who actually like those specials. Given the choice, as the vast majority are, they'll choose "Miami Vice" or MTV every time.

As difficult as it was at first, we persevered and resisted both kinds of peer pressure. We lived with the tears, the pleadings, the conniving. "Dad, my teacher says there is a special show on tonight that I have to watch. She said don't come to school tomorrow if you haven't seen the show," Elizabeth would say after supper.

After three months my wife and I began to see things happen that the Woods had predicted. Suddenly we had the time each night as a family to read aloud, to read to ourselves, to do homework at an unhurried pace, to learn how to play chess and checkers and Scrabble, to make the plastic models that had been collecting dust in the closet for two years, to bake cakes and cookies, to write thank-you notes to aunts and uncles, to do household chores and take baths and showers without World War II breaking out, to play on all the parish sports teams, to draw and paint and color, and—best of all—to talk with one another, ask questions and answer questions.

Our children's imaginations were coming back to life again.

For the first year, the decision was a heavy one for all of us. With time it grew lighter. Jamie, being younger, had never developed the acute taste for television that Elizabeth had over the years, and he lost the habit fairly easily. It took Elizabeth longer to adjust.

Over the years the plan was modified until it worked like this:

1. The television is turned off at supper time and not turned on again until the children are in bed, Monday through Thursday.

2. Each child is allowed to watch one school-night show a week (subject to parents' approval). Homework, chores, et cetera must be finished beforehand.

3. Weekend television is limited to any two of the three nights. The remaining night is reserved for homework and other activities. The children make their selections separately.

The suggestion to modify the original diet and allow one school night show a week came from my wife during the third year of the plan and it met with my immediate resistance. Only reluctantly did I agree to give it a try.

As it turned out, it was an excellent decision. By limiting the choice to one show a week, we forced the child to be discriminating in his or her selections, to distinguish worth from trash. They became very choosy, refusing to waste the privilege, and began using a critical eye in evaluating shows.

The habit of watching, however, continued to decrease while other interests expanded. By the time Elizabeth was a ninth-grade student, she didn't bother to use her school-night option more than three or four times in the course of the entire year. More than half the time Jamie forgot until the week was over. "Hey!" he'd say on Saturday. "I never watched my show this week. Why didn't somebody remind me?"

We structured the diet to allow the family to control the television and not the other way around. Perhaps this particular diet won't work for your family, but any kind of control is better than none. Some families allot their children a ration of poker chips (red for sixty minutes, white for thirty minutes) and they must deposit the appropriate chip in a jar atop the set. When the week's quota of chips runs out, no more TV. Those parents who feel such restrictions are cruel or unusual treatment might consider the "privileged" Park Avenue childhood that produced executive Michael Eisner, who has already headed ABC and Paramount, and now chairs the $10 billion Disney empire. "For every hour of television I watched, I had to read for two hours," Eisner recalls, and his movie viewing was so limited he didn't see his first Disney movie until several years after college. Fortunately for Eisner, his parents believed in "raising" a child, as opposed to "watching him grow up."

If you are going to require your children to curtail their TV viewing, if you are going to create a three-hour void in their daily lives, then *you* must make a commitment to fill that void. *You* have to produce the crayons and paper, *you* have to teach them how to play checkers, *you* have to help with the cookie mix. And most importantly, *you* must pick up those books—books to be read to the child, books to be read by the child, books to be read to yourself—even when you have a headache, even when you're tired, even when you're worried about your checkbook. You'll be surprised. Just as that book will take your child's mind off television, it also will take your mind off the headache or checkbook.

There is, however, a device that might save the addicted family a great deal of anguish. A parent in Hawaii told me how her children

had learned to read by watching Japanese movies on television—
with subtitles. I then began to wonder about the possibilities posed
by close-captioned TV, the process by which the audio portion of a
program is converted to subtitles on the screen. Originally designed
for the hearing-impaired, it is now being investigated with some
success by academics as a possible device for reaching slow or remedial readers,[27] and actively promoted by the National Captioning
Institute in Falls Church, Virginia, toward that goal.

Priced around $200 and available in a variety of retail outlets,
the TeleCaption 3000 decoder is hooked up to the set and the previously unseen captions become visible for more than 175 hours of
weekly programming. In addition, more than 1,100 videocassettes
are also close-captioned. "You want to watch 'The Cosby Show,'
kids? Fine—but you can only *watch* it. The sound is going off and
you'll have to read it with the decoder tonight." Now *that's* using
the technology instead of being used *by* it.

The need to protect children's unformed imaginations from the
stultifying effects of excessive television viewing was seen most dramatically in the psychological profiles done on the fifty-two American hostages after their release from 444 days of Iranian captivity.
The hostages (as did Vietnam POWs before them) paid repeated
tribute to the one psychological factor that appeared to be the savior
of their sanity: their imaginations. State Department doctors noted
the hostages developed intricate "daydreaming" which allowed them
to escape their tormenters many times a day—like the one who
fantasized a train trip from India to England, complete with a mental
script of seating arrangements, passenger descriptions, and dining
car menu.[28]

This "daydreaming" technique which allowed the hostages to
make daily fantasy trips home to their families gave them momentary
escape and served as a constant reminder of who they were and why
they were there. My point in mentioning this is to remind you that
a great many of our children face a future in which they will someday
be hostages: hostages to bad marriages, hostages to unhappy jobs
and careers, hostages to illnesses or neighborhoods. How well they
survive their captivity may well be determined by their imaginations,
their ability to dream and hold fast to those dreams.[29]

If we are ever going to dilute the negative impact of television, we will have to do it by educating the public. Several successful projects already are available for communities to copy.

By far the most extensive, successful, and famous model to date is the Farmington Turn-Off, a month-long campaign staged by the Farmington (CT) Public Library every January since 1984 and copied by hundreds of towns throughout North America. It also demonstrates the impact one person can have in his or her community—and beyond. Under the direction of children's librarian Nancy DeSalvo, the campaign is intended to make families aware (through temporary withdrawal) of television's addictive nature and give them alternative activities they can pursue instead of mindless viewing. The latter requires involvement by as many community agencies as possible—libraries, schools, churches, and park and recreation departments—which, in turn, heightens a sense of community among families.

The campaign has also generated extraordinary media coverage for schools and libraries. Farmington's coverage was worldwide, including features in *The New York Times* and the *Wall Street Journal;* a spot on "Entertainment Tonight"; and a week of on-the-air phone calls from David Letterman to Nancy DeSalvo in which he tried to persuade her with nearly $3,000 in prizes to break her TV fast and turn on his show. (She declined.)

If you are considering a TV Turn-Off project, the definitive handbook on the subject is Marie Winn's *Unplugging the Plug-In Drug* (Penguin). Regardless of how broad a turn-off campaign you plan (individual home, classroom, school, or entire community), everything you'll need to know is contained in this one resource—the experiences gained from other Turn-Offs, organization tips, activities, publicity, pitfalls, and charts.

It would be naïve, however, to assume that even half the parents will avail themselves of such awareness programs. Thus the best hope for changing America's television habits rests with the classroom teacher who is educating tomorrow's parents sitting in the classroom today. We're spending a great deal of time and money educating children to the dangers of alcohol and drug abuse, teenage pregnancy, and AIDS, but so far we've done *nothing* to teach them how to cope with television.

What we need are carefully constructed curriculums like that developed by educational development specialist Glenda Green with the Connecticut Department of Education. Her six-week curriculum for Southbury, Connecticut, elementary schools, "Watching Wisely," covered these themes: Second Grade—TV as teacher and salesman; Third Grade—How real are TV families; Fourth Grade—How TV characters solve their problems; Fifth Grade—TV violence; Sixth Grade—TV news versus the newspaper.

As long as Americans spend more time watching than reading, educators must address the need for critical *viewing* as well as critical *reading*. If readers are trained to read interpretively, so too must viewers be taught to look critically at TV. And if we succeed with this teaching, we'll have changed the present pattern in which 70 percent of what Americans hear in a political campaign consists of thirty- and sixty-second commercials consisting of half-truths and innuendo. The whole country benefits if we teach the next generation to know when the TV evangelist is talking about Almighty God and when he's talking about the almighty dollar, and how to spot the hidden commercials on talk shows ("Don, tell us about this clip from your special coming up this Thursday night . . ."). And they will also have a better chance of knowing when a congressional committee witness is acting instead of testifying, when he is manipulating the audience with grins and macho posturing.

As E. B. White noted a half century ago, television is "the test of the modern world." Used correctly, it can inform, entertain and inspire. Used incorrectly, television will control families and community, limiting our language, dreams, and achievements. It is our "test" to pass or fail.

With books-on-tape mushrooming each year (a $300 million market in 1987), the opportunities for reading aloud have broadened into areas and hours previously untouched. Salespeople are driving the breadth of the land listening to the classics they never got around to reading themselves; family car trips have grown noticeably calmer with children's stories in the tape deck. All are examples of how technology can be used to make us a more literate nation instead of an illiterate one.

The use of audiocassettes at home or in the classroom is of great benefit. While they are not a substitute for a live person who can hug a child and answer his questions, they can fill an important gap when the adult is not available. Even when a cassette is used as background noise while a child is playing, it is still enriching his vocabulary more than television, with its abbreviated sentences. So by all means begin your home and car cassette library of songs, rhymes, and stories. Community libraries and bookstores now have a wide assortment for all ages. Most producers of quality story cassettes are more than happy to send you their catalogues. Four of the best are:

• Caedmon Inc., 1995 Broadway, New York, NY 10023
• The Mind's Eye, P.O. Box 6727, San Francisco, CA 94101
• Weston Woods Studios, Dept. CAS, Weston, CT 06883
• Listening Library, Inc., One Park Ave., Old Greenwich, CT 06870.

Listening Library has also produced *Read Along! An Audio Handbook for Parents, Educators, and Librarians,* an excellent guide to more than four hundred award-winning children's stories now available as both books and audiocassettes, along with learning activities. It is available by writing to Listening Library at the above address.

Radio drama may have died on the airwaves but it is very much alive in libraries and bookstores on cassettes that include shows like "Superman," "The Green Hornet," "The Lone Ranger," "Sergeant Preston of the Yukon," and "Inner Sanctum." These are excellent stimulants to listening and imagining for children as young as nine because they require the listener to imagine what the people in the radio dramas look like, what they're wearing, what they're doing, and the landscape or setting. Such imagining is a long way from the passive nature of television.

You can take radio one step further and encourage the child or class to develop its own radio drama, complete with script, sound effects, background music, and actors—all facilitated by the tape recorder and an enthusiastic adult.

For older students, most public libraries now boast an extensive collection of long-playing records and cassettes featuring classical literature being read aloud. The readers include not only featured names of the theater like Alexander Scourby, Orson Welles, and

James Earl Jones but a host of literary figures reading their own works: Eudora Welty, John Cheever, John Updike, Shirley Jackson, and William Saroyan. These collections would also prove advantageous to those adults who wish to share the spoken word with a family or class but who themselves are not particularly good readers-aloud.

The cassette recorder could be the handiest listening device since the human ear. Its low cost and simple operation make it an item for every classroom and home and an object for both education and entertainment. In recent years, classroom teachers have begun to incorporate the recorder into their learning centers where the child listens to a story while following along in the book. This auditory reinforcement, when combined with the visual image of print, is extremely successful in breaking down barriers for intimidated beginning readers. Now we must share the success of this method with as many parents as possible.

Dr. Marie Carbo, a pioneer in reading styles research, taped stories and books for her students and achieved "phenomenal" results while working as a learning disabilities specialist during the 1970s. Her students ran the gamut of learning handicaps: disabled, educable-retarded, emotionally disturbed, and severely speech-impaired. By listening to Dr. Carbo's tape and following in the book, each child was free to move at his own pace and had a constant language model as companion—the tape. There was the additional reinforcement from repeated playing of the tape and the pace of the reader's voice was slow enough for the child to follow easily. As the child's reading ability improved, Carbo increased the pace of the story and the size of the word groupings.[30]

Describing a particular case, Dr. Carbo says, "The greatest gain in word recognition was made by Tommy, a sixth-grade boy reading on a 2.2 level. Prior to working with the tapes he had faltered and stumbled over second-grade words while his body actually shook with fear and discomfort. Understandably, he hated to read. Because a beloved teacher had once read *Charlotte's Web* to him, he asked me to record his favorite chapter from this book. I recorded one paragraph on each cassette side so that Tommy could choose to read either one or two paragraphs daily. The first time that he listened to a recording (five times) and then read the passage silently to himself (twice), he was able to read the passage to me perfectly with excellent expression and without fear. After this momentous event, Tommy worked hard. At last he knew he was capable of learning to read and was willing to give it all he could. The result was a fifteen-month gain in word recognition at the end of only three months. Every learning-disabled child in the program experienced immediate success with her or his individually recorded books," explains Dr. Carbo.

If such remarkable results are possible with learning-disabled children, imagine what can be done with children who have fewer disadvantages.

Do you remember the excitement you felt as a child when you saw one of your teachers outside the classroom setting—in the supermarket or waiting in line at the movies? It was like seeing a movie star on the street, wasn't it? And what most children would love to do is bring their teacher *home* with them—so their family could meet her and see how terrific she is. In one-room schoolhouses (see *Caddie Woodlawn,* by Carol Ryrie Brink) that was once possible, but not today. Or is it? Couldn't that be done vicariously through taped stories sent home with the child in a plastic Ziploc bag that also contained a paperback book of the story?

Hearing the teacher reading in his own home would inspire not only the child, it might also reach siblings, even the illiterate or semiliterate parent. Once, about a month after I'd spent a morning with a local fourth-grade class, the teacher brought in a recording I had done of *Ira Sleeps Over* and made it available to individual students whenever they finished their work. They not only listened to it then, they played it as a class *every* lunch hour for a month. (The principal told me he thought he was going to lose his mind if he heard it one more time.) It gave the class an opportunity to experience vicariously a return visit from me and it also initiated a strong enough connection between them and the book that many soon had it memorized.

For the traveling parent (or absentee grandparent), the tape recorder is an excellent surrogate storyteller. During a job change several years ago, Barry Lein of Sterling, Massachusetts, was separated from his wife, Cheryll, and two sons for long periods of time. Cheryll tells how "he used to read stories to Adam [age four] and

Matthew [age two] on cassettes and mail them home. Each night the boys would listen to their dad's voice, and they would be together—at least in spirit. When a new tape arrived, all play stopped until it was heard—not just by our sons but also by their cousins with whom we were staying."

She also recalls when, during this period, Adam was hospitalized with a severe asthma attack. "He was in an oxygen tent with his tape recorder playing when his doctor came. 'What's this?' he asked. When I told him that it was Adam's daddy reading stories to him, the doctor seemed amazed—and impressed."

I found another example of utilizing the family "entertainment center" to benefit family reading in the home of Bob and Kay Pranis in rural Chaska, Minnesota. Kay, who does most of the family's reading aloud, capitalized on the technological wizardry of her husband and had him fix the household stereo system so it could broadcast her readings into the upstairs and kitchen speakers. Thus she could sit beside the stereo and read to her husband and three teenage children on Saturday mornings as they did their household chores, much the way traveling sales reps have begun to listen to books on tape as they drive from one city to the next.

Along with making Saturday chores bearable, it created such devoted listeners that when one member is away from home during one of the readings, they insist that Kay tape the day's chapters so they can catch up later. Carrying it one step further, Bob Pranis even hooked up an amplifier system in the family van so Kay's car-trip readings can easily be heard in the front and back seats. (And fortunately for this family of readers and listeners, she doesn't suffer from car sickness when reading and riding.)

8. Sustained Silent Reading: Reading-Aloud's Natural Partner

With the tests, with the "methods," with the class structures, with the teacher's determination to teach . . . no one had ever had much time in school to just read the damn books. They were always practicing up to read, and the practice itself was so unnecessary, or so difficult, or so boring you were likely to figure that the task you were practicing for must combine those qualities and so reject it or be afraid of it.

—James Herndon, from
How to Survive in Your Native Land

After finishing my forty-five-minute career talk to the fourth-grade students at Brunton School in Springfield, Massachusetts, I debated whether to ask my usual question: What have you read lately? A week before, I'd asked the question of a fifth-grade class in the same school system and came away depressed by the lack of response. Only four children in the room had been able to think of anything they had read lately. I was embarrassed for the class, the teacher, the system, and the city. Reluctantly, I now asked the question again, dreading another disappointing response.

But those wonderful fourth-grade pupils surprised me. For

forty-five minutes they spouted the names of the books they had been reading. I could barely get a word in edgewise as their enthusiasm and excitement flooded the room.

Later, as I was leaving, I asked the teacher, Terri Cullinane, "What have you done to those kids? I haven't seen a class this excited by books in years."

"Two things," she answered. "We—the other teachers and I—read aloud to them every day, and SSR." (SSR is an abbreviation for Sustained Silent Reading.) "Every day when we go to lunch, each child leaves his library book on his desk. It is ready and waiting for him when he returns after lunch. We read quietly for ten minutes, close our books, and go on with classwork."

Terri explained that the SSR program had been in effect only a few months but already the faculty had seen a dramatic change in reading habits and attitude among the children.

"Ten minutes a day may not seem like much time but think of it this way: ten minutes a day for five days. That's almost a solid hour of reading and it puts the child well into the book, much further, by the way, then most of them would be if they were left to read it on their own time."

SSR is one of those commonsense ideas that is so obvious and uncomplicated it is often overlooked in today's complex educational scheme. I suppose if it were complicated, expensive, and gradeable, everyone would be pushing for it. Unfortunately, most school systems and homes either haven't heard about it or won't dare to try it.

SSR is the most commonly used but several other acronyms exist: DEAR (Drop Everything and Read), DIRT (Daily Individual Reading Time), SQUIRT (Sustained Quiet Un-Interrupted Reading Time). They all boil down to a simple principle: Reading is, among other things, a skill. And like all skills, the more you use it, the better you get at it. Conversely, the less you use it, the more difficult it is. The comparison is often made with swimming because, like swimming, once you learn to read you never forget it. But in order to get better at either skill, you must jump into the book or the water and do it over and over.

The truth is today's students don't read very much, a fact conceded by most teachers and unknown to most parents. Two comprehensive investigations of how 158 capable fifth-grade students spend their after-school time showed that 90 percent of those students devoted only 1 percent of their free time to reading books and 30 percent to watching television. Indeed, 50 percent read for an average of four minutes or less a day, 30 percent read two minutes a day, and 10 percent read nothing at all.[1]

"Well," says the parent, "they may not be reading much outside school but they certainly must be reading during the five hours they're in school!" Nice thought, but not true. The most comprehensive look at the American classroom is John Goodlad's seven-year study, *A Place Called School,* in which he reports that only 6 percent of class time is occupied by the act of reading in the elementary school, 3 percent in the middle school, and 2 percent in the high school.[2] (Yes, there are exceptions to these averages. If your child or school is the exception, consider yourself fortunate.)

Clearly, students are not reading much and therefore not getting much better at it. The important question is: *Why* are they not reading? The only logical answers are either because they don't like it or because they don't have the time. There are no other major reasons. Eliminate those two factors and you've solved the American literacy dilemma. Reading aloud goes to work on the first factor and SSR attacks the second.

Originally proposed in the early 1960s by Lyman C. Hunt, Jr., of the University of Vermont, SSR has received its biggest boost from reading experts Robert and Marlene McCracken.[3] Experimenting with a variety of techniques and schools, the McCrackens recommend the following procedures for SSR programs:

1. Children should read to themselves for a *limited* amount of time. Teachers and parents should adapt this to their individual class or family and adjust it with increasing maturity. Ten or fifteen minutes are the frequent choices for the classroom.

2. Each student should select his own book, magazine, or newspaper. No changing during the period is permitted. All materials must be chosen before the SSR period begins.

3. The teacher or parent must read also, setting an example. This cannot be stressed too strongly.

4. No reports are required of the student. No records are kept.

Administrators worried over the ungraded free-form nature of students reading library books, paperbacks, magazines, or newspapers should not consider it a departure from the curriculum just because no textbook is involved. SSR (by third grade) can be the student's most important vocabulary builder, more so than basal textbooks or even daily oral language. "Basal readers and textbooks do not offer the same richness of vocabulary, sentence structure, or literary form as do trade books. Analyses comparing stories in basal readers with trade books show that the ones in primary-grade basals have fewer plot complications, involve less conflict among and within characters, and offer fewer insights into characters' goals, motives, and feelings . . . A diet consisting only of basal stories probably will not prepare children well to deal with real literature."[4] Indeed, about half of the 3,000 most commonly used words are not even included in K-6 basals.[5]

In his exhaustive studies of the "basalization" of children's literature,[6] Kenneth Goodman points to this simple example of the differences between trade books and selections/revisions in basal readers:

Original text from one of Judy Blume's early books, *The One in the Middle Is the Green Kangaroo*):

> Freddy Dissel had two problems. One was his older brother Mike. The other was his younger sister Ellen. Freddy thought a lot about being the one in the middle. But there was nothing he could do about it. He felt like the peanut butter part of a sandwich, squeezed between Mike and Ellen.

Revised text from basal textbook (Holt, Level 8):

> Maggie had a big sister, Ellen.
> She had a little brother, Mike.
> Maggie was the one in the middle.
> But what could she do?

Though the last few years have seen serious efforts by some publishers to avoid this kind of emaciation, the pressures from special interest groups continue to leave us with textbooks that are written by committees, edited by committees, submitted to curriculum committees, and finally approved by school committees. The end result is a book with neither a voice nor texture but one that pleases a committee of adults and bores the child reader. Similar conclusions have been drawn in nearly all subject areas from primary grades through secondary,[7] to the point where California's Department of Education (as of 1989) has discontinued reading textbooks that are not based on *real* stories, on literature written by authors.

We could also be sending the wrong messages to students by the *way* we teach. Jeanne Jacobson of Western Michigan University, Kalamazoo, tells of working with a functionally illiterate man in his mid-twenties whose *only* experience with reading had been reading *out loud*. Every teacher he'd ever had required him to read out loud. Thus when his family was busy, he thought he couldn't practice reading because there was no one to listen to him. Among his many teachers and tutors, no one had ever modeled any other kind of reading to him. He saw no one in his home reading silently, no one at work. "The message in the media? Newscasters and talk show hosts . . . hide the fact they're reading. No one sees the cue cards or the TelePrompTer," Jacobson noted afterward.[8]

The other message we often send is this: "Boys and girls, when you finish your seatwork, you may go over to the window library and pick a book to read." Meaning: When you finish the important stuff, you can go waste time. Recreational reading becomes the filler in the curriculum.

SSR allows the child to read long enough and far enough so the act of reading becomes automatic. If one must stop to concentrate on each word—sounding it out and searching for meaning—then fluency is lost along with meaning. It is also fatiguing. Being able to do it automatically is the goal.[9] To achieve this, the Commission on Reading (*Becoming a Nation of Readers*) recommended two hours a week of independent reading and less time on skill sheets and workbooks.[10]

SSR also provides students with a new perspective on reading—as a form of recreation. Judging from the number of people (graduates of our schools) who come home from work at night and think they can relax only by watching television, there is a critical need for such lessons.

On the secondary level, there may not be a change in student skills, but there are positive attitudinal changes toward the library, voluntary reading, assigned reading, and the importance of reading. This affects the amount students read and thus their facility with the process.[11]

Younger readers, however, show significant improvement in both attitude and skills with SSR.[12] "Poor readers," points out Professor Richard Allington of the State University of New York, "when given ten minutes a day to read, initially will achieve five hundred words and quickly increase that amount in the same period as proficiency grows."

In a School District of Philadelphia–Federal Reserve Bank study made to determine which reading methods "worked," it was shown that among 1,800 Philadelphia fourth-grade students "the more minutes a week of sustained silent reading, the better the pupils achieved." The same study also indicated that the number of minutes a day of reading instruction that might be lost through SSR did not affect pupil achievement.[13]

Martha Efta offers a special example of SSR's worth. Ms. Efta taught a primary-level class of educable mentally retarded children in Westlake, Ohio. The children, ranging in age from seven to ten, were frequently hyperactive and nonreaders. When she heard of the SSR procedure in a graduate course, she was cautious about the idea despite the professor's wholehearted support for it. After all, she thought, the experts were talking about normal children, not the retarded.

With some trepidation, she explained the procedures to her students and reshaped the rules to fit her classroom. Because of their short attention spans, she allowed each student to choose as many as three books or magazines for the period. Students were allowed to sit any way and in any place they chose in the room. Ms. Efta initially kept the program to three minutes in length, then gradually increased it to thirteen minutes over a period of weeks. This was the class's limit.

"From the onset [of SSR]," Ms. Efta explained, "the students

have demonstrated some exciting and favorable behavior changes—
such as independent decision making, self-discipline, sharing . . .
and broadened reading interests. The enthusiastic rush to select their
day's reading materials following noon recess is indicative of the
children's interest and eagerness for SSR. The children seem to delight in the adult-like responsibility of selecting their own reading
matter."[14]

The McCrackens report that most of the instances where SSR
fails are due to teachers (or aides) who are supervising instead of
reading. The other problem area is where classes lack enough SSR
materials from which to choose.

Writing in *The Reading Teacher,* the McCrackens called attention
to the overwhelming part the teacher plays as a role model in SSR.[15]
Teachers reported widespread imitation by students of the teacher's
reading habits.

Students in one class noticed the teacher interrupting her reading
to look up a word in the dictionary and began doing the same. When
a junior high teacher began to read the daily newspaper each day,
the class began doing the same.

Linda Kuse, a primary teacher in Newburyport, Massachusetts,
brings an element of surprise to her SSR program. Each day she
picks a student to be in charge of the SSR alarm. The student can
set it for any time during the day. When the alarm sounds, the fifteen-
minute SSR period begins. The activity also teaches everyone how
to operate a wind-up clock.

At Maercker School in Westmont, Illinois, each day's school-
wide twenty-minute SSR period is begun by a student who an-
nounces (via the intercom) what he or she is reading and offers a
brief synopsis.

When teachers talk about what they are reading or describe a
spine-tingling section of their book, students are quick to follow suit
and share their reaction. By doing this, the McCrackens write, "they
are teaching attitudes and skills; they are teaching children that reading is communication with an author, an assimilation of and reaction
to an author's ideas."

At St. Louis King of France school in Metairie Park, Louisiana,
the principal explains the purpose of daily SSR in his newsletter: "It

is a serious effort to raise the student's awareness of reading. All in the school participate. Please do not call or come to school during that fifteen-minute span."

You say there isn't enough time in the curriculum for SSR? Then do what Randall School in Bassett, Wisconsin, did—they extended the school day by fifteen minutes. If you have time for gym, art, music, recess, assemblies, and field trips to the zoo, then you'd better find the time for reading real books. If you can't find the time in school, students won't find it outside school either.

The growing popularity of Pizza Hut's Book It! program is another hopeful sign. It was begun in the 1985–86 school year, and more than half the students in American elementary schools now can obtain coupons for free pizzas—depending on how many books they've read. And though the program costs Pizza Hut more than $100 million in free pizzas each year, the company says, "We believe a child's potential is not just everybody's business. It is everybody's future."[16] Imagine what we could accomplish if every corporation in America had the same philosophy.

The real impact of such incentive programs is not the commerce involved but the amount of reading they stimulate—which improves skills and attitudes. When Dr. Jerrome Goldberg, assistant superintendent in Natick, Massachusetts, initiated a reading incentive program there during children's out-of-school time, the public library reported an increase in circulation each year—but only in the children's department. These students are often willing to work more for recognition than for the value of the prize. Natick's prizes included pencils, bookmarks, and buttons with dinosaurs and bears on them.

Nonetheless, such incentive programs stir the ire of education purists who are squeamish about offering prizes to children for reading. Why, I ask, is there a separate set of standards for children? If incentive programs are good for adults (salespeople, insurance agents, and ballplayers), why not kids? The player who has a $50,000 incentive clause in his contract for winning the batting crown is going to try harder. And experience shows us that students will read longer for a pizza than they will for nothing. Many's the swimmer who was initially tricked into the water and then found out how much he liked it. But if the purists truly believe children would read and write for nothing more than the pleasure of the experience, then I suggest the first incentive they should remove is the report card. After all, most children are working in school to achieve that "grade"—not because they love the spelling and addition problems.

SSR works as well in the home as in the classroom. Indeed, considering that by the end of eighth grade, a child has spent only 9,000 hours in school compared to 95,000 outside school, it behooves parents to involve themselves in home SSR before they challenge a teacher on "why Johnny isn't doing better in reading this year."

The same SSR rules should apply in the home; that is, don't tell your child to go read for fifteen minutes while *you* watch television. You can, of course, tailor SSR to fit your family. For children who are not used to reading for more than brief periods of time it is important at first to limit SSR to ten or fifteen minutes. Later, when they are used to reading in this manner and are more involved in books, the period can be extended—often at the child's request. As in the classroom, it is important to have a variety of available material—magazines, newspapers, novels, picture books. A weekly trip to the library can do much to meet this need.

I should also note that the "Three B's" (Books, Bookracks, and Bedlamps) I mentioned on page 29 are invaluable to the success of SSR in the home.

The time selected for family SSR is also important. Involve the whole family in the decision, if possible. Bedtime seems to be the most popular time, perhaps because the child does not have to give up any activity for it except sleeping—and most children gladly surrender that.

9. How to Use the Treasury

The success we have in helping children become readers will depend not so much on our technical skills but upon the spirit we transmit of ourselves as readers. Next in importance comes the breadth and depth of our knowledge of the books we offer. Only out of such a ready catalogue can we match child and book with the sort of spontaneous accuracy that is wanted time and again during a working day.

—Aidan Chambers, from
"Talking About Reading,"
The Horn Book (October 1977)

An essential element in reading aloud is *what* you choose to read aloud. Not all books are worth reading aloud.

The style of writing—if it's convoluted or the sentence structure too complex for the tongue or ear—can make your choice unsuccessful. And reading aloud a boring book induces the same results as reading it silently. Boring is boring. Therefore, the aim of the Treasury is to list books whose subject matter, style, and structure make wonderful read-alouds.

There are two ways to use the Treasury. One way offers three hundred titles and synopses; the second way, however, will triple the number of titles. For example, when you look up *The Biggest Bear,* by Lynd Ward, in the picture book section, you will find not only a synopsis of that book; reading beyond the synopsis reveals another recommended book by Lynd Ward, ten related picture books (about the challenges of owning pets), three short novels, and three full-length novels. There is also a cross-reference to the book *Daisy Rothschild* (p), where more books are listed.

In the reference to *Daisy Rothschild* (p), the letter in parentheses refers to one of the categories into which the Treasury is divided: a listing of Wordless Books and Predictable Books; Picture Books (p); Short Novels (s); Novels (n); Poetry (po); and Anthologies (a). All books in the respective categories are listed alphabetically by title. The Author/Illustrator Index to the Treasury will also help you locate books.

In the synopses, I have tried to indicate wherever I thought certain books needed special attention from the reader-aloud. For example, Harry Mazer's *Snow-Bound* is a compelling novel about two teenagers fighting for their lives in a snowstorm. Many of my teacher friends read it to their middle-school classes each year and skip over the occasional four-letter words in the text. The story is one of the children's favorites and it would be a shame to deprive them of its excitement and values because of a dozen strong words. Nevertheless, the reader-aloud should be alerted to the situation.

I have noted "for experienced listeners" to indicate those books I feel would be poor choices for children just beginning the listening experience. These books should be read aloud only after the children's attention and listening spans have been developed with shorter books and stories.

The number of pages noted for each book should indicate to the reader the number of sittings the book requires. A children's book of thirty-two pages can be completed easily in one session.

What is the difference between those titles given main entries and those listed after the synopsis? Most of the time there is only a fine distinction, sometimes none. The problem in compiling the Treasury is there isn't enough room to give every book a main entry and synopsis.

Of the more than 2,000 children's books published each year, about 60 percent could be categorized as "fast food for the mind," and of minimal lasting value. Only about 10 percent of the year's crop could be rated Grade A.

This is not to say that fast-food books are worthless. On the contrary, they serve as hors d'oeuvres and build appetites (to say nothing of reading skills) for more nourishing books later. They also serve as valuable transition steps between textbook reading and leisure reading. Jacques Barzun, most recently a consultant to the Council for Basic Education, is the author of *Teacher in America* (written while he was professor of history and later provost of Columbia University), in which he comments on so-called junk reading by children: "Let me say at once that all books are good and that consequently a child be allowed to read everything he lays his hands on. Trash is excellent; great works . . . are admirable. . . . The ravenous appetite will digest stones unharmed. Never mind the need to discriminate; it comes in its own time."[1] (In using the word "trash," Barzun was referring to formula fiction like the Hardy Boys and Nancy Drew.)

The reader-aloud, however, offers an alternative for the child, allowing him to sample the "Grade A" books which may be beyond either his skills or his surface appetites. We should, therefore, in reading aloud concern ourselves primarily (though not exclusively) with books that will stimulate children's emotions, minds, and imaginations, stories that will stay with them for years to come, literature that will serve as a harbor light toward which a child can navigate.

Few parents and teachers have the time or opportunity to wade through the vast numbers of newly published books, not to mention the previous year's volumes. Librarians and booksellers can help in this chore, especially when they know the patron's needs and preferences. ("Mrs. Rostek, wait until you see the new dinosaur book that's just come in. Andy will love it!") But not everyone has access to such professional services, and I hope the Treasury will help in that regard.

I fully recognize the danger in compiling any "book list." There will always be those who see it as exclusive. ("If it's not mentioned in *The Read-Aloud Handbook*'s Treasury, it can't be that good!") As well-intentioned as such thinking may be, it is wrong. If Harvard and Stanford can't agree on which classics constitute the core curriculum, how could I come up with the ultimate list? And with more than 2,000 new children's books being issued this year, the best of those will already be missing from this revision and must wait for the revision four years from now. If you find someone using the list exclusively, please call this chapter to their attention.

I make no boast of the Treasury being a comprehensive list. It is intended only as a starter and time-saver. (I'd be willing to wager, in fact, that I've left your all-time favorite off the list.) Some books, like *Treasure Island* or *Tom Sawyer,* have not been listed here because they already are included in most school reading curriculums. Another obvious choice, the Bible, is omitted. As the world's greatest collection of stories, it is an obvious choice for reading aloud, but the multiplicity of sects makes the choice of one or even several texts impossible. Fortunately there is no shortage of books containing Bible stories for children, and their selection best rests in the hands of the individual parent or teacher.

I have tried to make the collection as balanced as possible between classical, traditional, and contemporary titles. It will not be as heavy with classics as the elitists would like. The idea is to create readers, not English professors. Some of the picture books are fifty years old, like *Mike Mulligan and His Steam Shovel;* others are only two years old, like *The Amazing Voyage of Jackie Grace.* Where you do not find single volumes of certain classics (like the Greek myths), you will often find them in one of the recommendations in the Anthologies or Poetry sections. I am also the beneficiary of a network of parents, teachers, and librarians whom I've met in my travels and who regularly give me tips on titles. ("Jim, you missed a wonderful book in your last edition, one I think you should know about. It's called . . .") I immediately think of two books in this edition that came to my attention this way: *Sideways Stories from Wayside School,* by Louis Sachar (many teachers and librarians recommended it), and *The Girl with the Silver Eyes,* by Willo Davis Roberts (from a Florida mother who said her daughter "would rather listen to that book than go to Disney World").

In making my selections, I use the following criteria:

1. I must have read the book. (After all these years of reading aloud, I can tell almost immediately if it works "aloud.")
2. The book must have a proven track record as a read-aloud

with children. Teachers, librarians, and other parents assist in such evaluations.

3. The book must be interesting enough to inspire children to want to read another one like it, or even the same book again.

Nearly all the books listed are strong on narrative. By and large, they have a story to tell in which there is a conflict, some drama, and a conclusion. Nothing consistently holds the attention of a classroom of children with divergent interests quite like fiction. I have purposely avoided books that are top-heavy with dialogue because (1) they are often too difficult to read aloud, and (2) they read more like television scripts than books.

Below the main entry for each book, you will find the name of the author and illustrator, along with the publisher, recommended grade level, and the number of pages.

In listing the publishers, the paperback publisher (if there is one) will always follow the hardcover publisher, separated by a semicolon. For example: Harper, 1960; Bantam, 1971. Where a particular publisher handles both the hardcover and paperback editions, the notation will be: Harper (both), 1972; 1975. Bear in mind, however, that the publishing data are subject to change as books go out of print or go into paperback. The most up-to-date listing on the availability of books is a reference guide called *Books in Print,* found in most libraries, along with *Paperback Books in Print.* Another of the great things about libraries is how you can often find books still on their shelves that are long out of print and not sold in bookstores.

The grade recommendations for each book refer to the "listening level" of the book; in other words, Gr. 1-3 means this book can be understood when read aloud to most children in grades one through three. There will be many first-graders who couldn't read it on their own but can certainly comprehend it when it is read to them. But I must emphasize that these grade recommendations are meant to be flexible guidelines, not rules. In addition to the numbered grade levels, the following codes are included:

Tod.—infants and toddlers up to three-year-olds
Pre-S.—from three-year-olds to five-year-olds
K—kindergartners

10. Treasury of Read-Alouds

Predictable Books

(These picture books contain word or sentence patterns that are repeated often enough to enable children to predict their appearance and thus begin to join in on the reading. Books marked with an * are described at length in the Picture Book section of the Treasury.)

Are You My Mother?, P. D. Eastman (Random House, 1960)
Ask Mister Bear, Marjorie Flack (Macmillan, 1986)
Brown, Brown Bear, What Do You See?, Bill Martin Jr. (Holt, 1983)

The Cake That Mack Ate, Rose Robart (Atlantic, 1986)
Chicken Soup with Rice, Maurice Sendak (Harper, 1962)
Do You Want to Be My Friend?, Eric Carle (Putnam, 1971)
Drummer Hoff, Ed Emberly (Prentice-Hall, 1967)
The Elephant and the Bad Boy, Elfrida Vipont (Putnam, 1986)
Fat Mouse, Harry Stevens (Viking, 1987)
*Goodnight Moon, Margaret Wise Brown (Harper, 1947)
The Gingerbread Boy, Paul Galdone (Clarion, 1975)
The Gunnywolf, A. Delaney (Harper, 1988)
Hattie and the Fox, Mem Fox (Bradbury, 1987)
Henny Penny, Paul Galdone (Clarion, 1968)
The House That Jack Built, Rodney Peppe (Delacorte, 1985)
It Looked Like Spilt Milk, Charles Shaw (Harper, 1947)
The Little Old Lady Who Was Not Afraid of Anything, Linda Williams
    (Crowell, 1986)
Mr. Magnolia, Quentin Blake (Salem House, 1980)
Old Mother Hubbard, Colin and Jacqui Hawkins (Putnam, 1985)
Over in the Meadow, Olive Wadsworth (Viking, 1985)
The Teeny Tiny Woman, Barbara Seuling (Puffin, 1978)
Three Blind Mice, John Ivimey (Clarion, 1987)
*The Three Little Pigs, Paul Galdone (Clarion, 1970)
*Tikki Tikki Tembo, Arlene Mosel (Holt, 1968) (p)
This Old Man: The Counting Song, Robin Koontz (Dodd, Mead, 1988)
The Wheels on the Bus, Maryann Kovalski (Little, Brown, 1987)
*Where's Spot?, Eric Hill (Putnam, 1980)

Wordless Books

(These picture books contain no words; the story is told entirely with
pictures arranged in sequence. Wordless books can be "read" not only by
pre- and beginning readers, but also by illiterate or semiliterate adults who
want to "read" to children. They "tell" the book, using the pictures for
clues to the emerging plot. Books marked with an * are described at length
in the Picture Book section of the Treasury.)

*The Adventures of Paddy Pork, John Goodall (Harcourt, 1968)
Ah-Choo!, Mercer Mayer (Dial, 1976)
Amanda and the Mysterious Carpet, Fernando Krahn (Houghton Mifflin, 1985)

The Angel and the Soldier Boy, Peter Collington (Knopf, 1987)
The Bear and the Fly, Paula Winter (Crown, 1976)
A Birthday Wish, Ed Emberley (Little, Brown, 1977)
Bobo's Dream, Martha Alexander (Dial, 1970)
A Boy, a Dog, and a Frog, Mercer Mayer (Dial, 1967)
Breakfast Time, Ernest and Celestine, Gabrielle Vincent (Greenwillow, 1982)
Bubble, Bubble, Mercer Mayer (Macmillan, 1973)
Changes, Changes, Pat Hutchins (Macmillan, 1971)
The Christmas Gift, Emily McCully (Harper, 1988)
Creepy Castle, John Goodall (Atheneum, 1975)
Deep in the Forest, Brinton Turkle (Dutton, 1976)
Do You Want to Be My Friend?, Eric Carle (Crowell, 1971)
Dreams, Peter Spier (Doubleday, 1986)
Ernest and Celestine's Patchwork Quilt, Gabrielle Vincent (Greenwillow, 1982)
Frog Goes to Dinner, Mercer Mayer (Dial, 1974)
Frog on His Own, Mercer Mayer (Dial, 1973)
Frog, Where Are You?, Mercer Mayer (Dial, 1969)
The Gift, John Prater (Viking, 1985)
Good Dog Carl, Alexandra Day (Green Tiger, 1985)
The Great Escape, Philippe Dupasquier (Houghton Mifflin, 1988)
The Grey Lady and the Strawberry Snatcher, Molly Bang (Four Winds, 1980)
The Hunter and the Animals, Tomie dePaola (Holiday, 1981)
Little Red Riding Hood, John Goodall (Atheneum, 1988)
The Midnight Adventures of Kelly, Dot, and Esmeralda, John Goodall
    (Atheneum, 1972)
Moonlight, Jan Ormerod (Lothrop 1982; Puffin, 1983)
The Mystery of the Giant Footprints, Fernando Krahn (Dutton, 1977)
Noah's Ark, Peter Spier (Doubleday, 1977)
One Frog Too Many, Mercer Mayer (Dial, 1975)
The Other Bone, Ed Young (Harper, 1984)
Paddy Goes Traveling, John Goodall (Atheneum, 1982)
Paddy's Evening Out, John Goodall (Atheneum, 1973)
Paddy to the Rescue, John Goodall (Atheneum, 1985)
Pancakes for Breakfast, Tomie dePaola (Harcourt, 1978)
Peter Spier's Christmas, Peter Spier (Doubleday, 1982)
Peter Spier's Rain, Peter Spier (Doubleday, 1982)
Rosie's Walk, Pat Hutchins (Macmillan, 1968)
Shrewbettina's Birthday, John Goodall (Harcourt, 1970)
The Silver Pony, Lynd Ward (Houghton Mifflin, 1973)
Sleep Tight, Alex Pumpernickel, Fernando Krahn (Little, 1982)

The Snowman, Raymond Briggs (Random, 1978)
A Story to Tell, Dick Bruna (Price, Stern, 1968)
Sunshine, Jan Ormerod (Lothrop, 1981; Puffin, 1983)
Up a Tree, Ed Young (Harper, 1983)
Up and Up, Shirley Hughes (Lothrop, 1986)
Where's My Monkey?, Dieter Schubert (Dial, 1987)

Reference Resources

(Here are four oversized, economical picture book reference sources relating to areas about which children show continuing interest.)

DO ANIMALS DREAM?
by Joyce Pope
Viking, 1986
96 pages
Information, illustrations, and charts to answer the nearly 100 questions children ask most often at the Natural History Museum.

HOW THE HUMAN BODY WORKS
by Giovanni Caselli
Grosset, 1987
64 pages
Dramatic allegorical illustrations to answer the most common questions about the human body. Also: *Why Do Our Bodies Stop Growing?,* by Drs. Philip and Ruth Whitfield.

THE KIDS' QUESTION & ANSWER BOOK
by the editors of *Owl* Magazine
Grosset, 1988
77 pages
Questions and answers on 100 topics—from dinosaurs and dizziness to sneezes and hiccups.

LIFE THROUGH THE AGES
by Giovanni Caselli
Grosset, 1987
64 pages
In hundreds of color illustrations, the great ideas and moments in history (from Stone Age to Space Age) are chronicled.

Picture Books

THE ADVENTURES OF PADDY PORK
by John S. Goodall
Harcourt, 1968
Pre-S.–2   60 (small) pages
This is the British counterpart (but more sophisticated in concept) of America's successful *Boy and Frog* series by Mercer Mayer. It is a series of wordless books that detail the adventures of a naughty pig and his bottomless curiosity. Because of the small format, it is best read with no more than three children at once. Sequels: *Ballooning Adventures of Paddy Pork; Creepy Castle; Jacko; The Midnight Adventures of Kelly, Dot, and Esmeralda; Naughty Nancy Goes to School; Paddy Goes Traveling; Paddy's Evening Out; Paddy Pork—Odd Jobs; Shrewbettina's Birthday.*

ALADDIN
Retold by Andrew Lang • Illustrated by Errol Le Cain
Viking, 1981; Puffin, 1983
Gr. 2 and up   30 pages
Here is the world-famous tale about the magic lamp that brings the poor Persian boy his heart's desire—but only after great trials. More such tales can be found in an excellent new edition of *Stories from the Arabian Nights,* retold by Naomi Lewis. Related books: *Inside My Feet* (s); *The Wish Giver* (n); *Do Not Open,* by Brinton Turkle; *The Secret in the Matchbox,* by Val Willis.

ALEXANDER AND THE TERRIBLE, HORRIBLE, NO GOOD, VERY BAD DAY
by Judith Viorst • Illustrated by Ray Cruz
Atheneum (both), 1972; 1976
K and up   34 pages

Everyone has a bad day once in a while but Alexander has the worst of all. Follow him from a cereal box without a prize to a burned-out night light. A modern classic for all ages to chuckle over and admit, "I guess we're all entitled to a terrible, horrible, no good . . ." Sequel: *Alexander Who Used to Be Rich Last Sunday*. Also by the author: see listing with *If I Were in Charge of the World and Other Worries* (po).

THE AMAZING VOYAGE OF JACKIE GRACE
by Matt Faulkner
Scholastic, 1987
Pre-S–Gr. 1   38 pages
Once he climbs into the bathtub, Jackie's imagination carries him away to the high seas where he battles pirates and a fierce storm in a book that does for bathtubs what *Where the Wild Things Are* does for bedrooms. Related books: *The Great Piratical Rumbustification* (s); *How I Hunted the Little Fellows* (p); *Obadiah the Bold*, by Brinton Turkle; *Regards to the Man in the Moon* (p); *Andrew's Bath*, by David McPhail; *And to Think That I Saw It on Mulberry Street*, by Dr. Seuss; *The Beast in the Bathtub*, by Kathleen Stevens; *Burt Dow, Deep-Water Man*, by Robert McCloskey; *Jack at Sea*, by Philippe Dupasquier; *King's Bidgood's in the Bathtub*, by Audrey Wood; and the following series by Edward Ardizzone: *Little Tim and the Brave Sea Captain; Lucy Brown and Mr. Grimes; Lucy in Danger; Ship's Cook Ginger; Tim All Alone; Tim and Charlotte; Tim and Ginger; Tim's Friend Towser; Tim in Danger; Tim's Last Voyage; Tim to the Lighthouse*.

AMELIA BEDELIA
by Peggy Paris • Illustrated by Fritz Seibel
Harper, 1963; Scholastic, 1970
K–4   24 pages
America's most lovable maid since "Hazel," Amelia is a walking disaster—thanks to her insistence on taking directions literally. She "dusts the furniture" with dusting powder; "dresses the turkey" in shorts; "puts the lights out" on the clothesline. She makes for a hilarious exploration of homonyms and idioms. Sequels: *Amelia Bedelia and the Baby; Amelia Bedelia and the Surprise Shower; Amelia Bedelia's Family Album; Amelia Bedelia Goes Camping; Amelia Bedelia Goes Shopping; Come Back, Amelia Bedelia; Good Work, Amelia Bedelia; Play Ball, Amelia Bedelia; Teach Us, Amelia Bedelia; Thank You, Amelia Bedelia*. Related books: *The Stupids Step Out* (p); *All of Our Noses Are Here and Other Noodle Tales*, retold by Alvin Schwartz; *I'm Telling You*

Now, by Judy Delton; *The King Who Rained,* by Fred Gwynne; *The McGoonys Have a Party,* by Brian Schatell.

THE AMINAL
by Lorna Balian
Abingdon (both), 1972; 1985
K–5   26 pages
A picture book story of how children's imaginations often run ahead of reality, particularly when accompanied by their fears. Also by the author: *The Sweet Touch; Humbug Rabbit.* Related books: *Wolf! Wolf!* (p); *How I Hunted the Little Fellows* (p); *And to Think That I Saw It on Mulberry Street,* by Dr. Seuss.

ARNOLD OF THE DUCKS
by Mordicai Gerstein
Harper (both), 1983; 1985
Pre-S.–Gr. 2   54 pages
A contemporary Mowgli, little Arnold disappears from his backyard wading pool one day and finds himself not only adopted by a family of ducks, but also thinking and acting like a duck. He even learns to fly. All goes well until the "call of home" drowns out the "call of the wild" in this poignant and often funny tale. Other unusual children can be found in: *The Silver Pony* (p); *Up and Up,* by Shirley Hughes; and *Avocado Baby,* by John Burningham.

BENNETT CERF'S BOOK OF ANIMAL RIDDLES
by Bennett Cerf • Illustrated by Roy McKie
Random, 1959
Pre-S.–2   62 pages
Joke books are an instant favorite with children. Because jokes are easily and willingly committed to memory, they offer the child an opportunity to display his cleverness when he recites them, thus building self-confidence and a sense of humor. Sequels: *Bennett Cerf's Book of Laughs; Bennett Cerf's Book of Riddles; More Riddles.* Related books: *Buggy Riddles,* by Katy Hall and Lisa Eisenberg; *Spooky Riddles,* by Marc Brown; *Ten Copycats in a Boat and Other Riddles,* by Alvin Schwartz; and these three riddle books by David Adler: *The Carsick Zebra and Other Animal Riddles; The Purple Turkey and Other Thanksgiving Riddles;* and *The Twisted Witch and Other Spooky Riddles.* For older children: *The Best Joke Book for Kids* and *The Best Joke Book for*

Kids #2, by Joan Eckstein and Joyce Gleit; *Haunted House* and *How Do You Get a Horse Out of the Bathtub?*, by Louis Phillips.

THE BIGGEST BEAR
by Lynd Ward
Houghton Mifflin (both), 1952; 1973
K–3   80 pages
Johnny adopts a bear cub fresh out of the woods and its growth presents problem after problem—the crises we invite when we tame what is meant to be wild. Also by the author: *The Silver Pony* (p). Related books: *The Carp in the Bathtub* (p); *The Mysterious Tadpole* (p); *Cappyboppy*, by Bill Peet; *Emily's Own Elephant*, by Philippa Pearce; *Faithful Elephants*, by Yukio Tsuchiya; *Harry's Dog*, by Barbara Ann Porte; *The Josephina Story Quilt*, by Eleanor Coerr; *No One Is Going to Nashville*, by Mavis Jukes; *Pelican*, by Brian Wildsmith; *Suleiman the Elephant*, by Margret Rettich; *Storm Boy*, a short novel by Colin Thiele; and (for older children): *The Animal Family* (n); *Gentle Ben* (n): *Mr. Popper's Penguins* (n); *Owls in the Family* (s); *Ferret in the Bedroom, Lizards in the Fridge*, by Bill Wallace; see also: *Daisy Rothschild* (p).

THE BOY WHO HELD BACK THE SEA
retold by Lenny Hort • Illustrated by Thomas Locker
Dial, 1987
K–5   26 pages
Complete with magnificent landscapes in the style of the Dutch masters, here is the classic tale of the determined Dutch boy who saves his sleeping village by plugging the hole in the leaking dike. Related books on courageous children: *Brave Irene* (p); *Wagon Wheels* (p); *The Emperor and the Kite*, by Jane Yolen; *Harald and the Giant Knight* and *Harald and the Great Stag*, by Donald Carrick; *The Lighthouse Keeper's Daughter*, by Arielle North Olson; and the following series by the great Edward Ardizzone: *Little Tim and the Brave Sea Captain; Lucy Brown and Mr. Grimes; Lucy in Danger; Ship's Cook Ginger; Tim All Alone; Tim and Charlotte; Tim and Ginger; Tim's Friend Towser; Tim in Danger; Tim's Last Voyage; Tim to the Lighthouse*. For older readers, see listing with *The Courage of Sarah Noble* (s).

BRAVE IRENE
by William Steig
Farrar (both), 1986; 1988
K–5   28 pages

When Irene's dressmaker mother falls ill and cannot deliver the dutchess's gown for the ball, Irene shoulders the huge box and battles a winter storm to make the delivery. For other books by this great artist/storyteller, see Index to Treasury. Related books: *A Chair for My Mother* (p); *Legend of the Bluebonnet* (p); *Belinda's Hurricane,* by Elizabeth Winthrop. For a list of books about courageous children, see *The Boy Who Held Back the Sea* (p).

BRODERICK
by Edward Ormondroyd • Illustrated by John Larrecq
Parnassus, 1969; Houghton Mifflin, 1984
Pre-S.–2   32 pages
Because they share problems in a world preoccupied with bigness, children seem to have an affinity for mice and their stories. Broderick is one of the best of the lot. Nestled away in a library where he searches for the meaning of his life while eating the bindings, he finally discovers the purpose of books—and a new world opens for him. Also by the author: *Theodore* and *Theodore's Rival*. For related stories about reading, see *Too Many Books* (p). Other mouse books: *Frederick* (p); *Island of the Skog* (p); *Amos and Boris* and *Dr. De Soto,* both by William Steig; *The Big Hungry Bear,* by Don and Audrey Wood; *Cathedral Mouse* by Kay Chorao; *Dudley and the Strawberry Shake* (series), by Judy Taylor; *If You Give a Mouse a Cookie,* by Laura Numeroff; *Loudmouse,* by Richard Wilbur; *The Mousewife,* by Rumer Godden; *Norman the Doorman,* by Don Freeman. For mice novels, see *Pearl's Promise* (n).

THE CARP IN THE BATHTUB
by Barbara Cohen • Illustrated by Joan Halpern
Lothrop, 1972
Gr. 1–4   48 pages
When Leah and Harry's mother brings a live carp home (to cook for Passover) and temporarily stores it in the bathtub, she never anticipates their adopting it as their best friend. With bittersweet humor, the story offers a nostalgic view of Passover customs. Also by the author: *Molly's Pilgrim;* for older children: *Thank You, Jackie Robinson* (n); *Benny; King of The Seventh Grade*. Related books: *The Biggest Bear* (p); *The Golem* and *Stories for Children,* both by Isaac Bashevis Singer; *The Mysterious Tadpole,* by Steven Kellogg.

A CHAIR FOR MY MOTHER
by Vera B. Williams
Greenwillow, 1982
K–3   30 pages
This is the first book in a trilogy of tender picture books about a family of three women: Grandma, Mama, and daughter Rosa (all written in the first person by the child). In this story, they struggle to save their loose change (in a glass jar) in order to buy a chair for the child's mother—something she can collapse into after her waitressing job. In *Something for Me*, the glass jar's contents are to be spent on the child's birthday present. What an important decision for a little girl to make! After much soul-searching, she settles on a used accordion. In *Music, Music for Everyone*, the jar is empty again. With all the loose change going for Grandma's medical expenses now, little Rosa searches for a way to make money and cheer up her grandma. Related books: *The Giving Tree* (p); *The Witch of Fourth Street* (s); *A Gift for Mama* (a short novel), by Esther Hautzig; see also Index to Treasury for books by Ezra Jack Keats.

CLOUDY WITH A CHANCE OF MEATBALLS
by Judi Barrett • Illustrated by Ron Barrett
Atheneum (both), 1978; 1982
Pre-S.–5   28 pages
In the fantasy land of Chewandswallow, the weather changes three times a day (at breakfast, lunch, and supper), supplying all the residents with food out of the sky. But suddenly the weather takes a turn for the worse; instead of normal size meatballs, it rains meatballs the size of basketballs; pancakes and syrup smother the streets. Something must be done! Also by the author: *Animals Should Definitely Not Act Like People; Animals Should Definitely Not Wear Clothing; Benjamin's 365 Birthdays.* Related books: *The Great Green Turkey Creek Monster*, by James Flora; *The Giant Jam Sandwich*, by John Lord.

THE COMPLETE ADVENTURES OF PETER RABBIT
by Beatrix Potter
Warne, 1982; Puffin, 1984
Tod.–1   96 pages
Here in one volume are the four original tales involving one of the most famous animals of all time—Peter Rabbit. In a vicarious way children identify with his naughty sense of adventure, and then thrill at his narrow escape from the clutches of Mr. McGregor. Much of the success of Beatrix Potter's

books is due to her sensitive illustrations as much as to the story line. For this reason I feel the recent editions of *The Tale of Peter Rabbit* illustrated by others fail by comparison. All twenty-three of the Potter books come in a small format (recently republished by Warne from the original artwork) that I think is ideal because young children feel more comfortable holding that size (3" × 5"). This volume, slightly larger, is the most economic choice while still retaining the Potter illustrations. Also by the author: *Hill Top Tales*. Related books: *The Easter Bunny That Overslept,* by Priscilla and Otto Friedrich; *Little Sister Rabbit,* by Ulf Nilsson.

CORDUROY
by Don Freeman
Viking, 1968; Puffin, 1976
Tod.–2   32 pages
The story of a teddy bear's search through a department store for a friend. His quest ends when a little girl buys him with her piggybank savings. Sequel: *A Pocket for Corduroy*. Also by the author: *Beady Bear; Bearymore; Dandelion; Mop Top; Norman the Doorman*. Toddlers will enjoy the board books *Corduroy's Day, Corduroy's Party,* and *Corduroy's Toys*. For other teddy bear books, see *Ira Sleeps Over* (p).

CRANBERRY THANKSGIVING
by Wende and Harry Devlin
Four Winds, 1971
K–4   30 pages
The first of a series of mystery-adventure tales set on the cranberry bog shores of Cape Cod. A regular cast of young Becky, her grandmother, and a retired old sea captain are supported by a variety of pratfalling villains and sheriffs. If possible, read the series in this order: *Cranberry Thanksgiving; Cranberry Christmas; Cranberry Halloween; Cranberry Valentine; Cranberry Easter; Cranberry Birthday; Cranberry Mystery*.

CURIOUS GEORGE
by H. A. Rey
Houghton Mifflin, (both); 1941; 1973
Pre-S.–1   48 pages
One of the classic figures in children's books, George is the funny little monkey whose curiosity gets the best of him and wins the hearts of his millions of fans. Among the more than twenty books in the series: *Curious George and the Dump Truck; Curious George at the Laundromat; Curious George*

Flies a Kite; Curious George Goes to a Restaurant; Curious George Goes to the Circus; Curious George Goes to the Hospital; Curious George Learns the Alphabet; Curious George Plays Baseball; and *Curious George Rides a Bike.*

THE CUT-UPS CUT LOOSE
by James Marshall
Viking, 1987; Puffin, 1989
K–2 30 pages
Armed with rubber snakes, spitballs, and stink bombs, Spud and Joe are the quintessential neighborhood and school cut-ups, and every reader/listener will love their antics in battling Mr. Spurgle—who not only lives in their neighborhood but is their school principal, too, in this sequel to *The Cut-Ups.* Also by the author: *George and Martha* (series); *Space Case* and *Miss Nelson Is Missing* (p) (with Harry Allard); and *The Stupids Step Out* (p). For related books about school, see *The Day Jimmy's Boa Ate the Wash* (p).

DAISY ROTHSCHILD: THE GIRAFFE THAT LIVES WITH ME
by Betty Leslie-Melville
Doubleday, 1987
Gr. 1–4 42 pages
This remarkable true story features a husband and wife in Africa who adopt nine-foot, 1,500-pound "Daisy." The adoptee is a three-month-old endangered species of giraffe and she turns out to be very much a "child," complete with security blanket and temper tantrums, who falls in love with "Dad" and exhibits sibling rivalry. For related books on the bittersweet joys that come when families "adopt" wild animals, try these five true stories: *The Goose Family Book,* by Sybille Kalas; *Julius* (chimpanzee), by T. B. Klingsheim; *Koko's Story* (Koko is the baby gorilla who learned to "sign" more than 500 vocabulary words) and *Koko's Kitten,* by Dr. Francine Patterson; *A Moose for Jessica* (the celebrated Vermont bull moose that fell in love with the Hereford cow), by Pat Wakefield and Larry Carrara. For other books on taming the naturally wild, see *The Biggest Bear* (p).

DAWN
by Molly Bang
Morrow, 1983
K–4 30 pages
In this modern adaptation of a Japanese fairy tale ("The Crane Wife"), a shipbuilder marries a mysterious woman who weaves magnificent sails for

him. Her only demand is that he never watch her while she weaves. All is well until he breaks his vow. The incorporation of a child and an upbeat ending make this adaptation especially successful. Also by the author: *The Gray Lady and the Strawberry Snatcher; Ten, Nine, Eight; Wiley and the Hairy Man*. Related books: *Arnold of the Ducks* (p); *The Crane Wife*, retold by Katherine Paterson; *The Selkie Girl*, by Susan Cooper; *The Wreck of the Zephyr*, by Chris Van Allsburg; and for older children, *The Animal Family* (n); *A Stranger Came Ashore* (n).

THE DAY JIMMY'S BOA ATE THE WASH
by Trinka Hakes Noble
Dial (both), 1980
Pre-S.–2   30 pages

In this hilarious disaster story, Jimmy brings his pet boa constrictor on the class trip to a farm. Slapstick abounds as animals, students, and teachers respond in character. In the sequel, *Jimmy's Boa Bounces Back*, Meggie's mother brings the boa to her garden club meeting with terrible results.

The following books (some funny, others serious) have classroom settings: *The Cut-Ups Cut Loose* (p); *Freckle Juice* (s); *Miss Nelson Is Missing* (p); *The Balancing Girl*, by Bernice Rabe; *The Boy Who Hated Valentine's Day*, by Sally Whitman; *Crow Boy*, by Taro Yashima; *My Teacher Sleeps at School*, by Leatie Weiss; *The Snake That Went to School* (short novel), by Lilian Moore; *The Secret in the Matchbox*, by Val Willis; *Starting School*, by Janet and Allan Ahlberg; *Teach Us, Amelia Bedelia*, by Peggy Parish; *That Dreadful Day*, by James Stevenson; *Timothy Goes to School*, by Rosemary Wells. Also, don't miss Miriam Cohen's series on one first-grade class's trials and triumphs: *Bee My Valentine!; Best Friends; First Grade Takes a Test; Jim's Dog Muffins; Jim Meets the Thing; Lost in the Museum; The New Teacher; No Good in Art; See You Tomorrow, Charles; So What?; Tough Jim; Will I Have a Friend?*

DEEP IN THE FOREST
by Brinton Turkle
Dutton (both), 1976; 1986
Pre-S.–2   30 pages

A wordless book reversing the conventional Goldilocks/Three Bears tale. This time the bear cub visits Goldilocks's family cabin with hilarious and plausible results. Also by the author: *Thy Friend, Obadiah* (p); and *Do Not Open*. For a list of other wordless books, see Wordless Books section of Treasury. Related books: *The Three Bears* by Paul Galdone and a contemporary version of *Goldilocks and the Three Bears* by James Marshall; and for experienced listeners, a clever fairy tale parody, *Jeremiah in the Deep Woods,* by Allan Ahlberg.

DINOSAUR BOB AND HIS ADVENTURES WITH THE FAMILY LIZARDO
by William Joyce
Harper, 1988
Pre-S.–4   30 pages
In this dinosaur fantasy book, the Lizardo family brings a dinosaur home from Africa with them and he proves to be the ultimate pet for home and community—after some initial misgivings by the police department. Also by the author: *George Shrinks.* Related books: *The Mysterious Tadpole* (p); *The Enormous Egg* (n); *My Father's Dragon* (s); *The Big Beast Book: Dinosaurs and How They Got That Way,* by Jerry Booth; *The Boy Who Was Followed Home,* by Margaret Mahy; *Big Old Bones: A Dinosaur Tale, Patrick's Dinosaurs,* and *What Happened to Patrick's Dinosaurs?,* all by Carol Carrick; *Digging Up Dinosaurs,* by Aliki; *Dinosaurs Are 568,* by Jean Rogers; *Little Grunt and the Big Egg,* by Tomie dePaola; and *Prehistoric Pinkerton,* by Steven Kellogg.

AN EVENING AT ALFIE'S
by Shirley Hughes
Lothrop, 1985
Pre-S.–2   28 pages
This is the classic "babysitter" story, describing the excitement for little Alfie, his baby sister and the babysitter on the night the water pipe burst. (This book and Peter Spier's *Noah's Ark* are a wonderful combination—read *Noah* first.) Other books in the series by one of England's most popular authors: *Alfie Gives a Hand; Alfie Gets in First; Alfie's Feet.* Also by the author/illustrator: for toddlers—*Bathwater's Hot; All Shapes and Sizes; Colors; Noisy; Out and About; Two Shoes, New Shoes; When We Went to the Park;* for Pre K. and up—*Dogger; Haunted House; Lucy and Tom's ABC; Lucy and Tom's Christmas; Lucy and Tom's Day; Sally's Secret; Up and Up* (wordless).

FABLES FROM AESOP
Retold by James Reeves • Illustrated by Maurice Wilson
Bedrick/Blackie, 1985
Gr. 2–6   123 pages
Here are fifty of the most famous lessons on the human condition, retold

by this distinguished English poet. Another excellent resource is *Anno's Aesop*, by Mitsumasa Anno. Related books: *Cry Wolf and Other Aesop Fables*, by Naomi Lewis; *Petunia* (p); *The Tales of Uncle Remus* (a); *Bo Rabbit Smart for True*, by Priscilla Jaquith; *Fables* (contemporary), by Arnold Lobel; *Frederick's Fables*, by Leo Lionni; see Index to Treasury for Bill Peet books.

FAIR IS FAIR
by Leon Garfield • Illustrated by S. D. Schindler
Doubleday, 1983
K–5   28 pages
Two street orphans follow a stray dog into an old English mansion where their meals are mysteriously provided each day. Set in eighteenth-century England in winter, the story brims with secrets, friendship, beautiful language, and dramatic illustrations—topped with a surprise ending. For experienced listeners. Related books: *A Lion to Guard Us* (s); *The Moon's Revenge* (p); *Sara Crewe* (s); *The Story of Holly and Ivy* (s).

FLASH, CRASH, RUMBLE AND ROLL
by Franklyn M. Branley • Illustrated by Barbara and Ed Emberly
Harper (both); 1985
K–3   30 pages
This nonfiction book about thunderstorms is done in the simple, insightful, and reassuring manner that makes the Harper series "Let's-Read-and-Find-Out Science Books" the best of its kind in publishing for pre- and beginning readers. There are more than 100 short picture books covering these topics: wildlife, computers, dinosaurs and prehistory, the environment, the human body, plants, and space travel. Their detailed pictures work best for reading aloud to a group no larger than six. A free catalogue is available by writing: Let's-Read-and-Find-Out-Books, Publicity Dept., JT, Harper Junior Books, Harper & Row, 10 East 53rd St., New York, NY 10022. For related books, see Reference Resources (p).

FOOLISH RABBIT'S BIG MISTAKE
by Rafe Martin • Illustrated by Ed Young
Putnam, 1985
Pre-S.–3   30 pages
One of the oldest versions of the "the sky is falling" tale, here it is a powerful narrative featuring rumor and panic until cooler heads prevail. The large illustrations are a perfect match to the dramatic text. Related books: *Tales*

from Uncle Remus (a); *Fables from Aesop* (p); *Bo Rabbit Smart for True: Folktales from the Gullah,* by Priscilla Jaquith; *Mr. Monkey and the Gotcha Bird,* by Walter Dean Myers.

FREDERICK
by Leo Lionni
Pantheon (both), 1966
Pre-S. and up   28 pages
Frederick is a tiny gray field mouse. He is also an allegorical figure representing the poets, artists, and dreamers of the world. While his brothers and sisters gather food against the oncoming winter, Frederick gathers the colors and stories and dreams they will need to sustain their hearts and souls in the winter darkness. Also by the author: *Alexander and the Wind-up Mouse; The Biggest House in the World; Fish Is Fish; Frederick's Fables: A Leo Lionni Treasury of Favorite Stories; Little Blue and Little Yellow; Nicholas, Where Have You Been?; Pezzetino; Swimmy; Tilly and the Wall.* For related books, see listing under *Broderick* (p).

FROG AND TOAD ARE FRIENDS
by Arnold Lobel
Harper (both), 1970; 1979
Pre-S.–2   64 pages
Using a simple early-reader vocabulary and fablelike story lines, the author-artist developed an award-winning series that is a must for young children. Generous helpings of humor and warm personal relationships are the trademarks of the series, each book containing five individual stories relating to childhood. Few author/illustrators sustained as high a quality of work through so many books as did Arnold Lobel. Sequels: *Days with Frog and Toad; Frog and Toad All Year; Frog and Toad Together.* Also by the author: *Fables; Giant John; Grasshopper on the Road; The Great Blueness and Other Predicaments; Gregory Griggs and Other Nursery Rhyme People; Mouse Soup; Mouse Tales; Owl at Home; Uncle Elephant; Whiskers and Rhymes.*

THE GIVING TREE
by Shel Silverstein
Harper, 1964
K–4   52 pages
A tender look at friendship, love, and sharing in a simple but unorthodox fashion. Also by the author: *Where the Sidewalk Ends* (po). Related books

on giving: *A Chair for My Mother* (p); *The Mountain That Loved a Bird* (p); *The Silver Pony* (p); *Babushka*, retold by Charles Mikolaycak; *Something for Me*, by Vera B. Williams; *Wilfred the Rat*, by James Stevenson.

GOODNIGHT MOON
by Margaret Wise Brown
Harper (both), 1947; 1977
Tod.–Pre-S.   30 pages
A classic tale for very young children on the bedtime ritual, sure to be copied by every child who hears it. Also by the author: *The Important Book; The Runaway Bunny*. Related bedtime books for infants and toddlers: *The Napping House* (p); *At This Very Minute*, by Kathleen Rice Bowers; *Goodnight, Goodnight*, by Eve Rice; *Hush Little Baby*, by Jeanette Winter; *Moonlight*, by Jan Ormerod; *A Story to Tell*, by Dick Bruna; *The Sun's Asleep Behind the Hill*, by Mirra Ginsburg; *Ten, Nine, Eight*, by Molly Bang; *The Tomorrow Book*, by Doris Schwerin. For older children, see *Ira Sleeps Over* (p).

GRANDADDY'S PLACE
by Helen Griffith • Illustrated by James Stevenson
Greenwillow, 1987
K–3   36 pages
On her first visit to her grandaddy's rural Georgia cabin, a young city girl is frightened by its strangeness. Soon, however, the old man's quiet charm begins to work its magic and a new world opens for the child. The book is divided into short six-page chapters. Sequel: *Georgia Music*. Also by the author, for experienced listeners: *Foxy*. Related grandparent books: *What's Under My Bed?* (p); *Always Gramma*, by Vaunda Nelson; *The Big Red Barn*, by Eve Bunting; *The Crack-of-Dawn Walkers* and *The Purple Coat*, by Amy Hest; *Grandma's House* and *Grandma's Promise*, by Elaine Moore; *The Grandma Mix-up*, by Emily McCully; *Knots on a Counting Rope*, by Bill Martin, Jr., and John Archambault; *No Bath Tonight*, by Jane Yolen; *Oma and Bobo*, by Amy Schwartz; *Tales of a Gambling Grandmother*, by Dayal Kaur Khalsa; *William and Grandpa*, by Alice Schertle; also these novels: *Stone Fox* (s); *The War with Grandpa*, by Robert K. Smith.

HANS ANDERSEN'S FAIRY TALES
translated by L. W. Kingsland • Illustrated by Rachel Birkett
Oxford, 1985
Gr. 1 and up   259 pages

Here are twenty-six of Andersen's best-known tales in a single volume, complete with color and black-and-white illustrations. A Puffin edition, edited by Naomi Lewis, is also excellent.

Highly recommended picture books of his individual tales:

The Emperor's New Clothes, illustrated by Virginia Lee Burton (Houghton, 1949; Scholastic, 1971), 42 pages.

The Little Mermaid, adapted by Anthea Bell, illustrated by Chihiro Iwasaki (Picture Book Studio, 1984), 32 pages.

The Princess and the Pea, illustrated by Dorothee Duntze (Holt, 1985), 32 pages.
  The Snow Queen, adapted by Naomi Lewis, illustrated by Angela Barrett (Holt, 1988), 42 pages.

The Steadfast Tin Soldier, illustrated by David Jorgensen (Knopf, 1986).

Thumbeline, translated by Anthea Bell, illustrated by Lisbeth Zwerger (Picture Book Studio, 1985) 28 pages.

The Ugly Duckling, retold and illustrated by Lorinda B. Cauley (Harcourt [both], 1979), 44 pages.

The Wild Swans, retold by Amy Ehrlich, illustrated by Susan Jeffers (Dial, 1981), 40 pages.

For preschool children being introduced to fairy tales for the first time, see Index to Treasury for Paul Galdone and Anne Rockwell books. For other fairy tale titles, see listings for Folk/Fairy Tales in Anthologies Section; also *The Jolly Postman* (p).

HARALD AND THE GREAT STAG
by Donald Carrick
Clarion, 1988
K–4   32 pages

When young Harald hears the Baron's huntsmen plan to hunt and kill the Great Stag, the boy purposely leads their dogs astray, only to find *himself* hunted instead. This story and its companion, *Harald and the Giant Knight,* bring to life the drama of life in the Middle Ages. For other Carrick books, see Index to Treasury. For related books on courage, see: *The Boy Who Held Back the Sea* (p). Books on the Middle Ages for more experienced listeners: *Otto of the Silver Hand* (n); *Robin Hood: His Life and Legend* (n); *The Search for Delicious* (n); *The Knights,* by Michael Gibson; *The Reluctant Dragon* (s); *Saint George and the Dragon,* retold by Margaret Hodges; *The Sword in the Tree* and *Wish at the Top,* by Clyde R. Bulla; and *A Tournament of Knights,* by Joe Lasker.

HARRY AND THE TERRIBLE WHATZIT
by Dick Gackenbach
Clarion (both), 1977; 1984
Pre-S.–3   32 pages
When his mother doesn't return immediately from her errand in the cellar, little Harry is positive she's been captured by the monsters he thinks live down there. A gentle lesson in courage and the need to confront our fears before they get out of hand. Also by the author: *A Bag Full of Pups; Claude the Dog; Do You Love Me?; The Princess and the Pea.* Related books: *Where the Wild Things Are* (p); *What's Under My Bed?* (p); *The Beast in the Bed,* by Barbara Dillon; *Donovan Scares the Monsters,* by Susan Whitlock; *The Little Old Lady Who Wasn't Afraid of Anything,* by Linda Williams; *Spiders in the Fruit Cellar,* by Barbara Joosse; *There's an Alligator Under My Bed* and *There's a Nightmare in My Closet,* by Mercer Mayer.

HARRY THE DIRTY DOG
by Gene Zion • Illustrated by Margaret B. Graham
Harper (both), 1956; 1976
Tod.–2   28 pages
This little white dog with black spots just might be the most famous dog in all of children's literature. All children identify with Harry—partly for his size, partly for his aversion to soap and water, partly for his escapades. The sentences are simple and expressive but it is the artwork that triumphs in the Harry books. The bold black outline of the characters easily enables very young children to see and understand the progress of the story. Sequels: *Harry and the Lady Next-Door; Harry by the Sea; No Roses for Harry.* Also by the author: *Dear Garbage Man.* Related books: *Curious George* (p); *Benjy and His Friend* and *Benjy and the Barking Bird,* by Margaret Graham.

HECKEDY PEG
by Audrey Wood • Illustrated by Don Wood
Harcourt, 1987
K–5   30 pages
A determined mother outsmarts a witch who has captured and bewitched her seven children. For other books by the Woods, see *The Napping House* (p). Related books: *A Special Trick* (p); *The Whingdingdilly* (p); *Do Not Open,* by Brinton Turkle; *Liza Lou and the Yeller Belly Swamp,* by Mercer Mayer; *The Pumpkinville Mystery,* by Bruce Cole; and *Sarah's Unicorn,* by Bruce Coville.

HENRY BEAR'S PARK
by David McPhail
Little, Brown, 1976; Puffin, 1978
Gr. 1–5   48 pages
This is so original, so dramatic, and so beautifully told and illustrated that few children will forget it. When Henry Bear's well-to-do father leaves suddenly on a ballooning adventure, he leaves Henry in charge of his newly purchased park. Henry, feeling the importance of filling in for his father, moves into the park as superintendent and excels in the position until the loneliness for his father begins to wear him down. In one little book, the author has made some poignant observations about the feelings we all have for "special places," the longing for our loved ones when they are away, the sadness when friends disappoint us, and the joy of being loved. Also by the author: *Andrew's Bath; The Bear's Toothache; Fix-It; Great Cat; Sisters; The Train.* Related books: *My Father's Dragon* (s); *Dear Daddy . . . ,* by Philippe Dupasquier; *A Father Like That,* by Charlotte Zolotow; *My Dad the Magnificent,* by Kristy Parker; *Uncle Elephant,* by Arnold Lobel.

HOUSEHOLD STORIES OF THE BROTHERS GRIMM
Translated by Lucy Crane • Illustrated by Walter Crane
Dover (paperback only), 1963
K and up   270 pages
This collection of fifty-three tales contains the Grimms' most popular works in a translation that is easily read aloud and includes more than 100 illustrations. The maturity and listening experience of your children should determine their readiness to handle the subject matter, complexity of plot, and language of these unexpurgated versions. Among the many picture books of tales of the Brothers Grimm are:

The Elves and the Shoemaker, retold by Freya Littledale, illustrated by Brinton Turkle (Four Winds, 1975; Scholastic, 1977), 30 pages.
Hansel and Gretel, retold by Rika Lesser, illustrated by Paul Zelinsky (Dodd, 1984), 36 pages.
Rapunzel, retold by Barbara Rogasky, illustrated by Trina Schart Hyman (Holiday, 1982), 32 pages.
Rumpelstiltskin, retold and illustrated by Paul O. Zelinsky (Dutton, 1986), 34 pages.
Sleeping Beauty, retold and illustrated by Trina Schart Hyman (Little, 1977), 48 pages; see also *Sleeping Ugly* by Jane Yolen.

Snow White, translated by Randall Jarrell, illustrated by Nancy Elholm Burkert (Farrar, 1982), 26 pages.

The Water of Life, retold by Barbara Rogasky, illustrated by Trina Schart Hyman (Holiday, 1986), 36 pages.

For preschool children being introduced to the fairy tale for the first time, *The Three Bears and 15 Other Stories,* by Anne Rockwell, is an excellent collection; see Index to Treasury for books by Paul Galdone and (K–4) Tomie dePaola, nearly all of which are based on folk/fairy tales. For other titles, see listings under Folk/Fairy Tales in Anthologies section; also *The Jolly Postman* (p). Novels written in the fairy tale/fantasy format are listed under *The Lion, the Witch and the Wardrobe* (n).

THE HOUSE ON EAST 88TH STREET
by Bernard Waber
Houghton Mifflin (both), 1962; 1975

Pre-S.–3 48 pages

When the Primm family discovers a gigantic crocodile in the bathtub of their new brownstone home, it signals the beginning of a wonderful picture book series. As soon as the Primms overcome their fright, they see him as your children will—as the most lovable and human of crocodiles. Sequels (in this order): *Lyle, Lyle, Crocodile; Lyle and the Birthday Party; Lyle Finds His Mother; Lovable Lyle;* and *Funny, Funny Lyle.* Also by the author: *Ira Sleeps Over* (p). Related books about animals with unusual powers: *Amos: The Story of an Old Dog and His Couch,* by Susan Seligson; *Cat and Canary,* by Michael Forman; *Fred,* by Posy Simmonds; *The Giraffe and the Pelly and Me,* by Roald Dahl; *Perfect the Pig,* by Susan Jeschke; *The Story of the Dancing Frog,* by Quentin Blake; see also Bill Peet books listed with *The Whing-dingdilly.*

HOW I HUNTED THE LITTLE FELLOWS
by Boris Zhitkov • Illustrated by Paul O. Zelinsky
Dodd, 1979

Gr. 1–6 48 pages

This is a dramatic though unconventional story of an overactive imagination. Forbidden to touch the ship model on his grandmother's mantel, the small boy imagines there is a tiny crew living aboard the craft. Finally he is so convinced of this that he takes apart the ship to find them. Just as he shamefully realizes his mistake, his grandmother returns home. There the story ends, unresolved because the author's sequel was lost years ago, but it does make for a wonderful opportunity for reader and listeners to discuss the possible contents of that sequel. Related books: *The Amazing Voyage of Jackie Grace* (p); *The Aminal* (p); *The Indian in the Cupboard* (n); *The Island of the Skog* (p); *The Littles* (s); *George Shrinks,* by William Joyce.

I CAN—CAN YOU?
by Peggy Parish
Greenwillow, 1980
Tod.   10 laminated pages
This is one in a series (See and Do books) that stimulates a baby's language, motor, and social skills through activities suggested by the text. For example, in this book children (multi-ethnic) are pictured touching toes, wiggling fingers, sticking out tongues—and the child is asked if he can do that activity. All the books in the series have the same title, the difference being a "level" number (1–4) on the cover that refers to the child's maturity level.

Here are toddler books that relate to physical and intellectual concepts children learn best at home in someone's lap:

Labeling their environment—*And So Can I!*, *The Early Words Picture Book,* and *The First Words Picture Book,* by Bill Gillham; *The Baby's Catalogue* by Janet and Allan Ahlberg; *Come to Town* and *In Our House,* by Anne Rockwell; *Jesse Bear, What Will You Wear?,* by Nancy W. Carlstrom; *The Sesame Street Word Book* (Golden); *Viking First Picture Dictionary,* by Brian Thompson.

Opposites—*Big and Little,* by Richard Scarry; *Fast-Slow, High-Low* by Peter Spier; *Here a Chick, There a Chick,* by Bruce McMillan; *Push Pull, Empty Full,* by Tana Hoban.

Colors and counting—*Counting Wildflowers* and *Growing Colors,* by Bruce McMillan; *Ten, Nine, Eight,* by Molly Bang.

Time—*The Tomorrow Book,* by Doris Schwerin.

Other concepts: *Spot Looks at Colors, Spot Looks at Shapes, Spot's Big Book of Words,* by Eric Hill; and this series by Shirley Hughes: *Bathwater's Hot; All Shapes and Sizes; Colors; Noisy, Out and About; Two Shoes, New Shoes;* and *When We Went to the Park;* see also *Pat the Bunny* (p) and *Playing* (p).

IF I RAN THE ZOO
by Dr. Seuss
Random (both), 1950; 1980
Pre-S.–4   54 pages

Little Gerald McGrew finds the animals in the local zoo pretty boring when compared with the wonderfully zany and exotic creatures that populate the zoo of his imagination. Children love to follow in the wake of Gerald's madcap safari around the world in search of Thwerlls, Chuggs, Gussets, Gherkins, and Seersuckers, species so rare only the words and pen of Dr. Seuss could describe them. Be sure to tell your audience that, in real life, Dr. Seuss's father was the zoo director in Seuss's hometown, Springfield, Massachusetts. Sequel: *If I Ran the Circus.*

Dr. Seuss is the best-selling author of children's books for the most deserving of reasons: children love his books. Whether it is because of the verbal gymnastics or the unbounded imagination evident in his drawings, the affection and excitement between child and book is unmistakable. Though Seuss's "limited vocabulary" books like *The Cat in the Hat* are excellent beginning readers, it is his storybooks that should receive the attention of readers-aloud. These include (in rhyming verse): *I Can Lick 30 Tigers Today and Other Stories; I Had Trouble in Getting to Solla Sollew; On Beyond Zebra; Scrambled Eggs Super;* and *Thidwick, the Big-Hearted Moose.* These five, along with *If I Ran the Zoo* and *If I Ran the Circus,* are available in large-format paperback.

Other Dr. Seuss books which make excellent read-alouds include: *And to Think That I Saw It on Mulberry Street; Bartholomew and the Oobleck; The Butter Battle Book; Did I Ever Tell You How Lucky You Are?; Dr. Seuss's Sleep Book; The 500 Hats of Bartholomew Cubbins; How the Grinch Stole Christmas; Horton Hatches the Egg; Horton Hears a Who; Hunches in Bunches; I Am NOT Going to Get Up Today!; The King's Stilts; The Lorax; McElligot's Pool; The Shape of Me and Other Stuff; The Sneetches and Other Stories;* and *Yertle the Turtle.*

Dr. Seuss fans will also enjoy Bill Peet books (see Index to Treasury).

IF YOU GIVE A MOUSE A COOKIE
By Laura Numeroff • Illustrated by Felicia Bond
Harper, 1985
Pre-S.–K   30 pages
In a funny cumulative tale that comes full circle, a little boy offers a mouse a cookie and ends up working his head off for the demanding little creature. For related mouse books, see *Broderick* (p). Related cumulative tale books: *The Napping House* (p); *The Big Sneeze,* by Ruth Brown; *The Cake That Mack Ate,* by Rose Robart; *The Elephant and the Bad Boy,* by Elfrida Vipont; *Fat Mouse,* by Harry Stevens; *The Gingerbread Boy,* by Paul Galdone; *The*

House That Jack Built, by Rodney Peppe; *The Little Old Lady Who Was Not Afraid of Anything,* by Linda Williams; see also the Predictable Books section of the Treasury.

IRA SLEEPS OVER
by Bernard Waber
Houghton Mifflin (both), 1972; 1975
K–6   48 pages

This is a warm, sensitive, and funny look at a boy's overnight visit to a friend's house. The tale centers on the child's personal struggle over whether or not to bring along his teddy bear. It makes for lively discussion about individual sleeping habits, peer pressures, and the things we all hold on to—even as grown-ups. In the sequel, *Ira Says Goodbye,* two best friends experience a dreaded childhood pain when Reggie moves away. Also by the author: *The House on East 88th Street* (p). Related books on teddy bears or dolls: *Corduroy* (p); *The Legend of the Bluebonnet* (p); *The Story of Holly and Ivy* (s); *William's Doll* (p); *Dogger,* by Shirley Hughes; *Don't Worry, I'll Find You,* by Anna Hines; *Good as New,* by Barbara Douglas; *Humphrey's Bear,* by Jan Wahl; *Snuggle Piggy and the Magic Blanket,* by Michele Stepto; *Theodore* and *Theodore's Rival,* both by Edward Ormondroyd; *Where's My Monkey?,* by Dieter Schubert. Highly recommended: the award-winning record/cassette "Unbearable Bears," by Kevin Roth (Marlboro Records, Kennett Square, PA) for a collection of favorite teddy bear songs.

THE ISLAND OF THE SKOG
by Steven Kellogg
Dial (both), 1973; 1976
Pre-S.–2   32 pages

Sailing away from city life, a boatload of mice discover the island of their dreams, only to be pulled up short by the appearance of a fearful monster already dwelling on the island. How imaginations can run away with us and how obstacles can be overcome if we'll just talk with others are central issues in this tale. Also by the author: *The Mysterious Tadpole* (p); three retellings of American legends: *Johnny Appleseed, Paul Bunyan,* and *Pecos Bill;* also *Best Friends; Can I Keep Him?; The Mystery Beast of Ostergeest; The Mystery of the Missing Mitten; Pinkerton, Behave!; Prehistoric Pinkerton; Ralph's Secret Weapon; A Rose for Pinkerton; Tallyho, Pinkerton!* Related books: *The Aminal* (p); *How I Hunted the Little Fellows* (p).

THE JOLLY POSTMAN
by Janet and Allan Ahlberg
Little, Brown
Gr. 1–4   14 pages
As the postman pedals his way through this book and makes his deliveries, the pages are ingeniously designed as envelopes inside of which is a letter or notice from The Three Bears, Goldilocks, a wicked witch, the wolf at Grandma's house, and Cinderella, all of whom receive a light-hearted ribbing from the authors. The book is an excellent introduction to writing: the envelopes contain letters, postcards, occupant junk mail, and even book club offerings. Because the letters are easily lost during circulation, libraries find it a difficult book to keep on the shelf but bookstores have great success with it. Also by the author/illustrators: *The Baby's Catalogue; Jeremiah in the Dark Woods* (another fairy parody); and *Starting School*. Related books: *Goldilocks and the Three Bears*, retold by James Marshall; *Jack and the Beanstalk, Lazy Jack,* and *The Three Pigs,* all by Tony Ross; *The Princess and the Frog,* by A. Vesey; *Sidney Rella and the Glass Sneaker,* by Bernice Myers; *Sleeping Ugly,* by Jane Yolen; *The Tough Princess,* by Martin Waddell. For serious fairy tale collections, see the Anthology section of the Treasury along with the Index to Treasury listings for Andersen and Grimm.

KATY AND THE BIG SNOW
by Virginia Lee Burton
Houghton Mifflin (both), 1973; 1974
Pre-S.–2   40 pages
The modern picture book classic about the brave, untiring tractor whose round-the-clock snowplowing saves the blizzard-bound city of Geoppolis. As much as this is the story of persistence, it is also a lesson in civics as Katy assists the local authorities in pursuing their duties. After reading this story, try Franklyn Branley's *Snow Is Falling*. Also by the author, see *Mike Mulligan and His Steam Shovel* (p). Related books: *The Little Engine That Could* (p); *Anna, Grandpa, and the Big Storm,* by Carla Stevens; *Grandma's Promise,* by Elaine Moore; *The Snowman Who Went for a Walk,* by Mira Lobe; *Something Is Going to Happen,* by Charlotte Zolotow; *Up North in Winter,* by Deborah Hartley; *White Snow Bright Snow* by Alvin Tresselt.

THE LEGEND OF THE BLUEBONNET
Retold by Tomie dePaola
Putnam (both), 1984
Pre-S.–4

Here is the legend behind the bluebonnets that blanket the state of Texas—the story of the little Comanche Indian orphan who sacrificed her only doll in order to end the drought that was ravaging her village. Related book by the author: *The Legend of the Indian Paintbrush;* for other titles relating to American Indians, see *Where the Buffaloes Begin* (p).

Tomie dePaola is one of America's most beloved and prolific author/illustrators. His books often treat the theme of the human spirit and are marked by rambunctious humor and warmth. Among his works featuring old legends or retellings: *Big Anthony and the Magic Ring; The Clown of God; Finn M'Coul: The Giant of Knockmany Hill; Francis: the Poor Man of God; The Friendly Beasts; Georgio's Village; Helga's Dowry; The Legend of Befana; Little Grunt and the Big Egg; The Prince of the Dolomites; Strega Nona; Strega Nona's Magic Lessons.*

His other books include: *The Comic Adventures of Old Mother Hubbard and Her Dog; Mother Goose; Oliver Button Is a Sissy; Tomie dePaola's Book of Poems; Watch Out for the Chicken Feet in Your Soup.* Two of his books deal with the elderly: *Nana Upstairs & Nana Downstairs* and *Now One Foot, Now the Other.*

LITTLE BEAR
by Else Holmelund Minarik • Illustrated by Maurice Sendak
Harper (both), 1957; 1978
Pre-S.–1   54 pages
This series of books uses the simple but important elements of a child's life (clothes, birthdays, playing, and wishing) to weave poignant little stories about a child–bear and his family. The series has won numerous awards and is regarded as a classic in its genre. A former first-grade teacher, the author uses a limited vocabulary at no sacrifice to the flavor of the story. The series, which can be read in any order, includes: *Little Bear; A Kiss for Little Bear; Father Bear Comes Home; Little Bear's Friend; Little Bear's Visit.* Also by the author: *No Fighting, No Biting!* Another outstanding "bear" series is by Frank Asch: *Bear's Bargain; Bear Shadow; Goodbye House; Happy Birthday, Moon; Mooncake; Popcorn; Sand Cake;* and *Skyfire.* See also Martha Alexander's *Blackboard Bear* books.

THE LITTLE ENGINE THAT COULD
by Watty Piper • Illustrated by George and Doris Hauman
Platt, 1961; Scholastic, 1979
Pre-S.–2   36 pages

One of the most famous children's picture books of the twentieth century, this is the 1930 story of the little engine that smiled in the face of an insurmountable task and said, "I'm not very big but I'll do my best, and I think I can—I think I can—I think I can." Related books: *Katy and the Big Snow* (p); *Nice Little Girls* (p); *The Big Book of Real Trains,* by Walter Retan; *The Carrot Seed,* by Ruth Krauss; *Little Toot,* by Hardie Gramatky; *Smokey,* by Bill Peet; and *The Train,* by David McPhail.

THE LITTLE HOUSE
by Virginia Lee Burton
Houghton Mifflin (both), 1942; 1978
Pre-S.–3   40 pages
This Caldecott Medal winner uses a little turn-of-the-century country house to show the urbanization of America. With each page, the reader/listener becomes the little house and begins to experience the contentment, wonder, concern, anxiety, and loneliness that the passing seasons and encroaching city bring. Many of today's children who daily experience the anxieties of city life will identify with the little house and her eventual triumph. Also by the author, see *Mike Mulligan and His Steam Shovel* (p). Related books: *Dear Daddy . . . ,* by Philippe Dupasquier; *Farewell to Shady Glade* and *Wump World,* by Bill Peet; *The Lorax,* by Dr. Seuss; *Lost and Found,* by Jill Paton Walsh; *New Providence: A Changing Cityscape,* by Tscharner and Fleming; *Tattie's River Journey,* by Shirley Murphy. And don't miss Charles Martin's enchanting books about the island children: *For Rent; Island Rescue; Island Winter; Sam Saves the Day;* and *Summer Business.*

LITTLE RED RIDING HOOD
retold by Trina Schart Hyman
Holiday House, 1983
Pre-S.–3   32 pages
It's hard to imagine a better illustrated version of this famous tale. The artist has given us a child and grandma who are *every* child and grandmother and a texture so rich you can almost smell the woods. Related books about children's forest adventures: *Owl Moon* (p); *Flossie and the Fox,* by Patricia McKissack; *The Ghost-Eye Tree,* by Bill Martin, Jr., and John Archambault; *The Gunnywolf,* retold by A. Delaney; *Henry the Explorer,* by Mark Taylor; *Liza Lou and the Yeller Belly Swamp,* by Mercer Mayer; *Once When I Was Scared,* by Helena Pittman; *Wiley and the Hairy Man,* by Molly Bang.

MADELINE
by Ludwig Bemelmans
Viking, 1939; Puffin, 1977
Pre-S.–2   54 pages
This series of six marvelous books is about a daring and irrepressible personality named Madeline and her eleven friends who all live together in a Parisian house. Because of the expressive illustrations and the originality of Madeline, the books are among the favorites of children around the world. The author's use of fast-moving verse, daring adventure, naughtiness, and glowing color keep it a favorite in early grades year after year. The other books in the series are: *Madeline and the Bad Hat; Madeline and the Gypsies; Madeline in London; Madeline's Rescue; Madeline's Christmas.* Related books: *Nice Little Girls* (p); *Liza Lou and the Yeller Belly Swamp,* by Mercer Mayer; *The Three Robbers,* by Tomi Ungerer.

MAKE WAY FOR DUCKLINGS
by Robert McCloskey
Viking, 1941; Puffin, 1976
Pre-S.–2   62 pages
In this Caldecott Award–winning classic, we follow Mrs. Mallard and her eight ducklings as they make a traffic-stopping walk across Boston to meet Mr. Mallard on their new island home in the Public Garden. Also by the author: *Homer Price* (n); *Blueberries for Sal; Burt Dow, Deep-Water Man; Lentil; One Morning in Maine.* Related books: *Arnold of the Ducks* (p); *Are You My Mother?,* by P. D. Eastman; *Dabble Duck,* by Anne Ellis; *The Story About Ping,* by Marjorie Flack.

MIKE MULLIGAN AND HIS STEAM SHOVEL
by Virginia Lee Burton
Houghton Mifflin (both), 1939; 1977
K–4   42 pages
A modern classic, this is the heartwarming story of the demise of the steam shovel and how one shovel found a permanent home. Also by the author: *The Emperor's New Clothes; Katy and the Big Snow* (p); *The Little House* (p); *Choo-Choo.* Related books: *The Big Book of Real Trucks,* by Walter Retan; *Dear Garbage Man,* by Gene Zion; *Giant Work Machines,* by Thea Feldman; *Smokey,* by Bill Peet; *Tony's Hard Work Day,* by Alan Arkin.

MILLIONS OF CATS
by Wanda Gag
Coward, McCann (both), 1928; 1977
Pre-S.–2   30 pages
For more than fifty years this tale has enchanted children everywhere. An old man, in search of a cat to cure his loneliness, can't make up his mind which one he likes best and ends up taking a herd of cats home to his wife. Eventually the cats solve the problem themselves. Also by the author: *The Earth Gnome; Gone Is Gone; The Sorcerer's Apprentice*. Related books: *All the Cats in the World,* by Sonia Levitin; *The Boy Who Was Followed Home,* by Margaret Mahy; *Captain Whiz-Bang,* by Diane Stanley; *The King's Stilts,* by Dr. Seuss.

MISS NELSON IS MISSING
by Harry Allard • Illustrated by James Marshall
Houghton Mifflin, 1977; Scholastic, 1978
Pre-S.–4   32 pages
Poor, sweet Miss Nelson! Kind and beautiful as she is, she cannot control her classroom—the worst-behaved children in the school. But when she is suddenly absent, the children begin to realize what a wonderful teacher they had in Miss Nelson. Her substitute is the wicked-looking, strict Miss Viola Swamp, who works the class incessantly. Wherever has Miss Nelson gone and when will she return? A copy of this book should be in the hand of every elementary-level substitute teacher. Sequels: *Miss Nelson Is Back; Miss Nelson Has a Field Day*. Also by the author: *The Stupids Step Out* (p). For related books, see *The Day Jimmy's Boa Ate the Wash* (p).

MISS RUMPHIUS
by Barbara Cooney
Viking, 1982; Puffin, 1985
Pre-S. and up   30 pages
I cannot think of a book with art and prose that match more perfectly, nor a story more poignant than this tale of one woman's personal odyssey through life in search of fulfilling her grandfather's wish that she do something to make the world more beautiful. Her search begins in childhood, continues through world travels, and finally, in old age, she finds fulfillment in the seeds of flowers she spreads throughout her village by the sea. Related flower/garden stories: *The Legend of the Bluebonnet* (p); *The Legend of the Indian Paintbrush,* by Tomie dePaola; *Linnea's Windowsill Garden,* by Chris-

tina Bjork; *The First Tulips in Holland,* by Phyllis Krasilovsky; *Soup for Supper,* by Phyllis Root; *A Tree Is Nice,* by Janice M. Udry; and *Vegetable Soup,* by Jeanne Modesitt.

THE MOON'S REVENGE
by Joan Aiken • Illustrated by Alan Lee
Knopf, 1987
Gr. 2–7   28 pages
A young boy inadvertently earns the wrath of the moon which curses his newborn sister with muteness until the boy achieves an almost impossible task seven years later. In one of Joan Aiken's most haunting tales, the boy and his fiddle become the constant companions of the girl as the story builds to a dramatic conclusion when a ferocious sea monster threatens their tiny coastal village. For experienced listeners. Also by the author: *The Wolves of Willoughby Chase* (n). Related books: *The Reluctant Dragon* (s); *The Search for Delicious* (n); *The Dragon, Giant, and Monster Treasury,* selected by Caroline Royds; *The Ghost of Skinny Jack,* by Astrid Lindgren; *The Deliverers of Their Country* and *The Book of Dragons,* by E. Nesbit; *The Wish Giver* (n); *The Mirrorstone,* by Michael Palin.

MOSS GOWN
by William H. Hooks • Illustrated by Donald Carrick
Clarion, 1987
Gr. 1–5   48 pages
One of the more than 400 versions of Cinderella, this centuries-old Southern version adds elements of King Lear to make an enchanting tale of family rejection and triumph amidst the plantations of the Old South. Other versions: *Cinderella* (traditional), by John Fowles; *Mufaro's Beautiful Daughters* (African), by John Steptoe; *Yeh-Shen* (Chinese), by Ai-Ling Louie. Related books: *Little Daylight,* George MacDonald's fairy tale adapted to picture-book format by Erick Ingraham.

MOTHER GOOSE, A TREASURY OF BEST LOVED RHYMES
by Watty Piper • Illustrated by Tim and Greg Hildebrandt
Platt, 1972
Tod.–2   66 pages
Of the two dozen nursery rhyme books available today, this volume—with easy-to-view, large-format illustrations that portray present- and olden-day children in the 102 rhymes—is my favorite for extended use with children. The determining factors in selecting this from the dozens of Mother Goose

collections are its choice of rhymes, illustration sizes and the vividness of their colors, and the weight of the book (not too heavy). My second choice would be *Gyo Fujikawa's Original Mother Goose. Tomie dePaola's Mother Goose* is excellent and also available in a smaller paperback version, *Hey Diddle Diddle*. Related books: Timeless finger/hand rhymes (complete with diagrams) are collected and illustrated by Marc Brown in *Finger Rhymes; Hand Rhymes;* and *Play Rhymes;* also *Mother Goose,* illustrated by William Joyce and *Whiskers and Rhymes,* by Arnold Lobel.

THE MOUNTAIN THAT LOVED A BIRD
by Alice McLerran • Illustrated by Eric Carle
Picture Book Studio, 1985
K–5   24 pages
A barren stone mountain is visited one day by a passing bird who gives the lonely mountain warm company and solace. Unable to stay because there is no environment to support him, the bird does return each spring, eventually bringing a tiny seed. In this allegory on the cycles and common needs of all living things, the mountain's tears for the bird become a stream that waters the seed that leads to new life for bird and mountain. Related books: *Frederick* (p); *The Giving Tree* (p); *The Very Hungry Caterpillar* (p); *The Sun, The Wind and the Rain,* by Lisa Peters.

THE MYSTERIOUS TADPOLE
by Steven Kellogg
Dial (both), 1977; 1979
Pre-S.–4   30 pages
When little Louis's uncle in Scotland sent him a tadpole for his birthday, neither of them had any idea how much havoc and fun the pet would cause in Louis's home, classroom, and school swimming pool. The tadpole turns out to be a direct descendant of the Loch Ness Monster (but what a cuddly monster this is!). Don't miss the tucked-away name of the junior high school. For other books by the author, see Index to Treasury. Related books: *Dinosaur Bob* (p); *The Boy Who Was Followed Home,* by Margaret Mahy; *The Great Green Turkey Creek Monster,* by James Flora; *The Red Carpet,* by Rex Parkin; *Patrick's Dinosaur,* by Carol Carrick; *The Pumpkinville Mystery,* by Bruce Cole; *The Secret in the Matchbox,* by Val Willis; *Who Wants a Cheap Rhinoceros?,* by Shel Silverstein.

NADIA THE WILLFUL
by Sue Alexander • Illustrated by Lloyd Bloom
Pantheon, 1983
Gr. 2–6   48 pages

Unable to cope with his grief at his son's death, an Arab sheik bitterly decrees that none may utter his son's name again. It falls to his willful daughter to convince her father that memories are the only way we can keep the dead alive, a task she accomplishes with great poignancy. Also by the author: *Dear Phoebe; World Famous Muriel.*

The following books relate to the subject of grief and can be useful in helping children cope with the loss of pets or loved ones: *The Accident*, by Carol Carrick (pet); *The Big Red Barn*, by Eve Bunting (mother); *Everett Anderson's Goodbye*, by Lucille Clifton (father); *Harry's Mom*, by Barbara Ann Porte (mother); *I Had a Friend Named Peter*, by Janice Cohn (friend); *I'll Always Love You*, by Hans Wilhelm (pet); *My Grandson Lew*, by Charlotte Zolotow, *Saying Good-Bye to Grandma*, by Jane Resh Thomas, and *Nana Upstairs & Nana Downstairs*, by Tomie dePaola (grandparents); *The Tenth Good Thing About Barney*, by Judith Viorst (pet). For older children, see listing with *A Taste of Blackberries* (s).

THE NAPPING HOUSE
by Audrey Wood • Illustrated by Don Wood
Harcourt, 1984
Tod.–Pre-S.   28 pages

This is one of the cleverest and most beautiful books for children. Its simple tale depicts a cozy bed on which are laid in cumulative rhymes a snoring granny, dreaming child, dozing dog, and a host of other sleeping characters until the surprise ending at daybreak. The subtle lighting changes on the double-page illustrations show the gradual passage of time during the night and the clearing of a storm outside. (Cumulative rhymes are among the most powerful vocabulary builders for children.) Also by the author and illustrator: *Heckedy Peg* (p); *The Big Hungry Bear; King Bidgood's in the Bathtub; Quick as a Cricket.* For other cumulative tales, see *If You Give a Mouse a Cookie* (p); also Predictable Books section of Treasury.

NICE LITTLE GIRLS
by Elizabeth Levy • Illustrated by Mordicai Gerstein
Delacorte (paperback only), 1978
Pre-S.–2   44 pages

Jackie has a problem with her new school: her teacher insists upon stereotyping classroom assignments as "boy" or "girl" jobs. Told with humor and warmth, Jackie's liberated views help the teacher and class to realize that tool boxes and train sets are for *everyone*. The relationship between Jackie and her parents is especially warm and reassuring. Also by the author: *Something Queer at the Library* (series). Related books: *Airmail to the Moon*, by Tom Birdseye; *Crow Boy*, by Taro Yashima; *Free to Be You and Me* (a); *Miss Rumphius* (p); *The Story of Ferdinand* (p); *William's Doll* (p); *The Balancing Girl*, by Berniece Rabe; *Like Jake and Me*, by Mavis Jukes; *Oliver Button Is a Sissy*, by Tomie dePaola; *Once Upon a Test: Three Light Tales of Love*, by Vivian Vande Velde; *Sleeping Ugly*, by Jane Yolen; *Sloppy Kisses* and *Tough Eddie*, by Elizabeth Winthrop; *The Story of the Dancing Frog*, by Quentin Blake; *Tammy and the Gigantic Fish*, by Catherine and James Gray; *World Famous Muriel*, by Sue Alexander.

NO JUMPING ON THE BED
by Tedd Arnold
Dial, 1987
Pre-S.–2
Warned that he mustn't jump on his bed or he might crash through the floor into the apartment below, Walter can't resist the temptation. The exaggerated results are hilarious and just when you think he dreamed it all . . . Related books: *The Amazing Voyage of Jackie Grace* (p); *Ira Sleeps Over* (p); *What's Under My Bed?* (p); *Barn Dance*, by Bill Martin, Jr., and John Archambault; *Bedtime for Frances*, by Russell Hoban; *Go to Sleep, Nicholas Joe*, by Marjorie Sharmat; *I Am NOT Going to Get Up Today!*, by Dr. Seuss; *I Don't Want to Go to Bed*, by Astrid Lindgren; *In the Night Kitchen*, by Maurice Sendak; *Winifred's New Bed*, by Lynn and Richard Howell.

OLD MOTHER WITCH
by Carol and Donald Carrick
Clarion, 1975
Gr. 1–6   32 pages
A group of boys out trick-or-treating on Halloween decide to tease the cranky old woman who lives on their street—only to find a frightening surprise waiting for them. The old woman has suffered a heart attack and is lying unconscious on the porch. A young boy's brush with near tragedy and the sobering effect it has upon him will reach all children, inspiring a new sensitivity to the elderly in their neighborhoods. For other books by the author, see *Sleep Out* (p). Related books on the elderly: *Miss Rumphius*

(p); *Always Gramma,* by Vaunda Nelson; *Annie and the Old One,* by Miska Miles; *Ella,* by Bill Peet; *I Know a Lady,* by Charlotte Zolotow; *Miss Maggie,* by Cynthia Rylant; *Now One Foot, Now the Other,* by Tomie dePaola; *Wilfred Gordon McDonald Partridge,* by Mem Fox. For grandparent books, see *Grandaddy's Place* (p).

OWL MOON
by Jane Yolen • Illustrated by John Schoenherr
Philomel, 1987
Pre-S.–3   30 pages
In this suspenseful and poignant Caldecott Award–winner, a young girl and her father hike through the snow and into the woods one cold, moonlit night to call owls. Jane Yolen is the author of more than 100 books, including *The Girl Who Loved the Wind, No Bath Tonight,* and *Sleeping Ugly.* Related books: *The Man Who Could Call Down Owls,* by Eve Bunting; *The Owl-Scatterer,* by Howard Norman; *Owls in the Family* (s); *Sleep Out,* by Carol Carrick; *Up North in Winter,* by Deborah Hartley.

PAT THE BUNNY
by Dorothy Kunhardt
Golden, 1962
Tod.   18 pages
This book is intended to involve actively the child's senses—patting a bunny picture that has a piece of furry material attached to it; smelling a scented flower picture; lifting a cloth flap on the page to play peek-a-boo with the boy beneath; turning the pages of the tiny book glued to one of the pages. This is a popular and important favorite of very young children. Sequel: *Pat the Cat,* by Dorothy Kunhardt's daughter, Edith. For related toddler books, see listing at end of *Playing* (p).

PETER SPIER'S RAIN
by Peter Spier
Doubleday (both), 1982; 1987
Tod.–1   36 pages
This magnificent wordless book traces the activities of brother and sister through a rainy day and night, inside and outside the house. Spier is a master observer of family and neighborhood life, and his eighty-four illustrations capture every feeling a child could possibly experience on a rainy day. His holiday book *Peter Spier's Christmas* uses the same successful formula.

Peter Spier's books have a universal appeal. In helping us find beauty in the commonplace or in simplifying the complex, Spier bridges all ages with a variety of perspectives. The three-year-old looking at the garage scene in *Bored—Nothing to Do!*, where the boys are building a life-size airplane from house scraps, will enjoy the color and fun in the boys' task while a fifth-grade child will see the same page as a dream come true and appreciate the magnitude of the task. Other Spier books for all ages: *Dreams; Noah's Ark; People.*

For toddlers through kindergarten: *Crash! Bang! Boom!; Fast-Slow, High-Low; Gobble, Growl, Grunt.*

K–5: *The Book of Jonah; Erie Canal; Fox Went Out on a Chilly Night; London Bridge Is Falling Down; Oh, Were They Ever Happy; The Star-Spangled Banner; We, The People.* Because of the minute details of his illustrations, the Spier books are best read to small groups where the art can be appreciated up close.

PETUNIA THE SILLY GOOSE STORIES
by Roger Duvoisin
Knopf, 1988
Pre-S.–2   145 pages
Collected here are five of the classic Petunia books featuring the scatter-brained but lovable goose. The stories, done in a large format, have the perfect blend of the humor and wisdom that characterize fables. Related books: *Fables from Aesop* (a); *Frederick's Fables,* by Leo Leonni; see also Bill Peet books in the Index to the Treasury.

THE PIED PIPER OF HAMELIN
Retold by Barbara Bartos-Hoppner • Illustrated by Annegert Fuchshuber
Lippincott, 1987
K–5   26 pages
The consequences of breaking your word are dramatically portrayed here in this 700-year-old tale of enchantment when the Pied Piper rids Hamelin of its rat infestation but is denied his reward. Related books about mysterious strangers: *Dawn* (p); *A Special Trick* (p); *The Magician,* by Uri Shulevitz; *Old Henry,* by Joan Blos; *The Paper Crane,* by Molly Bang; *Paper John,* by David Small; *The Pumpkinville Mystery,* by Bruce Cole; *The Selkie Girl,* retold by Susan Cooper; *The Stranger* and *The Wreck of the Zephyr,* by Chris Van Allsburg; *Ty's One-Man Band,* by Mildred P. Walter.

188 | THE NEW READ-ALOUD HANDBOOK

PLAYING
by Helen Oxenbury
Wanderer, 1981
Tod.   14 laminated pages
In a small boardbook format, we see a toddler playing with important items
in his environment. Other books by the author/artist include *All Fall Down;
Clap Hands; Family, Friends; I Can; I Hear; I See; I Touch; Say Goodnight;
Tickle, Tickle; Tom and Pippo Go for a Walk; Tom and Pippo Make a Mess;*
and *Tom and Pippo Read a Story.*

A set of washable, nontoxic cloth books is also a must for toddlers:
from Random House—*Baby Animals Say Hello,* by Norman Gorbaty; *Baby's
Cradle Songs,* by Roberta Beasley; *Baby's Favorite Things,* by Marsha Cohen.
Other related books: *I Can—Can You?* (p); *Mother Goose* (p); *Pat the Bunny*
(p); *The Early Words Picture Book* and *The First Words Picture Book,* both by
Bill Gillham.

Three other outstanding series: by Rosemary Wells—*Max's Birthday;
Max's Breakfast; Max's Christmas; Max's First Word; Max's New Suit; Max's
Ride;* and *Max's Toys;* by Barbro Lindgren—*Sam's Ball; Sam's Bath; Sam's
Car; Sam's Cookie; Sam's Lamp; Sam's Potty; Sam's Teddy Bear;* and *Sam's
Wagon;* by Jan Ormerod—*Bend and Stretch; Dad's Back; Making Friends;
Messy Baby; Mom's Home; Reading;* and *Sleeping;* by Harriet Ziefert—*Me
Too! Me Too!* and *Chocolate Mud Cake.* For other toddler books, see listings
with *I Can—Can You?* (p); *Snuffy* (p); and *Where's Spot?* (p).

THE POKY LITTLE PUPPY
by Janette S. Lowrey • Illustrated by Gustaf Tenggren
Golden, 1942
Tod.–K   24 pages
One of the all-time best-sellers in the Golden Books mass-market line, here
is the puppy-dog version of *The Adventures of Peter Rabbit.* The puppy keeps
tripping over his curiosity and ends up late or left out. Sequels: *The Poky
Little Puppy and the Lost Bone; Poky Little Puppy & the Patchwork Blanket;
Poky Little Puppy at the Fair.* Other related books: *Sam's Cookie* (p); *Snuffy*
(p); *Where's Spot?* (p).

THE POLAR EXPRESS
by Chris Van Allsburg
Houghton Mifflin, 1985
K and up   32 pages

For believers and nonbelievers, here is the magical story of a young boy who boards a mythic train for the North Pole one Christmas eve and returns later that night with a gift that lasts a lifetime. Like all the Van Allsburg books, this one is marked with a dreamlike enchantment. Also by the author: *Ben's Dream* (wordless); *The Garden of Abdul Gusazi; Jumanji; The Mysteries of Harris Burdick* (nearly wordless book and excellent for creative writing classes); *The Stranger; The Wreck of the Zephyr; Two Bad Ants; The Z Was Zapped* (alphabet book).

Other winter holiday books: *Babushka*, retold by Charles Mikolaycak; *Fair Is Fair* (p); *A Certain Small Shepherd* (s); *The Story of Holly and Ivy* (s); *The Chanukkah Tree*, by Eric Kimmel; *The Elves and the Shoemaker*, retold by Freya Littledale; *Father Christmas*, by Raymond Briggs; *How the Grinch Stole Christmas*, by Dr. Seuss; *Just Enough Is Plenty: A Hanukkah Tale*, by Barbara Goldin; *The Legend of Old Befana*, by Tomie dePaola; *The Night Before Christmas*, illustrated by Tomie dePaola; *The Nativity* (with *very* unusual illustrations by Julie Vivas); *The Night After Christmas*, by James Stevenson; *Peter Spier's Christmas*, by Peter Spier; *The Power of Light: Eight Stories for Hanukkah*, by Isaac B. Singer; *Santa Claus and His Elves*, by Mauri Kunnas; *Star Mother's Youngest Child*, by Louise Moeri; *With Love at Christmas*, by Mem Fox.

REGARDS TO THE MAN IN THE MOON
by Ezra Jack Keats
Four Winds, 1981
Tod.–3   32 pages

When the neighborhood children tease Louie about the junk in his backyard, his father shows him how a little imagination can convert that rubbish into a spaceship that will take him to the farthest galaxies. The next day, Louie and his friend Susie hurtle through space in their glorified washtub and discover that not even gravity can hold back a child's imagination.

Children experiencing the joys and discoveries of early childhood will find themselves cast as the central characters in Ezra Jack Keats's books. The settings for his stories are largely inner-city but the emotions are those of all children in all settings: the pride of learning how to whistle, the excitement of outwitting older children. His works also include *Apt. 3; Goggles; Hi, Cat; Jenny's Hat; John Henry; A Letter to Amy; Louie; Maggie and the Pirates; Peter's Chair; Pet Show; The Snowy Day; The Trip;* and *Whistle for Willie*. Ezra Jack Keats fans will enjoy the books of Martha Alexander and Charlotte Zolotow (see Index to Treasury). Related books: *The Aminal* (p); *How I Hunted the Little Fellows* (p); *Airmail to the Moon,* by Tom Birdseye; *And to Think That I Saw It on Mulberry Street,* by Dr. Seuss; *Bored—Nothing to Do!,* by Peter Spier.

RIP VAN WINKLE
by Washington Irving, retold and illustrated by John Howe
Little, Brown, 1988
Gr. 1–5   30 pages

The classic tale of the Dutchman who slept for twenty years is told in glorious illustrations with a text that makes the story very accessible for today's child. For older children, the original Washington Irving text (with N. C. Wyeth illustrations) is once again available from publisher William Morrow. Related books: the French short story "The Magic Thread" in *Fairy Tales,* by Nikolai Ustinov; *The Legend of Sleepy Hollow,* retold by Diane Wolkstein; *Little Daylight,* George MacDonald's fairy tale adapted by Erick Ingraham.

THE SHRINKING OF TREEHORN
by Florence Parry Heide • Illustrated by Edward Gorey
Holiday House, 1971; Dell, 1980
Gr. 4–8   60 pages

When a young boy mentions to his social-climbing parents that he's begun to shrink, he's ignored. When he calls it to the attention of his teachers, his words fall on deaf ears. Day by day he grows smaller and day by day the adults continue to talk around him and his problem. Finally he must solve it himself. All children will recognize themselves here, but various age levels will bring different senses of humor and sympathy to the tale. Sequels: *Treehorn's Treasure; Treehorn's Wish.* (The *Shrinking* and *Treasure* books are included in one paperback volume under the Dell title *The Adventures of Treehorn.*) The author also has written two very funny novels: *Banana Twist* and *Banana Blitz.*

THE SILVER PONY
by Lynd Ward
Houghton Mifflin, 1973
Pre-S.–4   176 pages

The classic wordless book, this is the heartwarming story of a lonely farm boy and the flights of fancy he uses to escape his isolation. His imaginative trips take place on a winged pony and carry him to distant parts of the world to aid and comfort other lonely children. Also by the author: *The Biggest Bear* (p). Related books: *The Mountain That Loved a Bird* (p); *Up and Up,* by Shirley Hughes.

SLEEP OUT
by Carol Carrick • Illustrated by Donald Carrick
Clarion (both), 1973; 1982
K–5   30 pages
Christopher and his dog achieve that one great triumph that all children dream of accomplishing: they sleep out alone in the woods one night. This is the first in a series of six books about Christopher and his family. While the books can be enjoyed separately, they work best when read in sequence after *Sleep Out: Lost in the Storm*—Christopher searches for his lost dog after a long night's storm; *The Accident*—Christopher must come to terms with his grief after his dog is killed; *The Foundling*—Christopher adjusts to the idea of starting life anew after the dog's death; *The Washout*—Christopher and his new dog, Ben, rescue Christopher's stranded mother after a storm; *Ben and the Porcupine*—Christopher and his dog confront a neighborhood nuisance; *Dark and Full of Secrets*—Christopher timidly discovers the wonders of lake snorkeling; *Left Behind*—Christopher is accidentally separated from his classmates during a class trip.

Other books by one or both members of this talented husband-and-wife team include *Old Mother Witch* (p); *Big Old Bones: A Dinosaur Tale; The Climb; The Crocodiles Still Wait; Harald and the Giant Knight; Harald and the Great Stag* (p); *Morgan and the Artist; Octopus; Patrick's Dinosaur; Paul's Christmas Birthday; What Happened to Patrick's Dinosaur;* and three novels: *The Elephant in the Dark, Stay Away from Simon,* and *What a Wimp!*

SNUFFY
by Dick Bruna
Price, Stern, 1984
Tod.–Pre-S.   24 (small) pages
After Mother Goose, one of Dick Bruna's books should be the next read-aloud for infants and toddlers, even preschoolers who are being introduced to books or read aloud to for the first time. These books also make excellent first readers for children just learning to read. *Snuffy* is typical of Bruna's style: a little dog canvasses the neighborhood until he finds a neighbor's lost little girl. Simple drawings, bright colors, and easily discernible emotions in an uncomplicated story are the ingredients of Bruna's books, which

have sold almost 48 million copies around the world. Among his more than fifty titles are *Animals; The Apple; The Fish; I Can Count; I Can Dress Myself; I Can Read; I Know About Numbers; Lisa and Lynn; The Little Bird; Miffy; Miffy at the Seaside; Miffy at the Playground; Miffy at the Zoo; Miffy Goes Flying; Miffy in the Hospital; Miffy in the Snow; Miffy's Birthday; Miffy's Dream; Snuffy and the Fire; When I'm Big.*

A SPECIAL TRICK
by Mercer Mayer
Dial (paperback only), 1976
Pre-S.–5   32 pages
When the magician's houseboy discovers a dictionary of magic spells while he is dusting one day, he can't resist trying his hand at the art. Before he can say, "Sprittle sprattle, nattle tattle," the room is overrun with slithering tooth-gnashing monsters. Fortunately, little Elroy's spunk is up to the challenge. A story told with great color, imagination, and humor.

Mercer Mayer's books run from simple wordless books to daringly complicated fairy tales. His works are characterized by glowing watercolors and stories with a strong flavor of magic and fantasy.

His wordless books include *Ah-Choo!; A Boy, a Dog, and a Frog* (the first in a five-book wordless series that also includes: *Frog Goes to Dinner; Frog on His Own; Frog, Where Are You?; One Frog Too Many*); and *Bubble, Bubble.*

His picture books for preschoolers to early-elementary grades include *If I Had; There's an Alligator Under My Bed; There's a Nightmare in My Closet; Terrible Troll;* and *What Do You Do with a Kangaroo?*.

His books for early-elementary to middle-school grades include *East of the Sun, West of the Moon; Liza Lou and the Yeller Belly Swamp;* and *The Sleeping Beauty.*

In addition, Mayer has been the illustrator for these books written by others: *Beauty and the Beast* (by Marianna Mayer); *The Crack in the Wall and Other Terrible Weird Tales* (by George Mendoza); *Everyone Knows What a Dragon Looks Like* (by Jay Williams).

THE STORY OF FERDINAND
by Munro Leaf • Illustrated by Robert Lawson
Viking, 1936; Puffin, 1977
Pre-S.–2   68 pages
This world-famous tale of a great Spanish bull who preferred sitting peacefully among the flowers to fighting gloriously in the bullring is one of early childhood's classics. It is illustrated by Robert Lawson in a simple black-

and-white style that further enhances children's comprehension of the story about one of the world's most famous pacifists. Related books: *Ira Sleeps Over* (p); *Nice Little Girls* (p); *William's Doll* (p); *Oliver Button Is a Sissy*, by Tomie de Paola.

THE STUPIDS STEP OUT
by Harry Allard • Illustrated by James Marshall
Houghton Mifflin (both), 1974; 1977
Gr. 1–4   30 pages
The title alone is enough to intrigue children, and the pictures and text will more than live up to their expectations. The family of Stanley Q. Stupid is aptly named: when their behavior isn't stupid, it is at the very least silly— and children will love them. Because of the need to explore the pictures carefully in search of the humor, small groups are best suited for this read-aloud. Sequels: *The Stupids Die; The Stupids Have a Ball.* Also by the author: *Miss Nelson Is Missing* (p). Related books: *Amelia Bedelia* (p); *All of Our Noses Are Here and Other Noodle Tales,* retold by Alvin Schwartz.

SYLVESTER AND THE MAGIC PEBBLE
by William Steig
Simon & Schuster, 1969; Windmill, 1969
Pre-S.–4   30 pages
In this contemporary fairy tale that won the Caldecott Medal, young Sylvester finds a magic pebble that will grant his every wish as long as he holds it in his hand. When a hungry lion approaches, Sylvester wishes himself into a stone. Since stones don't have hands with which to hold pebbles, the pebble drops to the ground and he cannot reach it to wish himself normal again. The subsequent loneliness of Sylvester and his parents is portrayed with deep sensitivity, making all the more real their joy a year later when they are happily reunited. Also by the author: *Brave Irene* (p); *The Real Thief; The Amazing Bone; Doctor De Soto.* Related books: *Arnold of the Ducks* (p); *The Chocolate Touch* (n); *The Whingdingdilly* (p). For grades 1–4, see *Bella Arabella* (s).

THE THREE LITTLE PIGS
by Paul Galdone
Clarion (both), 1970; 1984
Tod.–1   36 pages
The classic tale of how the clever and industrious member of the pig family outwitted the wicked wolf. Many of the simpler folktales of Joseph Jacobs,

the Brothers Grimm, and Hans Christian Andersen have been made into picture books by author–illustrator Paul Galdone. His versions are not meant as replacements for the originals but merely as introductions to the fairy tale for very young children. Between first and second grades, the child's maturity and listening span should be developed enough to warrant longer, more complicated tales. (See Chapter 3 for a discussion of fairy tales.) Galdone's most popular books include: *Cinderella; The Gingerbread Boy; The Greedy Old Fat Man; Henny Penny; The Hungry Fox and the Foxy Duck; Little Red Riding Hood; The Monster and the Tailor; Puss in Boots; Rumpelstiltskin; The Steadfast Tin Soldier; The Teeny-Tiny Woman; The Three Bears; Three Billy Goats Gruff;* and *The Turtle and the Monkey.* Related books: *The Three Bears and 15 Other Stories* (a); *Mr. and Mrs. Pig's Night Out,* by Mary Rayner.

THOMAS' SNOWSUIT
by Robert Munsch • Illustrated by Michael Martchenko
Annick (both), 1985
Pre-S.–4   24 pages
Thomas *hates* his new snowsuit, much to the dismay of his mother, teachers, and principal—all of whom find him a most determined fellow. But children find the situation just plain *funny!* Robert Munsch is as popular with Canadian children as Shel Silverstein (see *Where the Sidewalk Ends* [p]) is in the U.S. Among his books now available in the U.S.: *The Boy in the Drawer; The Dark; David's Father; 50 Below Zero; I Have to Go!; Jonathan Cleaned Up—Then He Heard a Sound; Love You Forever; Millicent and the Wind; Moira's Birthday; Mortimer; Mud Puddle; The Paperbag Princess.*

THY FRIEND, OBADIAH
by Brinton Turkle
Viking, 1969; Puffin, 1982
Pre-S.–2   38 pages
This is one in a series of books about a six-year-old boy and his colonial family on the island of Nantucket. The adventures deal with friendship, honesty, and courage while weaving a subtle history lesson. (Several of the titles may be out of print but can still be found in libraries.) Others in the series include *The Adventures of Obadiah; Obadiah the Bold; Rachel and Obadiah.* Also by the author: *Deep in the Forest* (wordless); *Do Not Open;* and the following seasonal books: *Over the River and Through the Wood* (Thanksgiving); *The Elves and the Shoemaker* (Christmas). For related books in a historical setting, see listing with *Wagon Wheels* (p).

TIKKI TIKKI TEMBO
by Arlene Mosel • Illustrated by Blair Lent
Holt, 1968; Scholastic, 1972
Pre-S.–3   40 pages
This little picture book tells the amusing legend of how the Chinese people changed from giving their firstborn sons enormously long first names and began giving all children short names. Related books: *Crow Boy*, by Taro Yashima; *The Emperor and the Kite*, by Jane Yolen; *The Five Chinese Brothers*, by Claire Bishop; *Shen of the Sea* (a collection of Chinese folk/fairy tales), by Arthur Bowie Chrisman; *Yeh-Shen: A Cinderella Story from China*, retold by Ai-Ling Louie.

TINTIN IN TIBET
by Hergé
Little, Brown (paperback only), 1975
Gr. 2–4   62 pages
When you've been in print for more than fifty years, been translated into twenty-two languages, and praised in *The Times* of London and *The New York Times,* you must be special. Tintin is just that. He's the boy detective who hopscotches the globe in pursuit of thieves and smugglers. Loaded with humor, adventure, and marvelous artwork (700 pictures in each issue), Tintin's special appeal for parents who want to assist their child in reading is the fact that each Tintin contains more than 8,000 words. Having heard Tintin read aloud, children will want to obtain his other adventures and read them by themselves, oblivious to the fact that they are reading 8,000 words in the process. Because of the size of the pictures, Tintin is best read aloud to no more than two children at a time. There are more than twenty different adventures in the series, sold primarily in select bookstores. Keep in mind that students who enjoy the Tintin comic format can be lured easily into these hardcover books with a similar format: *The Amazing Voyage of Jackie Grace* (p); *Fred,* by Posy Simmonds; *Jack at Sea,* by Philippe Dupasquier; *Where's Waldo* (p). The Tintin series includes: *The Black Island; The Calculus Affair; The Castafiore Emerald; Cigars of the Pharaohs; The Crab with the Golden Claws; Destination Moon; Explorers of the Moon; Flight 714; King Ottokar's Sceptre; Land of Black Gold; Prisoners of the Sun; Red Rackham's Treasure; The Red Sea Sharks; The Secret of the Unicorn; The Seven Crystal Balls; The Shooting Star;* and *Tintin and the Picaros.*

TOO MANY BOOKS
by Caroline Feller Bauer • Illustrated by Diane Paterson
Warne, 1984; Puffin, 1986
Pre-S.–2   32 pages

A wonderful introduction to the birth of a book-lover, this fanciful story follows Maralou from her infant love of books through learning to read, discovering the library, receiving her first book as a gift, and then developing an insatiable love of books that infects the entire town. Also by the author: *My Mom Travels a Lot*. Related titles on the subject of reading: *Broderick* (p); *The Amazing Voyage of Jackie Grace* (p); *The Great Piratical Rumbustification & The Librarian and the Robbers* (s); *Andy and the Lion,* by James Dougherty; *Arthur's Prize Reader,* by Lillian Hoban; *Aunt Lulu,* by Daniel Pinkwater; *Check It Out! The Book About Libraries,* by Gail Gibbons; *Clara and the Bookwagon,* by Nancy Levinson; *The Wednesday Surprise,* by Eve Bunting; *Dinosaurs Are 568,* by Jean Rogers; *Fix-It,* by David McPhail; *Grover Learns to Read,* by Dan Elliott; *How a Book Is Made,* by Aliki; *I Can Read,* by Dick Bruna; *I Can Read with My Eyes Shut,* by Dr. Seuss; *Least of All,* by Carol Purdy; *The Man Who Loved Books,* by Jean Fritz.

THE VERY HUNGRY CATERPILLAR
by Eric Carle
Philomel/Putnam (both), 1969; 1986
Tod.–1   38 pages

What an ingenious book! It is, at the same time, a simple, lovely way to teach a child the days of the week, how to count to five, and how a caterpillar becomes a butterfly. First, this is a book to look at—bright, bright pictures. Then it is something whose pages beg to be turned—pages that have little round holes in them made by the hungry little caterpillar. And as the number of holes grow, so does the caterpillar.

In a slightly more complicated book, *The Grouchy Ladybug,* Carle uses pages of various sizes to show the passage of time and growth in size of the ladybug's adversaries. In the middle of it all there's a little science lesson. Also by the author: *Eric Carle's Treasury of Classic Stories for Children* (a); *Do You Want to Be My Friend?; Have You Seen My Cat?; A House for a Hermit Crab; The Mixed-up Chameleon; The Secret Birthday Message; The Very Busy Spider.*

WAGON WHEELS
by Barbara Brenner • Illustrated by Don Bolognese
Harper (both), 1978; 1984
Pre-S.–3   64 small pages
In four short chapters, this story, based on a true incident, can be read either as a long picture book or as an introduction to chapter books. Three young black brothers follow a map to their father's homestead on the western plains. The trio braves storms, fires, and famine to achieve their goal. Two other black families' travels are depicted in *The Drinking Gourd*, by F. N. Monjo, a story of the underground railroad, and *The Gold Cadillac*, by Mildred Taylor, a family's car ride through the South in 1950. Related historical fiction: *The Courage of Sarah Noble* (s); *Charlie's House*, by Clyde R. Bulla; *Going West*, by Martin Waddell; *If You Traveled West in a Covered Wagon*, by Ellen Levine; *The Josephina Story Quilt*, by Eleanor Coerr; *Lost and Found*, by Jill Paton Walsh; *The Lucky Stone*, by Lucille Clifton; *My Prairie Year*, by Brett Harvey; *Watch the Stars Come Out*, by Riki Levinson; and the following easy-reader history books: *George the Drummer Boy* and *Sam the Minuteman*, both by Nathaniel Benchley. More historical fiction is listed with *A Lion to Guard Us* (s).

WHAT'S UNDER MY BED?
by James Stevenson
Greenwillow, 1983; Puffin, 1984
Pre-S.–2   30 pages
In this ongoing series, Stevenson gives us a most endearing combination: two innocent but slightly worried grandchildren turn again and again for reassurance to their grandfather, who concocts imaginative tales about his childhood that make their worries pale by comparison. They've yet to invent the Superhero who can equal the hilarious heroics and hair-raising escapades of Grandpa as a child. Also in the series: *Could Be Worse!; Grandpa's Great City Tour; The Great Big Especially Beautiful Easter Egg; No Friends; That Dreadful Day; That Terrible Halloween Night; We Can't Sleep; Worse Than Willy!; We Hate Rain!; Will You Please Feed Our Cat?* Also by the author: *Are We Almost There?; If I Owned a Candy Factory; The Night After Christmas; The Supreme Souvenir Factory; Wilfred the Rat; The Wish Card Ran Out.*

WHEN THE NEW BABY COMES I'M MOVING OUT
by Martha Alexander
Dial (both), 1979; 1981
Pre-S.–1   28 pages

Jealousy surfaces for a little boy as he anticipates the arrival of a new baby in the house and that all the attention will be diverted from him. His anger is soothed when his mother tells him the special roles and privileges of big brothers. This is a companion book to *Nobody Asked Me If I Wanted a Baby Sister*.

With her gentle humor, Martha Alexander is especially adept at depicting preschoolers' concerns and their eventual resolution. Her books (most are in paperback) and themes include *Bobo's Dream* (courage); *I'll Be the Horse If You'll Play with Me* (sibling rivalry); *I'll Protect You from the Jungle Beasts* (nightmares); *Marty McGee's Space Lab* (sex roles); *Maybe a Monster* (anxiety); *Move Over Twerp* (bullying); *No Ducks in Our Bathtub* (pets); *We Never Get to Do Anything* (stubbornness). In addition, Alexander has a set of four books that deal with a blackboard bear that comes to life in aid of a little boy squabbling with older playmates: *Blackboard Bear; And My Mean Old Mother Will Be Sorry, Blackboard Bear; I Sure Am Glad to See You, Blackboard Bear; We're in Big Trouble, Blackboard Bear.*

WHERE THE BUFFALOES BEGIN
by Olaf Baker • Illustrated by Stephen Gammell
Warne (both), 1981; 1983
Gr. 2 and up   46 pages
After hearing the tribal legend of the sacred lake where the buffaloes begin their life, a young Great Plains Indian boy daringly sets off in search of the spot—only to end up on a fearful ride to save his own life and his tribe. For experienced listeners. An update on the fate of the buffalo can be found in *Buffalo: The American Bison Today*, by Dorothy Patent. Related Indian picture books: *Annie and the Old One*, by Miska Miles; *The Double Life of Pocahontas* and *The Good Giants and the Bad Pukwudgies*, both by Jean Fritz; *How Rabbit Stole the Fire*, by Joanna Troughton; *Knots on a Counting Rope*, by Bill Martin, Jr., and John Archambault; *The Legend of the Bluebonnet* and *The Legend of the Indian Paintbrush*, both by Tomie dePaola; *Not Just Any Ring*, by Danita Haller; *Small Wolf*, by Nathaniel Benchley; and these legends told by Paul Goble: *Beyond the Ridge; Buffalo Woman; Death of the Iron Horse; The Gift of the Sacred Dog; The Girl Who Loved Wild Horses; The Great Race; Her Seven Brothers*. Also *North American Legends*, a collection by Virginia Haviland; and these novels: *The Courage of Sarah Noble* (s); *The Indian in the Cupboard* (n); *The Sign of the Beaver* (n); *Sing Down the Moon* (n); and *Stone Fox* (s).

WHERE'S SPOT?
by Eric Hill
Putnam, 1980
Tod.−2   20 pages
In looking for her missing puppy, Spot's mother searches every corner and niche of the house. As she peeks into closets and pianos, under beds and rugs, the reader and listeners can imitate her search by lifting page flaps to find an assortment of animals in hiding. The flaps are reinforced and the pages durable enough to be handled by young children. The book is an entertaining introduction to household names, animals, and the concept of "No." Sequels (in order): *Spot's Big Book of Words; Spot's Birthday Party; Spot's First Walk; Spot's First Christmas; Spot's First Easter; Spot Goes to the Beach; Spot Goes to the Circus; Spot Goes to the Farm; Spot Goes to School.* Other lift-the-flap books allowing active involvement between child and book: *Pat the Bunny* (p); *Winifred's New Bed,* by Lynn and Richard Howell; and the following books by Harriet Ziefert: *Bear All Year; Bear's Busy Morning; Bear Gets Dressed; Bear Goes Shopping; Birthday Card, Where Are You?; Daddy, Can You Play with Me?; Don't Cry, Baby Sam;* and *Mommy, Where Are You?* Other toddler books are listed at the end of *Playing* (p).

WHERE'S WALDO?
by Martin Handford
Little, Brown, 1987
K−4   26 pages
Waldo is a hiker on a worldwide trek who plays hide-and-seek with the reader/viewer who has to find him as he threads his way through thousands of people who populate a dozen different landscapes. Children will spend hours searching the pages for Waldo and the list of more than 300 items check-listed at the end of the book. Also note that in each scene Waldo loses one of his twelve personal items. Books like this stretch children's attention spans while polishing visual discrimination. Sequel: *Find Waldo Now!* Related books: *But Where Is the Green Parrot?,* by Thomas and Wanda Zacharias; *Each Peach Pear Plum,* by Janet and Allan Ahlberg; *My First Book of Puzzles,* from Platt and Munk; *What's Missing* and *What's Silly,* by Niki Yektai; *Where's Wallace?,* by Hilary Knight; for older children—*Opt: An Illusionary Tale,* by Arline and Joseph Baum.

WHERE THE WILD THINGS ARE
by Maurice Sendak
Harper (both), 1963; 1984
K–3   28 pages
This is the picture book that changed the course of modern children's literature. Sendak creates here a fantasy about a little boy and the monsters that haunt all children. The fact that youngsters are not the least bit frightened by the story, that they love it as they would an old friend, is a credit to Sendak's insight into children's minds and hearts. It was the 1964 winner of the Caldecott Medal. Actress Tammy Grimes does a magnificent reading of this book, along with selections from other Sendak works, on Caedmon recording No. CP1531, "Where the Wild Things Are and Other Stories." Also by the author: *Higglety Pigglety Pop!; In the Night Kitchen; Maurice Sendak's Really Rosie: Starring the Nutshell Kids;* the Nutshell library (which includes *Alligators All Around; Chicken Soup with Rice; One Was Johnny;* and *Pierre); Outside Over There; The Sign on Rosie's Door.* Related books: *The Amazing Voyage of Jackie Grace* (p); *Harry and the Terrible Whatzit* (p); *Andrew's Bath* and *The Bear's Toothache,* by David McPhail; *The Beast in the Bed,* by Barbara Dillon; *Humphrey's Bear,* by Jan Wahl; *In the Attic,* by Hiawyn Oram; *Moon Tiger,* by Phyllis Root; *There's a Nightmare in My Closet,* by Mercer Mayer. For a listing of books about bedtime antics, see *No Jumping on the Bed* (p).

THE WHINGDINGDILLY
by Bill Peet
Houghton Mifflin (both), 1970; 1982
Pre-S.–5   60 pages
Discontented with his life as a dog, Scamp envies all the attention given to his beribboned neighbor—Palomar the wonder horse. But when a backwoods witch changes Scamp into an animal with the feet of an elephant, the neck of a giraffe, the tail of a zebra, and the nose of a rhinoceros, he gets more attention than he bargained for: He ends up a most unhappy circus freak. Happily, all ends well, and tied into the ending is a subtle lesson for both Scamp and his readers: Be yourself! For a list of related books, see *Nice Little Girls* (p).

Bill Peet is one of the most popular of the contemporary author-illustrators, and his picture books never fail to instruct, stimulate, and amuse children. Neither the text (often in rhyming verse) nor the art rests in the shadow of the other—they complement each other beautifully. Though never heavy-handed, many of his books have a fablelike quality. Two of his works—*Wump World* and *Farewell to Shady Glade*—were among the first children's books to call attention to the environmental crises during the 1960s. A sampling of his various themes includes: ambition (*Chester the Worldly Pig*); arrogance (*Big Bad Bruce*); aging (*Encore for Eleanor*); conceit (*Ella*); courage (*Cowardly Clyde*); environment (*The Knats of Knotty Pine*); hope (*The Caboose Who Got Loose*); loyalty (*Jennifer and Josephine*). His *Bill Peet: An Autobiography* is a most unusual 190-page book for young readers. (Yes, there are pictures on *every* page.)

Other Bill Peet titles include *Buford the Little Bighorn; Capyboppy* (short novel); *Cyrus the Unsinkable Sea Serpent; Eli; How Droofus the Dragon Lost His Head; Hubert's Hair-Raising Adventure; Huge Harold; Jethro and Joel Were a Troll; Kermit the Hermit; The Kweeks of Kookatumdee; The Luckiest One of All; No Such Things; Pamela Camel; The Pinkish Purplish Egg; Randy's Dandy Lions; Smokey; The Spooky Tail of Prewitt Peacock;* and *Zella, Zack and Zodiac.*

WILLIAM'S DOLL
by Charlotte Zolotow • Illustrated by William Pène du Bois
Harper, (both), 1972; 1985
Pre-S.–4   32 pages

William's father wants him to play with his basketball or trains; William, to the astonishment of all, wishes he had a doll to play with. "Sissy," say his brother and friends. But William's grandmother says something else— something very important—to William, his father, and his brother. The message is one that all children and their parents should hear. For a list of related books, see *Nice Little Girls* (p); *When the New Baby Comes, I'm Moving Out* (p).

One of the most prolific (more than fifty books since 1944) and successful authors for children, Charlotte Zolotow is also one of the most beloved. She writes quiet little books with quiet simple sentences and her work is always illustrated by the best artists available. Few writers have their finger on the pulse of children's emotions as this author does. You'll have no trouble finding the many Zolotow books in your library—she has almost the entire "Z" shelf to herself. Your personal knowledge of your child's or class's emotional maturity should guide you in your Zolotow selections.

Here is a partial listing of her popular read-alouds: *Big Sister and Little Sister* (siblings); *Do You Know What I'll Do?* (siblings); *A Father Like That* (fatherless boy); *The Hating Book* (anger); *I Know a Lady* (old age); *I Like to Be Little; If It Weren't for You* (siblings); *If You Listen* (loneliness); *Janey* (friend moves away); *May I Visit?* (family, future); *Mr. Rabbit and the Lovely*

Present (sharing); *My Grandson Lew* (death); *Over and Over* and *Something Is Going to Happen* (seasons); *The Quarreling Book* (family friction); *Someone New* and *But Not Billy* (maturing); *Some Things Go Together* (rhymes); *The Storm Book* (weather); *The Summer Night* (bedtime, family); *Timothy Too!* (siblings); *Wake Up and Goodnight* (bedtime); *When I Have a Little Boy* and *When I Have a Little Girl* (parenting); *The White Marble* (friendship).

WOLF! WOLF!
by Elizabeth and Gerald Rose
Faber, 1984 (paperback only)
Pre-S.–2   30 pages
The classic tale of the naughty shepherd boy who cried "Wolf!" as a practical joke and found that nobody believed him when he eventually told the truth. Related books: *The Boy Who Held Back the Sea* (p); *A Big Fat Enormous Lie,* by Marjorie Sharmat; *Nobody Listens to Andrew,* by Elizabeth Guilfoile.

Short Novels

AMONG THE DOLLS
by William Sleator
Dutton, 1975
Gr. 4–6   70 pages
A spooky psychological thriller about a girl who receives an old dollhouse for a birthday present, and finds herself drawn into the house and tormented by the very dolls she'd mistreated the day before. A spellbinder. For older students, William Sleator is also the author of *Run*, a novel about three teenagers, alone in a beach house, stalked by a stranger in the night, and *The Duplicate,* a haunting science fiction novel. Related books: *The Indian in the Cupboard* (n); *Prisoners at the Kitchen Table* (n); *The Dollhouse Murders,* by Betty Wright.

BE A PERFECT PERSON IN JUST THREE DAYS!
by Stephen Manes
Clarion, 1982; Bantam, 1984
Gr. 3–6   76 pages
This is a laughing-aloud book. It is far from great literature but very close to the funny bone. A young boy, tired of bearing the brunt of everyone's taunts, begins a do-it-yourself course in becoming perfect—with hilarious

and unpredictable results. Also by the author: *The Great Gerbil Roundup*. Related books: *The Shrinking of Treehorn* (p); *Sideways Stories from Wayside School* (s); *Skinnybones* (n).

THE BEARS' HOUSE
by Marilyn Sachs
Dutton, 1987; Avon, 1988
Gr. 4–6   82 pages
A perfect vehicle for a discussion of values in the classroom, this novel deals with a ten-year-old girl whose mother is ill and can no longer care for the family after the father deserts. The girl decides to tend the family, all the while suffering the taunts of classmates because she sucks her thumb, wears dirty clothes, and smells. To escape, she retreats to the fantasy world she has created in an old dollhouse in her classroom. The need for greater under-standing and patience among classmates is an inherent part of this read-aloud. Sequel: *Fran Ellen's House*. Related books: The title story from *The Three Bears and 15 Other Stories*, by Anne Rockwell; *Bella Arabella* (s); *J.T.* (s); *Mrs. Fish, Ape, and Me, the Dump Queen* (n); and *The Story of Holly and Ivy* (s).

BELLA ARABELLA
by Liza Fosburgh
Four Winds, 1985; Bantam, 1987
Gr. 1–4   102 pages
Neglected by her wealthy, often-married mother, ten-year-old Arabella finds a substitute family and affection among the servants and cats in the family mansion. But the idea of boarding school is too much for her and she conspires with her best friend, Miranda the cat, and turns into a cat, something she discovers is far from enjoyable. For experienced listeners. Related books: For grades four and up, check your library for Paul Gallico's (now out-of-print) book about a boy turned into a cat, *The Abandoned*. Related books: *Arnold of the Ducks* (p); *The Monster's Ring* (s); *Rasmus and the Vagabond* (n); *The Wish Giver* (n); *The Night Watchman*, by Helen Cress-well.

THE BEST CHRISTMAS PAGEANT EVER
by Barbara Robinson
Harper, 1972; Avon, 1973
Gr. 2–6   80 pages
What happens when the worst-behaved family of kids in the town—the ones no mother would think of allowing her kids to play with—comes to

Sunday school and muscles into all the parts for the Christmas pageant? The results are zany and heartwarming; a most unusual Christmas story. Related books: *"Hey, What's Wrong with This One?"* (s); *The Polar Express* (p); *Skinnybones* (n); *The Random House Book of Humor for Children* (a).

A BLUE-EYED DAISY
by Cynthia Rylant
Bradbury, 1985; Dell, 1987
Gr. 4–8   99 pages

Take the time to experience the warm yet bittersweet year in the life of this eleven-year-old girl and her family in the hills of West Virginia as she experiences her first kiss, her first brush with death, comes to understand her good but hard-drinking father, and begins to grow into the person you'd love to have as a relative. Also by the author: *But I'll Be Back Again: Childhood of a Writer; The Relatives Came; Waiting to Waltz: A Childhood* (poetry). Related books: *Bridge to Terabithia* (n); *Ida Early Comes over the Mountain* (n); *Miracle at Clement's Pond* (n); (s); *Us and Uncle Fraud* (n); *Introducing Shirley Braverman* (n); *Pinch,* by Larry Callen; *Sarah, Plain and Tall,* by Patricia MacLachlin.

CALL IT COURAGE
by Armstrong Sperry
Macmillan (both), 1940; 1971
Gr. 2–6   94 pages

Set in the South Seas before the traders or missionaries arrived, this story describes the struggle of a boy to overcome his fear of the sea. Finally the taunts of his peers drive him into open confrontation with his fears. A Newbery Award–winning study of fear and courage. Related books: *The Cay* (n); *The Long Journey* (n); *Toliver's Secret* (n).

A CERTAIN SMALL SHEPHERD
by Rebecca Caudill • Illustrated by William P. du Bois
Holt, 1965; Dell, 1987
Gr. 2–6   48 pages

A mute child, assigned to the role of a shepherd in the school Christmas pageant, is heartbroken when a blizzard cancels the pageant. However, two visitors during the storm stir the depths of the child's soul and bring the story to a dramatic and touching end. Related books: *Child of the Silent Night* (n); *The Half-a-Moon Inn* (s); *The Story of Holly and Ivy* (s).

CHOCOLATE FEVER
by Robert K. Smith
Dell (paperback only), 1978
Gr. 1–5   94 pages
Henry Green is a boy who loves chocolate—he's insane over it. He even has chocolate sprinkles on his cereal and chocolate cake for breakfast. He thus becomes a prime candidate to come down with the world's first case of chocolate fever. Zany but with a subtle message on moderation in our eating habits. *Jelly Belly,* also by the author, uses humor and insight to describe the self-image problems of an overweight child. In *Jelly Belly,* as well as in *The War with Grandpa,* Smith paints a powerful picture of the relationship between child and grandparent. Also by the author: *Mostly Michael.* Related books: *The Chocolate Touch* (n); *Charlie and the Chocolate Factory,* by Roald Dahl; *The Kids' Book of Chocolate,* a book of chocolate history and facts by Richard Ammon.

THE COURAGE OF SARAH NOBLE
by Alice Dalgliesh • Illustrated by Leonard Weisgard
Macmillan (both), 1986; 1987
K-3   54 pages
At the beginning of the eighteenth century, an eight-year-old girl journeyed many miles from home into the colonial wilderness with her father. With her family's instructions—"Keep up your courage!"—ringing in her ears, she faces the dangers of the dark forest while Father builds their new cabin. Just when she feels she has confronted all her fears, her father asks her to stay in the Indian village while he returns for the rest of the family. Based on a true incident, the story is an excellent introduction to the historical novel in a short form. Also by the author: *The Thanksgiving Story.* A similar tale for older children can be found in *The Sign of the Beaver* (n). Related books on courage: *The Boy Who Held Back the Sea* (p); *A Lion to Guard Us* (s); *Stone Fox* (s); *Toliver's Secret* (n); *Twenty and Ten* (s); *Wagon Wheels* (p); *The Drinking Gourd,* by F. N. Monjo.

FANTASTIC MR. FOX
by Roald Dahl • Illustrated by Tony Ross
Puffin, 1988 (paperback only)
K-4   62 pages
When three contemptuous farmers antagonize their local fox, they take on more than they ever bargained for. And nobody writes about such situations

with more color and wit than Roald Dahl, author of *James and the Giant Peach* (n).

THE FRIENDSHIP
by Mildred Taylor
Dial, 1987
Gr. 4 and up   53 pages
The Logan children (from *Roll of Thunder, Hear My Cry*) witness the searing cruelty of racial bigotry during this story set in 1933 in rural Mississippi where two men (one white, one black) see their friendship threatened by violence when the black man breaks the rules and calls the other by his first name. Other books by the author set in this period: *The Song of the Trees* (short novel); the Newbery Award–winning *Roll of Thunder, Hear My Cry* (n); and *The Gold Cadillac*. Related books: *Marching to Freedom* (s); *The Lucky Stone,* by Lucille Clifton.

THE GREAT PIRATICAL RUMBUSTIFICATION & THE LIBRARIAN AND THE ROBBERS
by Margaret Mahy
Godine, 1986
Gr. 3–6   63 pages
Here are two wickedly clever short novels by one of the most versatile writers for children today. In the first story, a band of retired but restless pirates answers a babysitting ad in hopes of staging a giant pirate party. In the second tale, a band of aliterate robbers kidnaps a librarian (who happens to be a devotee of *reading aloud*), and she turns her captors into readers. Also by the author: *The Boy Who Was Followed Home*. Related books: *Jacob Two-Two Meets the Hooded Fang* (s).

THE HALF-A-MOON INN
by Paul Fleischman
Harper, 1980; Scholastic, 1982
Gr. 2–6   88 pages
A chilling fantasy-adventure story about a mute boy separated from his mother by a blizzard and later kidnapped by the wicked proprietress of a village inn. Fast-moving, white-knuckle reading. Also by the author: *Path of the Pale Horse* (n); *The Birthday Tree*. Related books: *Among the Dolls* (s); *A Certain Small Shepherd* (p); *Child of the Silent Night* (n).

HELP! I'M A PRISONER IN THE LIBRARY
by Eth Clifford
Houghton Mifflin, 1979; Scholastic, 1985
Gr. 1–4   106 pages
When their father's car runs out of gas in a blizzard, Mary Rose and Jo-Beth are told to stay in the car while Dad goes for help. The two sisters, however, soon leave in search of a bathroom and end up mysteriously locked into an empty old stone library. Before long, the lights go out, the phone goes dead, and a threatening voice cries out, "Off with their heads!" Dreadful moans emanate from the second floor. Sequels: *The Dastardly Murder of Dirty Pete; Just Tell Me When We're Dead!; Scared Silly*. Also by the author: *Harvey's Horrible Snake Disaster; The Man Who Sang in the Dark*. Related books: *Old Mother Witch* (p); *Anna, Grandpa, and the Big Storm*, by Carla Stevens.

"HEY, WHAT'S WRONG WITH THIS ONE?"
by Maia Wojciechowska
Harper, 1969
Gr. 3–6   96 pages
The wacky and hilarious adventures of three brothers who tire of their widowed father's reluctance to find a new wife. Taking matters into their own hands, they decide to find one for him. Amid the hilarity, some tender moments. Related books: *Us and Uncle Fraud* (n); *Be a Perfect Person in Just Three Days!* (s); *The Best Christmas Pageant Ever* (s); *Skinnybones* (n); *The Not-Just-Anybody Family*, by Betsy Byars.

THE HUNDRED DRESSES
by Eleanor Estes
Harcourt (both), 1944; 1974
Gr. 3–6   78 pages
Wanda Petronski comes from the wrong side of the tracks and is the object of class jokes until her classmates sadly realize their awful mistake and cruelty. But by then it's too late. Related books: *The Bears' House* (s); *Sara Crewe* (s); *Mrs. Fish, Ape, and Me, the Dump Queen* (n); *What If They Knew?* by Patricia Hermes.

INSIDE MY FEET: THE STORY OF A GIANT
by Richard Kennedy
Harper, 1979
Gr. 3–5   72 pages

In an age of *Star Wars* and revivals of *King Kong,* it is a rare story that can chill middle-graders, especially a story about a giant. But this tale of a frightened but determined child's battle to rescue his parents from an invisible giant will have children on the edge of their seats. This giant is no pushover—he's mean-spirited and awesome—yet he carries a heavy heart. To experience one of our great storytellers, pick up *Richard Kennedy: Collected Stories* (a), which includes this story as well as fifteen others. Related books: *Aladdin* (p); *Among the Dolls* (s); *The Iron Giant* (s); *The Monster's Ring* (s); *The Dragon, Giant, and Monster Treasury,* selected by Caroline Royds.

THE IRON GIANT: A STORY IN FIVE NIGHTS
by Ted Hughes
Harper (both), 1987
K–4   58 pages
The appeal and diversity of this story are such that it has been labeled science fiction, fantasy, a modern fairy tale—take your pick but don't miss it. With suspense dripping from every page, it describes an invincible iron giant— a robot without master—that stalks the land. Suddenly the earth faces a threat far greater than from the giant when an alien creature lands—forcing the iron man into a fight for his life. Related books on magic gone awry: *Aladdin* (p); *The Monster's Ring* (s); *The Moon's Revenge* (p); *The Dragon, Giant, and Monster Treasury,* selected by Caroline Royds; *The Mirrorstone,* by Michael Palin.

ISAAC CAMPION
by Janni Howker
Greenwillow, 1986
Gr. 7 and up   84 pages
From the pen of one of England's most promising writers for young adults comes this novel in the form of an old man's grim but compassionate recollections of his life as a twelve-year-old in 1901. Beginning with his idolized brother's accidental death as a result of a dare, Isaac's story traces his own hard relationship with his father, the harshness of life in those times, the obsessive blood feud between his father and a neighbor, and finally his coming of age. For experienced listeners. Related books: *Building Blocks* (n); *A Day No Pigs Would Die* (n); *The December Rose,* by Leon Garfield; *Flyaway,* by Lynn Hall.

JACOB TWO-TWO MEETS THE HOODED FANG
by Mordecai Richler
Knopf, 1975; Bantam, 1977
Gr. 3–5   84 pages
For the crime of insulting a grown-up, Jacob is sent to Children's Prison where he must confront the infamous Hooded Fang. A marvelous tongue-in-cheek adventure story, sure to delight all. Related books: *The Bunjee Venture,* by Stan McMurtry; *The Great Piratical Rumbustification* (s).

LAFCADIO, THE LION WHO SHOT BACK
by Shel Silverstein
Harper, 1963
Gr. 2–6   90 pages
Lafcadio decides he isn't satisfied being a lion—he must become a marksman and man-about-town and painter and world traveler and . . . Well, he tries just about everything and anything in hopes of finding happiness. If only he'd try being himself. A witty and thought-provoking book. Also by the author: see listing under *Where the Sidewalk Ends* (po). Related books: see list of picture books under *Nice Little Girls* (p).

LAURA INGALLS WILDER: GROWING UP IN THE LITTLE HOUSE
by Patricia Reilly Giff
Viking Kestrel, 1987; Puffin, 1988
Gr. 3–6   56 pages
This volume explores the life struggles of a woman whose life spanned the pioneer days and jet age, who gave millions of young readers (and TV viewers) the *Little House* series. This outstanding series (Women of Our Time) consists of short biographies ranging from sports and entertainment figures to politics and science. Another excellent biography series for even younger students is Childhood of Famous Americans (Macmillan), which focuses on the subjects' early years. Details on each of these series are available by writing the Children's Book Marketing Departments at Viking Penguin (see copyright page) and Macmillan at 866 Third Avenue, New York, NY 10022.

A LION TO GUARD US
by Clyde Robert Bulla
Crowell, 1981
K–4   117 pages

In a simple prose style that is rich in character and drama, one of America's most noted writers for children gives us a poignant tale of the founding fathers of the Jamestown colony and the families they left behind in England. Here we see a plucky heroine named Amanda and her determination to hold fast to her brother and sister despite the grim agonies of her mother's death, poverty, and shipwreck—all while she clings to the dream that some-day she will find the father who left them all behind. Few authors can write so intelligently and movingly for so young an audience. In another historical piece, *Charlie's House,* Bulla provides us with another New World face—this time a dreamy English boy turned out by his family and eventually indentured to Colonial farmers around 1750. Though his tale is sometimes told with grim realism, Charlie is a moving tribute to youthful determi-nation and courage. Also by the author: *Shoeshine Girl* (s); *Almost a Hero; The Chalk Box Kid; Daniel's Duck; Dexter; A Grain of Wheat: A Writer Begins* (forty-nine small pages describing Bulla's childhood efforts at writing); *Sword in the Tree; The Wish at the Top.* Related historical books for young listeners: *The Courage of Sarah Noble* (s); *Wagon Wheels* (p); *Lost and Found,* by Jill Paton Walsh; *Time Cat,* by Lloyd Alexander; for older readers, see also listings with *Jump Ship to Freedom* (n).

THE LITTLES
by John Peterson
Scholastic (paperback only), 1970
Gr. 1–4   80 pages
Children have always been fascinated with the idea of "little people"—from leprechauns to Lilliputians, from Thumbelina to hobbits. Unfortunately, much of the famous fantasy literature is often too sophisticated for reading aloud to young children. The Littles series is the exception—short novels that provide fast-paced reading. While not great literature, they serve as excellent introductions to the notion of "chapters" in books, and are ideal springboards to more complicated literature.

The series centers on a colony of six-inch people who live inside the walls of the Bigg family's home. Their dramatic escapades with gigantic mice, cats, gliders, and telephones, while keeping their existence a secret, are a stimulant for reading appetites.

The Littles series also includes *The Littles and the Big Storm; The Littles and Their Friends* (a guidebook to the series, complete with maps and anec-dotes); *The Littles and the Trash Tinnies; The Littles Go to School; The Littles Have a Wedding; The Littles' Surprise Party; The Littles to the Rescue; Tom Little's Great Halloween Scare.* Related books: *The Indian in the Cupboard* (n);

The Borrowers and *Poor Stainless,* by Mary Norton; *Stuart Little,* by E. B. White; *Tangle and the Firesticks,* by Benedict Blathwayt; *Thumbeline,* illustrated by Lisbeth Zwerger; *Tom Thumb,* by Charles Perrault (illustrated by Linda Postma).

MARCHING TO FREEDOM: THE STORY OF MARTIN LUTHER KING, JR.
by Joyce Milton
Dell, 1987 (paperback only)
Gr. 2–5   92 pages
In twelve fast-moving chapters, the great civil rights leader's life is detailed from his first public confrontation with racism at age fourteen until his assassination. Related books on black history: *The Friendship* (s); *Wagon Wheels* (p); *The Lucky Stone,* by Lucille Clifton; *Mary McLeod Bethune,* by Milton Meltzer; *The Story of George Washington Carver,* by Eva Moore; *Wanted Dead or Alive: The True Story of Harriet Tubman,* by Ann McGovern; for older, experienced listeners: *Jump Ship to Freedom* (n); *Roll of Thunder, Hear My Cry* (n); *Words by Heart* (n); *Narrative of the Life of Frederick Douglass: An American Slave,* by Frederick Douglass.

THE MONSTER'S RING
by Bruce Coville
Pantheon, 1982; Pocket Books, 1987
Gr. 2–4   87 pages
Just the thing for Halloween reading, this is a Dr. Jekyll/Mr. Hyde story of timid little Russell and the magic ring he buys that can turn him into a monster—not a make-believe monster but one with hairy hands, fangs and claws, one that roams the night, one that will make short order of Eddie the bully, and one that will bring out the worst in Russell. An exciting fantasy of magic gone awry. Also by the author: *Sarah's Unicorn* (p). Related books: *Among the Dolls* (s); *Bella Arabella* (s); *Black and Blue Magic,* by Zilpha K. Snyder; *The Bunjee Venture,* by Stan McMurtry; *The Mirrorstone,* by Michael Palin.

MY FATHER'S DRAGON
by Ruth S. Gannett
Knopf (both), 1948; 1987
K–2   78 pages
Here is a three-volume series bursting with fantasy, hair-raising escapes, and evil creatures. The tone is dramatic enough to be exciting for even

mature preschoolers but not enough to frighten them. The narrator relates the tales as adventures that happened to his father when he was a boy. This is an excellent transition series for introducing children to longer stories with fewer pictures. The series, in order, also includes *Elmer and the Dragon* and *The Dragons of Blueland*. For related books, see listing with *The Reluctant Dragon* (s); *Dinosaur Bob and His Adventures with the Family Lizardo* (p); *The Knight and the Dragon,* by Tomie dePaola.

ON MY HONOR
by Marion Dane Bauer
Clarion, 1986; Dell, 1987
Gr. 5–9   90 pages
When his daredevil best friend drowns in a swimming accident, young Joel tells no one and returns home to deny the reality and truth of the tragedy. This gripping drama of conscience and consequences is also a story of choices—the ones we make and those we refuse to make. Also by the author: *Rain of Fire* (n). Related books: *Death Run* (n); *Killing Mr. Griffin* (n); *Wolf Rider* (n); *Terpin,* by Tor Seidler.

OWLS IN THE FAMILY
by Farley Mowat
Little, Brown, 1961; Bantam, 1981
Gr. 2–6   108 pages
No child should miss this experience of reliving with the author his rollicking boyhood on the Saskatchewan prairie, raising dogs, gophers, rats, snakes, pigeons, and—most dramatically of all—owls. It is an era we will never see again; the next best thing is to bask in it secondhand through this piece of nostalgia, filled with childhood's laughter and adventure. Also by the author: *Lost in the Barrens.* For related books, see listings with *The Biggest Bear* (p); *Daisy Rothschild* (p); *Gentle Ben* (n); *My Side of the Mountain* (n); and *Storm Boy,* by Colin Thiele.

THE RELUCTANT DRAGON
by Kenneth Grahame • Illustrated by Ernest H. Shepard
Holiday House (both), 1938; 1989
Gr. 3–5   54 pages
The author of the classic *Wind in the Willows* offers us here a simple tale; simple in size (just an oversized short story); and simple in scope (a dragon, a boy, and a knight). But for all its simplicity, it is deep in charm. The dragon is not a devouring dragon but a reluctant dragon who wants nothing

to do with violence. The boy is something of a local scholar, well-versed in dragon lore and torn mightily between his desire to view a battle between the dragon and the knight and his desire to protect his friend the dragon. And the knight—he's no simple knight at all. He's the one and only St. George the Dragon Killer. This 1938 story is a charming introduction to a legendary time and place. For experienced listeners. Related books: *The Story of Ferdinand* (p); *Weird Henry Berg* (n); *The Dragon of Og,* by Rumer Godden; *Everyone Knows What a Dragon Looks Like,* by Jay Williams; and *Saint George and the Dragon,* by Margaret Hodges.

SARA CREWE
by Frances Hodgson Burnett
Scholastic, 1986 (paperback only)
Gr. 3–6   79 pages
This tale, as powerful today as it was nearly one hundred years ago when it was written, is the classic story of the star boarder at Miss Minchin's exclusive London boarding school who is suddenly orphaned and becomes a ward of the cruel headmistress. Now friendless, penniless, and banished to the attic as a servant, Sara holds fast to her courage and dreams—until at last she finds a friend and deliverance in a heart-warming surprise ending. Try comparing this story with that of the orphan child in *Peppermints in the Parlor* (n). *Sara Crewe* was expanded into an equally successful longer novel called *A Little Princess;* both are for experienced listeners. Also by the author: *The Secret Garden* (n); *Little Lord Fauntleroy*. Related books: *Mrs. Fish, Ape, and Me, the Dump Queen* (n); *Understood Betsy* (n).

SHOESHINE GIRL
by Clyde Robert Bulla
Crowell, 1975; Harper, 1989
Gr. 2–4   84 pages
A spoiled and greedy little girl learns something about life, money, and friendship when she becomes a shoeshine girl. For other books by the author, see *A Lion to Guard Us* (s). Related books: *Mrs. Fish, Ape, and Me, the Dump Queen* (n); *The Pinballs* (n); *Sara Crewe* (s); *The Most Beautiful Place in the World,* by Ann Cameron.

SOUP
by Robert Newton Peck
Knopf, 1974; Dell, 1979
Gr. 4–6   96 pages

Two Vermont pals share a genius for getting themselves into trouble. The stories are set in the rural 1930s when life was simpler and the days were longer. But the need for a best friend was just as great then as now. Sequels: *Soup and Me; Soup for President; Soup in the Saddle; Soup on Fire; Soup on Ice; Soup on Wheels; Soup's Drum; Soup's Goat; Soup's Uncle.* Also by the author, for older children: *A Day No Pigs Would Die* (n). Related books: *Homer Price* (n); *The Great Brain* (n); *Owls in the Family* (s); *The Not-Just-Anybody Family,* by Betsy Byars; *Tramp Steamer and the Silver Bullet,* by Jeffrey Kelly.

STONE FOX
by John R. Gardiner
Crowell, 1980; Harper, 1983
Gr. 1–7   96 pages
Here is a story that, like its ten-year-old hero, never stands still. It is filled to the brim with action and determination, the love of a child for his grandfather, and the loyalty of a great dog for his young master. Based on a Rocky Mountain legend, the story describes the valiant efforts of young Willy to save his ailing grandfather's farm by attempting to win the purse in a local bobsled race. The figure of Stone Fox, the towering favorite for the race, is an unusual departure from the Indian stereotype in children's literature. Pulsing with action, emotion, and originality. Also by the author: *Top Secret.* Related books: *Where the Red Fern Grows* (n); *Dexter,* by Clyde R. Bulla.

THE STORIES JULIAN TELLS
by Ann Cameron
Pantheon, 1981; Knopf, 1987
Gr. K–3   72 pages
The author takes six short stories involving little Julian and his family and weaves them into a fabric that glows with the mischief, magic, and imagination of childhood. Though centered on commonplace subjects like desserts, gardens, loose teeth, and new neighbors, these stories of family life are written in an uncommon way that will both amuse and touch young listeners.

Don't miss the opportunity to incorporate related activities into these readings: everyone can enjoy pudding while listening to the dessert story, or make pudding afterwards; order seeds from a catalog or plant a garden after the garden story; measure everyone's height after the birthday fig tree story. Sequels: *Julian's Glorious Summer; Julian, Secret Agent; More Stories*

Julian Tells. Also by the author: *The Most Beautiful Place in the World.* Related books: *Philip Hall Likes Me, I Reckon Maybe,* by Bette Greene.

THE STORY OF HOLLY AND IVY
by Rumer Godden • Illustrated by Barbara Cooney
Viking (both), 1985; 1988
K–5 31 pages
This is the loving tale of a lonely, runaway orphan girl, an unsold Christmas doll, and a childless couple on Christmas Eve. But with Rumer Godden's talent combined with Barbara Cooney's large-format color illustrations, it is so much more. It is unforgettable. For related books, see *Bella Arabella* (s); *The Polar Express* (p); *Rasmus and the Vagabond* (n); *The Velveteen Rabbit* (s).

A TASTE OF BLACKBERRIES
by Doris B. Smith • Illustrated by Charles Robinson
Crowell, 1973; Harper, 1986
Gr. 4–7 52 pages
One of the first of contemporary authors to look at death from the child's point of view, Ms. Smith allows us to follow the narrator's emotions as he comes to terms with the death of his best friend, who died as a result of an allergic reaction to bee stings. The sensitivity with which the attendant sorrow and guilt are treated makes this an outstanding book. It blazed the way for many others which quickly followed, but few have approached the place of honor that this one holds. Also by the author: *Return to Bitter Creek.* For a list of related picture books on grief, see *Nadia the Willful* (p); for older children: *A Day No Pigs Would Die* (n); *Tuck Everlasting* (n); *Where the Red Fern Grows* (n); *Dead Birds Singing,* by Marc Talbert; *The Kids' Book About Death and Dying,* by Eric Rofes; *The Magic Moth,* by Virginia Lee; *My Twin Sister Erika,* by Ilse-Margaret Vogel.

TWENTY AND TEN
by Claire H. Bishop
Viking, 1952; Puffin, 1978
Gr. 3–6 76 pages
Set in occupied France during World War II, this book depicts the courage and ingenuity of twenty fifth-graders in hiding ten Jewish refugee children. The story is filled with high drama and history. Adult readers might give a brief explanation of the ration card system—as a control system both in peacetime (gas rationing) and wartime (food)—before reading the novel to

children. Related books: *North to Freedom* (n); *The Golem,* by Isaac Bashevis Singer; *The Little Riders,* by Margaretha Shemin; *Smoke and Ashes: The Story of the Holocaust,* by Barbara Rogasky; *Snow Treasure,* by Marie McSwigan.

THE VELVETEEN RABBIT
by Margery Williams • Illustrated by David Jorgensen
Knopf, 1985
Gr. 2–7   48 pages
The classic tale of how the long-loved nursery toy rabbit becomes real through the love of a little boy. Because of the sophisticated point of view and writing, older audiences (especially children who have bid good-bye to stuffed animals) tend to appreciate this tale more than younger ones. This edition comes with an excellent audiocassette with Meryl Streep narrating. For a related tale, see *The Story of Holly and Ivy* (s).

THE WHIPPING BOY
by Sid Fleischman
Greenwillow, 1986
Gr. 3–6   90 pages
The brattish medieval prince is too spoiled ever to be spanked, so the king regularly vents his anger on Jeremy, a peasant "whipping boy." When circumstances lead the two boys to reverse roles, each learns much about friendship and sacrifice. Painted with Fleischman's broad humor, this is a fast-paced melodrama with short, cliff-hanger chapters. For other books by the author, see *Humbug Mountain* (n). For related medieval titles, see *Harald and the Great Stag* (p).

THE WITCH OF FOURTH STREET
by Myron Levoy
Harper (paperback only), 1972
Gr. 2–5   110 pages
What a glorious collection of read-aloud short stories! Both its readability and subject matter make it must reading in every classroom and home. All the stories are set among the tenements of New York's Lower East Side during the early 1900s and deal with the daily crises, hopes, fears, laughter, and customs of a neighborhood melting pot of Russian, Polish, Irish, Italian, German, Protestant, Catholic, and Jewish families. Eight stories in all, approximately thirteen pages each. Related books: *A Chair for My Mother* (p); *In the Year of the Boar and Jackie Robinson* (n); *Ike and Mama and the Once-in-a-Lifetime Movie,* by Carol Snyder; *Watch the Stars Come Out,* by Riki Levinson.

WOLF STORY
by William McCleery
Shoe String Press, 1988
K–3 82 pages

Now back in print after a long absence, this is one of the ultimate chapter-book read-alouds. It is a story on two tracks: (1) the lovable contest of wills between a five-year-old and his father as the latter attempts to tell a bedtime story and the child insists on editing the tale; and (2) the bedtime story itself in which a crafty wolf tries to outwit an equally determined hen.

THE WONDERFUL STORY OF HENRY SUGAR & SIX MORE
by Roald Dahl
Puffin, 1988 (paperback only)
Gr. 4–7 226 pages

Here is a seven-story collection by Roald Dahl for experienced listeners. Two stories—"Lucky Break" and "A Piece of Cake"—are not good read-alouds. However, the other five pieces are excellent, especially the title story, one of the most imaginative tales I've ever read to myself or to a child. For other books by Roald Dahl, see *James and the Giant Peach* (n).

Novels

THE ADVENTURES OF PINOCCHIO
by Carlo Collodi • Illustrated by Roberto Innocenti
Knopf, 1988
Gr. 1–5 144 pages

Unfortunately, whatever familiarity the modern child may have with this 1892 classic most often comes from having seen it emasculated in the movie version. Treat your children to the real version of the poor woodcarver's puppet who faces all the temptations of childhood, succumbs to most, learns from his follies, and gains his boyhood by selflessly giving of himself for his friends. The Knopf edition, perhaps the most lavishly illustrated ever, is the *real* Pinocchio. Related books: *Bella Arabella* (s); *The Story of Holly and Ivy* (s); *The Bad Times of Irma Baumlein,* by Carol R. Brink; and *The Real Thing,* by William Steig.

AND NOBODY KNEW THEY WERE THERE
by Otto Salassi
Greenwillow, 1984
Gr. 4–8   179 pages
As a publicity stunt, a demonstration squad of Marines disappears from a Houston fairground. With the news media and military officials debating their whereabouts, the nine men plan to walk 450 miles in twenty-six days and suddenly show up for a Fourth of July celebration in Mississippi. Their route is a nervy one—directly through Louisiana and Texas towns, farms, and woods, always under the cover of darkness. What they don't figure on is being discovered by two irrepressible thirteen-year-old boys, who quickly join the troop and prove themselves a hardy match for the Marines. Set up a map of the area and plot the journey as you read this one. Related books: *Good Old Boy* (n); *No Promises on the Wind,* by Irene Hunt.

THE ANIMAL FAMILY
by Randall Jarrell
Pantheon (both), 1965; 1987
Gr. 3–7   180 pages
In a beautiful allegory on the need for community, a lonely hunter brings a mermaid home to his island cabin. Over time they adopt a bear cub, a lynx, and, finally, an orphaned child. Jarrell, an honored poet, wraps the growth of this unconventional family in the warm humor and love that permeate the best of family/community situations. Though no great plot unfolds, the reader/listener is drawn into the characters so deeply you begin to care for them as family. As one teacher described the book: "It's like a warm glove." For experienced listeners. Related books: *Charlotte's Web* (n); *Pearl's Promise* (n); *Mrs. Frisby and the Rats of NIMH* (n).

BRIDGE TO TERABITHIA
by Katherine Paterson
Crowell, 1977; Harper, 1987
Gr. 4–7   128 pages
Few novels for children have dealt with so many emotions and issues so well: sports, school, peers, friendship, death, guilt, art, and family. A Newbery Award–winner, this book deserves to be read or heard by everyone. Also by the author: *The Great Gilly Hopkins.* Related books: *Miracle at Clement's Pond* (n); *A Taste of Blackberries* (s); *King Kong and Other Poets,* by Robert Burch; *My Twin Sister Erika,* by Ilse-Margaret Vogel.

BUILDING BLOCKS
by Cynthia Voigt
Atheneum, 1984
Gr. 6 and up   128 pages
Disgusted by what he considers his spineless father, young Brann falls asleep one day and, unlike Rip Van Winkle, wakes thirty-seven years *earlier*, mysteriously transported to another time and place where he finds a new playmate—a ten-year-old boy who turns out to be his father as a child. Their few days together give Brann a new understanding of his father's adulthood. For experienced listeners. Related books: *A Blue-Eyed Daisy* (s); *Isaac Campion* (s); *Flyaway,* by Lynn Hall.

CADDIE WOODLAWN
by Carol Ryrie Brink
Macmillan (both), 1935, 1970; 1973
Gr. 4–6   286 pages
You take *The Little House on the Prairie;* I'll take *Caddie Woodlawn.* Ten times over, I'll take this tomboy of the 1860s with her pranks, her daring visits to Indian camps, her one-room schoolhouse fights, and her wonderfully believable family. Try to pick up the 1973 revised edition with Trina Schart Hyman's sensitive illustrations. For experienced listeners. Sequel: *Magical Melons.* For an interesting comparative study, see *Introducing Shirley Braverman* (n). Related books: *Understood Betsy* (n); *Hannah's Farm: The Seasons on an Early American Homestead,* by Michael McCurdy; *Sarah, Plain and Tall,* by Patricia MacLachlin.

THE CALL OF THE WILD
by Jack London
Grosset, 1965; Bantam, 1969; Scholastic, 1970; Puffin, 1982
Gr. 6 and up   126 pages
This 1903 dog story, set amidst the rush for gold in the Klondike, depicts the savagery and tenderness between man and his environment in unforgettable terms. For experienced listeners. Read pages 10–32 in Irving Stone's biography *Jack London, Sailor on Horseback* for a portrait of London's deprived childhood and eventual awakening to books and writing. Also by the author: *White Fang.* Related books: *Lassie-Come-Home* (n); *The Cremation of Sam McGee* (po) and *Best Tales of the Yukon,* by Robert W. Service; *Kavik the Wolf Dog,* by Walt Morey; *Danger Dog,* by Lynn Hall.

THE CASE OF THE BAKER STREET IRREGULAR
by Robert Newman
Atheneum (both), 1978; 1984
Gr. 4–8   216 pages
This finely crafted mystery novel is an excellent introduction for young readers to the world of Sherlock Holmes. A young orphan is suddenly pitted against the dark side of turn-of-the-century London when his tutor-guardian is kidnapped. Complete with screaming street urchins, sinister cab drivers, bombings, murder, back alleys, and a child's-eye view of the great sleuth himself—Sherlock Holmes. For experienced listeners. Also by the author: *The Case of the Etruscan Treasure; The Case of the Frightened Friend; The Case of the Somerville Secret; The Case of the Threatened King; The Case of the Vanishing Corpse; The Case of the Watching Boy.* Related books: *The Curse of the Blue Figurine* (n); *Peppermints in the Parlor* (n); *The December Rose,* by Leon Garfield.

THE CAY
by Theodore Taylor
Doubleday, 1969; Avon, 1977
Gr. 2–6   144 pages
An exciting adventure about a blind white boy and an old black man shipwrecked on a tiny Caribbean island. The first chapters are slow but it builds with taut drama to a stunning ending. Related books: *Call It Courage* (s); *Hatchet* (n); *The Iceberg Hermit,* by Arthur Roth; *Swept in the Wave of Terror,* by Gloria Skurzynski; *The Voyage of the Frog,* by Gary Paulsen.

CHARLOTTE'S WEB
by E. B. White • Illustrated by Garth Williams
Harper (both), 1952
Gr. K–4   184 pages
One of the most universally acclaimed books in contemporary children's literature, it is loved as much by adults as by children. The tale centers on the barnyard life of a young pig who is slated to be butchered in the fall. The animals of the yard (particularly a haughty gray spider named Charlotte) conspire with the farmer's daughter to save the pig's life. While there is much humor in the novel, the author brings in wisdom and pathos in developing his theme of friendship within the cycle of life. Also by the author: *Stuart Little.* Related books: *The Animal Family* (n); *The Story of Doctor Doolittle* (n); *Pearl's Promise* (n); *Mrs. Frisby and the Rats of NIMH* (n); *The Cricket in Times Square,* by George Selden.

CHILD OF THE SILENT NIGHT: THE STORY OF LAURA BRIDGMAN
by Edith Fisher Hunter
Houghton Mifflin, 1963
Gr. 3–5   124 pages
When Charles Dickens visited the United States in 1842, the person he most wished to see was a thirteen-year-old girl in Boston named Laura Bridgman. And no wonder. This child's story is an inspiration to all who heard it then or hear it now. It was the triumphant efforts of this child and her teachers that eventually paved the way for another deaf, mute, and blind child nearly forty years later—Helen Keller. Related books: *A Certain Small Shepherd* (s); *The Half-a-Moon Inn* (s); *Helen Keller: From Tragedy to Triumph,* by Katharine Wilkie; *The Man Who Sang in the Dark,* by Eth Clifford.

THE CHOCOLATE TOUCH
by Patrick Skene Catling
Morrow, 1979; Bantam, 1981
Gr. 1–4   122 pages
Here is a new and delicious twist to the old King Midas story. Young John learns a dramatic lesson in self-control when everything he touches with his lips turns to chocolate—toothpaste, bacon and eggs, water, pencils, trumpet. What would happen, then, if he kissed his mother?

Either before or after reading this story, read or tell the original version, "The Golden Touch," which details King Midas's bout with greed and regret. For fifth grade and up, the tale is included as one of the stories in Nathaniel Hawthorne's *A Wonder Book* (a). Related books: *Chocolate Fever* (s); *The Search for Delicious* (n); *The Kids' Book of Chocolate,* a book of chocolate history and facts by Richard Ammon.

THE CURSE OF THE BLUE FIGURINE
by John Bellairs
Dial, 1983; Bantam, 1984
Gr. 4–8   200 pages
Except for Joan Aiken, nobody writes the Gothic chiller for middle-grade students like Bellairs. In this book, Johnny Dixon removes a small figurine from the basement of his church, only to be haunted by the evil spirits attached to it. Johnny and his professor friend continue their spine-tingling exploits down twisted tunnels in *The Mummy, the Will and the Crypt; The Revenge of the Wizard's Ghost;* and *The Spell of the Sorcerer's Skull.* Another series includes young Anthony and the local librarian: *The Dark Secret of*

Weatherend; The Treasure of Alpheus Winterborn; and *Lamp from the Warlock's Tomb.* Related books: *The Case of the Baker Street Irregular* (n); *Peppermints in the Parlor* (n); *The December Rose,* by Leon Garfield.

DANNY THE CHAMPION OF THE WORLD
by Roald Dahl
Knopf, 1975; Puffin, 1988
Gr. 3–6   196 pages
This is the exciting and tender story of a motherless boy and his father—"the most wonderful father who ever lived"—and their great adventure together. Teachers and parents should explain the custom and tradition of "poaching" in England before going too deeply into the story. Try comparing the experiences of Danny with those of Leigh Botts, a fatherless boy in *Dear Mr. Henshaw* (n). For other books by the author, see *James and the Giant Peach* (n).

A DAY NO PIGS WOULD DIE
by Robert Newton Peck
Knopf, 1972; Dell, 1986
Gr. 6 and up   150 pages
Set among Shaker farmers in Vermont during the 1920s, this poignant story deals with the author's coming of age at 13, his adventures, fears, and triumphs. As a novel of life and death, it should be read carefully by the teacher or parent before it is read aloud to children. A very moving story by the author of the Soup series (s). For experienced listeners. Related books: *Isaac Campion* (s); *Where the Red Fern Grows* (n); *Words by Heart* (n); *Old Yeller,* by Fred Gipson.

DEAR MR. HENSHAW
by Beverly Cleary
Morrow, 1983; Dell, 1984
Gr. 3–6   134 pages
In this 1984 Newbery Medal winner, Beverly Clearly departs from her *Ramona* format to write a very different but every bit as successful book—perhaps the finest in her thirty-year career. Using only the letters and diary of a young boy (Leigh Botts), the author traces his personal growth from first grade to sixth. We watch the changes in his relationship with his divorced parents, his schools (where he always ends up the friendless "new kid"), an author with whom he corresponds over the years, and finally with himself. There is wonderful humor here but there is also much sen-

sitivity to the heartaches that confront the growing number of Leigh Bottses in our homes and classrooms, and here too is a worthy role model in courage and perseverance. And, as icing on the cake, this book might do more for children's creative writing efforts than any textbook or classroom lesson you can offer. Also by the author: *Ramona the Pest* (series); *The Mouse and the Motorcycle* (series). Related books: *Danny the Champion of the World* (n); *J.T.* (n); *Rasmus and the Vagabond* (n); *Thank You, Jackie Robinson* (n); *The Amazing Memory of Harvey Bean*, by Molly Cone; *Mostly Michael*, by Robert K. Smith.

DEATH RUN
by Jim Murphy
Clarion, 1982
Gr. 7 and up   174 pages
To all appearances, the death of the high school basketball player appeared to be an accident, the result of a seizure suffered alone in the park. But Brian knows otherwise. He was one of the four boys involved in the prank that ended in death. And like Raskolnikov's in *Crime and Punishment,* his guilt and anxiety drive him into suspicious eccentricities that arouse the curiosity of a police detective. A suspenseful study of guilt, peer pressure, and a conscience struggling to be heard. Related books: *Killing Mr. Griffin* (n); *Wolf Rider* (n); *Pursuit,* by Michael French; *Run,* by William Sleator; *Terpin,* by Tor Seidler; *To Be a Killer,* by Jay Bennett.

A DOG CALLED KITTY
by Bill Wallace
Holiday, 1980; Archway, 1984
Gr. 1–5   137 pages
In this first-person narrative, a young boy struggles to overcome the deep-seated fear of dogs caused by his traumatic experience with a vicious dog during early childhood. Don't be misled by the cutesy-sweet title of this book; it is a powerfully moving story of childhood and family, written by an Oklahoma elementary school principal. Contrast the conflict in this book with the equally effective *Danger Dog,* by Lynn Hall, in which a young boy attempts to "deprogram" a trained attack dog. Also by the author: *Ferret in the Bedroom, Lizards in the Fridge; Trapped in Death Cave; Shadow on the Snow.* Related books: *Hurry Home, Candy* (n); *Where the Red Fern Grows* (n); *Foxy,* by Helen V. Griffith.

THE DOG DAYS OF ARTHUR CANE
by T. Ernesto Bethancourt
Holiday House, 1976
Gr. 5–8   160 pages
When an affluent high school boy is mysteriously transformed into a mongrel dog, he discovers exactly what is meant by the expression "a dog's life." Surviving on the streets of New York by his wits and the skin of his teeth, Arthur faces all the modern canine perils—dogcatchers, poisoned meat, speeding cars, even the gas chamber. Though the book has its humorous moments, much of its strength is in sheer drama. Readers may want to be alert to an occasional four-letter word. An equally effective story (for Gr. 4 and up) about a boy who becomes a cat is Paul Gallico's *The Abandoned,* now out of print but still found in the adult section of many libraries. Related books: *Bella Arabella* (s); *Incident at Hawk's Hill* (n); *Lassie-Come-Home* (n).

FROM THE MIXED-UP FILES OF MRS. BASIL E. FRANKWEILER
by E. L. Konigsburg
Macmillan, 1967; Dell, 1986
Gr. 4–7   162 pages
A bored and brainy twelve-year-old girl talks her nine-year-old brother into running away with her. To throw everyone off their trail, Claudia chooses the Metropolitan Museum of Art in New York City as a refuge, and amid centuries-old art they sleep, dine, bathe, and pray in regal secret splendor. An exciting story of hide-and-seek and a marvelous art lesson to boot. For experienced listeners. In related runaway books: a city boy hides in the wilderness—*My Side of the Mountain* (n); a city boy hides in the subway system—*Slake's Limbo* (n).

GENTLE BEN
by Walt Morey
Dutton, 1965; Avon, 1976
Gr. 3–6   192 pages
A young boy adopts a huge brown bear and brings to his family in Alaska all the joys and tears attendant to such a combination. Though the struggle to save animals from ignorant but well-intentioned human predators is one that has been written many times over, Morey's handling of characters, plot, and setting makes an original and exciting tale. He supports the pace of his story with many lessons in environmental science—from salmon runs

to hibernation. For related titles on taming the naturally wild, see listings with *Daisy Rothschild* (p) and *The Biggest Bear* (p). Also: *Call of the Wild* (n); *The Midnight Fox* (n); *My Side of the Mountain* (n); *Danger Dog,* by Lynn Hall; *The Grizzly,* by Annabel and Edgar Johnson.

THE GIRL WITH THE SILVER EYES
by Willo Davis Roberts
Atheneum, 1980; Scholastic, 1982
Gr. 4–8 181 pages
There is something about nine-year-old Katie that sets her apart—other than the strange silver pupils in her eyes. Her secret is that she has paranormal powers as a result of her mother being exposed to certain factory chemicals during pregnancy. Written as a suspense story, it's also a powerful study of a child who marches to a different drummer and the pain that comes with the march. Also by the author: *View from the Cherry Tree, The Magic Book.* Related book: *The Secret Life of Dilly McBean,* by Dorothy Haas.

GOOD NIGHT, MR. TOM
by Michelle Magorian
Harper (both), 1981; 1986
Gr. 6 and up 318 pages
This is the longest novel in this list of recommended titles; it might also be the most powerful. Adults should preview it carefully before reading aloud. Simply put, this is the story of an eight-year-old boy evacuated during the London blitz to a small English village, where he is reluctantly taken in by a grumpy old man. The boy proves to be an abused child, terrified of everything around him. With painstaking care, the old man—Mr. Tom— begins the healing process, unveiling to the child a world he never knew existed—a world of kindness, friendships, laughter, and hope. For experienced listeners. Also by the author: *Back Home.* Related books: *North to Freedom* (n); *Slake's Limbo* (n); *Understood Betsy* (n); *So Far from the Bamboo Grove,* by Yoko Watkins.

GOOD OLD BOY
by Willie Morris
Yoknapatawpha Press (both), 1981
Gr. 5–8 128 pages
If Tom Sawyer had lived in the 1940s, this would have been the story Mark Twain would have written. In this funny and suspenseful boyhood memoir

(based in part upon his award-winning *North Toward Home*), one of the South's finest writers tells us about growing up in the South. Originally published by Harper and Avon, it is now available only through Yoknapatawpha Press, P.O. Box 248, Oxford, MS 38655, where it is so beloved they boast of keeping it in print "forever." Related books: *And Nobody Knew They Were There* (n); *Soup* (s); *The Great Brain* (n).

THE GREAT BRAIN
by John D. Fitzgerald
Dial, 1967; Dell, 1988
Gr. 5 and up   175 pages
This is the first book in a series dealing with the hilarious—and often touching—adventures of an Irish–Catholic family surrounded by Utah Mormons in 1896. Seen through the eyes of a younger brother, Tom Fitzgerald is part boy genius and part conman, but in command of every situation. The series reads well on many levels, including a perspective of daily life at the turn of the century. For experienced listeners. Sequels (in order): *More Adventures of the Great Brain; Me and My Little Brain; The Great Brain at the Academy; The Great Grain Reforms; The Return of the Great Brain; The Great Brain Does It Again*. Related books: *Good Old Boy* (n); *Tramp Steamer and the Silver Bullet*, by Jeffrey Kelly.

HANG TOUGH, PAUL MATHER
by Alfred Slote
Lippincott, 1973; Harper, 1985
Gr. 5–7   156 pages
A moving sports story about a boy with leukemia and his struggle to win—against both his disease and his baseball opponents. After reading this aloud, encourage your listeners to read on their own the many other Alfred Slote sports books. Related books: *Winning Kicker* (n); *Benny*, by Barbara Cohen; *It's a Mile from Here to Glory*, by Robert C. Lee.

HATCHET
by Gary Paulsen
Bradbury, 1987; Puffin, 1988
Gr. 7 and up   195 pages
The lone survivor of a plane crash in the Canadian wilderness, this thirteen-year-old boy carries only three things away from the crash: a fierce spirit, the hatchet his mother gave him as a gift, and the secret knowledge that his mother was unfaithful to his father. All play an integral part in this

Newbery Honor survival story for experienced listeners. It's also filled with enough environmental science to qualify as a science class read-aloud. Related books: *The Cay* (n); *My Side of the Mountain* (for younger readers) (n); *The Sign of the Beaver* (n); *Snow-Bound* (n).

HOLDING ME HERE
by Pam Conrad
Harper, 1986
Gr. 6 and up   184 pages
When fourteen-year-old Robin secretly reads the diary of the new boarder at her mother's home, she uncovers more than she bargained for. The woman writes of the pain she is suffering after abandoning her husband and two young children, and Robin decides to bring them together—unaware the woman has been badly abused. A gripping drama, it is also a compassionate novel about divorce, families, sharing, and the risks of invading others' privacy. (Note: a few four-letter words.) Also by the author, an excellent young-adult love story, *What I Did for Roman*. Related books: *Wolf Rider* (n); *Miracle at Clement's Pond* (n); *Cracker Jackson*, by Betsy Byars; *Flyaway*, by Lynn Hall.

HOMER PRICE
by Robert McCloskey
Viking Kestrel, 1943; Puffin, 1976
Gr. 2–5   160 pages
A modern classic, this is a hilarious collection of stories about a small-town boy's neighborhood dilemmas. Whether it's the story of Homer's foiling the bank robbers with his pet skunk or the tale of his uncle's out-of-control doughnut maker, these six Homeric tales will long be remembered. Sequel: *Centerburg Tales*. Related books: *Humbug Mountain* (n); *The Great Brain* (n); *Soup* (s); *Pinch*, by Larry Callen; *Tramp Steamer and the Silver Bullet*, by Jeffrey Kelly.

HUMBUG MOUNTAIN
by Sid Fleischman
Little, Brown (both), 1978; 1988
Gr. 4–6   172 pages
Overflowing with humor, suspense, and originality, here are the captivating adventures of the Flint family as they battle outlaws, crooked riverboat pilots, ghosts, and their creditors on the banks of the Missouri River in the late 1800s. Very reminiscent of Mark Twain. Also by the author: *The*

Whipping Boy (s); *By the Great Horn Spoon; Chancy and the Grand Rascal; Jingo Django; Mr. Mysterious and Company.* Related books: *Homer Price* (n); *The Wish Giver* (n).

HURRY HOME, CANDY
by Meindert DeJong
Harper (both), 1953
Gr. 2–6   244 pages
With a childlike sense of wonder and pity, this book describes the first year in the life of a dog—from the moment she is lifted from her mother's side, through the children, adults, punishments, losses, fears, friendships, and love. Related books: *A Dog Called Kitty* (n); *Lassie-Come-Home* (n); *Foxy,* by Helen Griffith.

IDA EARLY COMES OVER THE MOUNTAIN
by Robert Burch
Viking, 1980; Avon, 1982
Gr. 2–6   145 pages
During the Depression, an ungainly young woman shows up to take over the household chores for Mr. Sutton and his four motherless children. The love that grows between the children and the unconventional Ida is, like Ida's tall tales, a joyous experience. She has been rightly described as a Mary Poppins in the Blue Ridge Mountains. Sequel: *Christmas with Ida Early.* Also by the author: *King Kong and Other Poets; Queen Peavy.* Related books: *Mrs. Fish, Ape, and Me, the Dump Queen* (n).

INCIDENT AT HAWK'S HILL
by Allan W. Eckert
Little, Brown, 1971; Bantam, 1987
Gr. 6 and up   174 pages
An extremely timid six-year-old who wandered away from his family's farm in 1870 is adopted by a ferocious female badger, à la Mowgli in the *Jungle Books.* The boy is fed, protected, and instructed by the badger through the summer until the family manages to recapture the now-wild child. Definitely for experienced listeners. Reading this aloud, I would paraphrase a large portion of the slow-moving prologue. Related books: *Bella Arabella* (s); *The Dog Days of Arthur Cane* (n).

THE INDIAN IN THE CUPBOARD
by Lynne Reid Banks
Doubleday, 1981; Avon, 1983
Gr. 2–6   182 pages

A witty, exciting, and poignant fantasy tale of a nine-year-old English boy who accidentally brings to life his three-inch plastic American Indian. Once the shock of the trick wears off, the boy begins to realize the immense responsibility involved in feeding, protecting, and hiding a three-inch human being from another time (1870s) and culture. An excellent values-clarification model. Readers-aloud should note beforehand that the miniature cowboy in the story occasionally uses the word "damn" in his exclamations. Also by the author: *Return of the Indian; I, Houdini.* For related Indian books, see listing with *Where the Buffaloes Begin* (p); other books: *The Littles* (s); *The Borrowers,* by Mary Norton; *The Steadfast Tin Soldier,* by Hans C. Andersen; *Down the Long Hills,* by Louis L'Amour.

IN THE YEAR OF THE BOAR AND JACKIE ROBINSON
by Bette Bao Lord • Illustrated by Marc Simont
Harper' (both), 1984; 1986
Gr. 1–5   169 pages

Over the course of the year 1947, we watch a little Chinese girl as she and her family begin a new life in Brooklyn. Told with great warmth and humor and based on the author's own childhood, Shirley Temple Wong's cultural assimilation will ring true with any child who has had to begin again—culturally or socially. To know this little girl is to fall in love with her—and her neighbors and classmates. Two comparative studies can be done with this book: one with Frances Hodgson Burnett's classic *Little Lord Fauntleroy,* in which a poor American boy is confronted with the cultural adjustment of moving into his grandfather's English estate; the other with *Homesick,* an autobiographical novel by Jean Fritz about her childhood in China. Related books: *Introducing Shirley Braverman* (n); for Gr. 4 and older: *The Voyage of the Lucky Dragon,* by Jack Bennett.

INTRODUCING SHIRLEY BRAVERMAN
by Hilma Wolitzer
Farrar (both), 1975; 1987
Gr. 3–5   154 pages

This novel covers slightly less than a year in the life of a Brooklyn, N.Y., girl during World War II. In twenty-two short, fast-paced chapters, we glimpse family life as it is affected by the war (air-raid practices, letters

from soldier neighbors, telegrams from the War Department, the triumphant return of peace) and family life as it is usually lived: spelling bee
competitions, visiting Grandpa in the nursing home, curing your little
brother of his timidity, facing down the neighborhood bully, and dress–up
games on rainy days. This book makes a sensitive and enlightening comparative study with *Caddie Woodlawn*. Many similar family and community
situations appear in the two novels, and the nearly 100-year difference in
their settings offers a unique social and cultural study. Related books: *Ramona the Pest* (n); *Us and Uncle Fraud* (n); *In the Year of the Boar and Jackie
Robinson* (n).

JAMES AND THE GIANT PEACH
by Roald Dahl • Illustrated by Nancy Ekholm Burkert
Knopf, 1961; Puffin, 1988
Gr. 1–6   120 pages
Young James, orphaned, is sent to live with his mean aunts and appears
resigned to spending the rest of his life as their humble servant. It is just
about then that a giant peach begins growing in the backyard. Waiting
inside that peach is a collection of characters that will captivate your audience
as well as they did James. Few books hold up over six grade levels as well
as this one does. It's my all–time favorite. The book also has been adapted
as a dramatization: *James and the Giant Peach: A Play,* by Richard George
(Puffin). Also by the author: *Danny the Champion of the World* (n); *Fantastic
Mr. Fox* (s); *The Wonderful Story of Henry Sugar* (s); *The BFG; Charlie and
the Chocolate Factory; The Enormous Crocodile; The Giraffe and the Pelly and
Me; Matilda*. Related books: *The Mighty Slide* (po).

J.T.
by Jane Wagner • Photographs by Gordon Parks
Dell (paperback only), 1971
Gr. 3–5   124 pages
J.T. is an inner-city black child, harassed by neighbors and teenagers and
the despair of his mother. He is, in fact, tottering on the brink of delinquency
when an old, one-eyed alley cat brings out his sensitivity and responsibility.
Excellent book about inner–city life, individual responsibility, life and death.
Related books: *Dear Mr. Henshaw* (n); *The Stories Julian Tells* (s); *The Most
Beautiful Place in the World,* by Ann Cameron.

JUMP SHIP TO FREEDOM
by James L. Collier and Christopher Collier
Delacorte, 1981; Dell, 1986
Gr. 5–9   200 pages
This is the first book in an award-winning historical trilogy that describes the troubles and triumphs in the black experience during the post–Revolutionary War period. It deals with Daniel Arabus, a courageous young slave, attempting to recover money earned by his father during the Revolution, money that will buy freedom for himself and his mother. The second book, *War Comes to Willy Freeman*, portrays the struggles of a young free black girl (disguised as a boy) as she searches for her mother who has been captured by the British. *Who Is Carrie?*, the third book, covers the further adventures of Dan Arabus and Carrie, a kitchen slave in the household of President Washington. All three novels are fast-paced and present a vivid picture of the slavery issues confronting the new nation. Readers-aloud are advised to first read the authors' note at the end of each book and their remarks regarding the use of the word "nigger." Another Revolutionary War book by the same authors: *My Brother Sam Is Dead* (n). Related books: *Listen Children* (a); *North to Freedom* (n); *Roll of Thunder, Hear My Cry* (n); *Sarah Bishop* (n); *Words by Heart* (n).

KILLING MR. GRIFFIN
by Lois Duncan
Little, Brown, 1978; Dell, 1980
Gr. 7 and up   224 pages
This young-adult story offers a chilling dissection of peer pressure and group guilt. Because of the subject matter and occasional four-letter words, care should be used in its presentation. The story deals with five high school students who attempt to scare their unpopular English teacher by kidnapping him. When their carefully laid plans slowly begin to unravel toward a tragic catastrophe, they find themselves unable to handle the situation. For a discussion of this book's use in the classroom, see Chapter 3. For experienced listeners. Also by the author: *Ransom; I Know What You Did Last Summer*. Related books: *Death Run* (n); *On My Honor* (s); *Someone Is Hiding on Alcatraz Island* (n); *Wolf Rider* (n); *Flyaway*, by Lynn Hall; *To Be a Killer*, by Jay Williams.

LASSIE-COME-HOME
by Eric Knight
Holt, 1940, 1971 (revised); Dell, 1972
Gr. 4 and up   200 pages
This is one of the greatest dog stories you could ever hope to read. It reads so easily, the words ring with such feeling, that you'll find yourself coming back to it year after year. As is the case with most dog stories, there are the usual sentiments of loss, grief, courage, and struggle. But here these feelings are presented in such a way that most other dog stories pale by comparison. Set between the Scottish Highlands and Yorkshire, England, in the early 1900s, the novel describes the triumphant struggle of a collie dog to return the 100 miles to her young master. Unfortunately, Hollywood and television have badly damaged the image of this story with their tinny, affected characterization. This is the original Lassie story. Related books: *The Call of the Wild* (n); *The Dog Days of Arthur Cane* (n); *Hurry Home, Candy* (n); *Stone Fox* (s); *Where the Red Fern Grows* (n); *Foxy,* by Helen Griffith.

THE LION, THE WITCH AND THE WARDROBE
by C. S. Lewis
Macmillan (both), 1950; 1970
Gr. 3–6   186 pages
Four children discover that the stuffy wardrobe closet in an empty room leads to the magic kingdom of Narnia—a kingdom filled with heroes, witches, princes, and intrigue. The first of seven enchanting books called the Narnia Chronicles. The sequels, in order, are: *Prince Caspian; The Voyage of the "Dawn Treader"; The Silver Chair; The Horse and His Boy; The Magician's Nephew;* and *The Last Battle.* Related books written in the fantasy/fairy tale genre: *The Ordinary Princess* (n); *The Search for Delicious* (n); *The Wonderful Wizard of Oz* (n); *Redwall,* by Brian Jacques; *Rumpty-Dudget's Tower,* by Julian Hawthorne.

THE LONG JOURNEY
by Barbara Corcoran
Atheneum (paperback only), 1974
Gr. 3–6   188 pages
In a desperate effort to aid her stricken grandfather, thirteen-year-old Laurie sets off on horseback in search of her uncle at the other end of Montana. Skirting cities and towns for fear of trouble, this gritty heroine encounters both unexpected danger and friendship in a fast-paced contemporary story.

Related books: *Call It Courage* (n); *North to Freedom* (n); *Toliver's Secret* (n); *Trouble River,* by Betsy Byars; *The Voyage of the Lucky Dragon,* by Jack Bennett.

THE MIDNIGHT FOX
by Betsy Byars
Viking, 1968; Puffin, 1981
Gr. 4–6   160 pages
From the very beginning, young Tommy is determined he'll hate his aunt and uncle's farm where he must spend the summer. His determination suffers a setback when he discovers a renegade black fox. His desire to keep the fox running free collides with his uncle's wish to kill it, and the novel builds to a stunning moment of confrontation and courage. An excellent book about values, with superb character development. Also by the author: *The Pinballs* (n); *The Burning Questions of Bingo Brown; A Blossom Promise; The Blossoms Meet the Vulture Lady; The Cartoonist; Cracker Jackson; The Not-Just-Anybody Family; Trouble River; Summer of the Swans; The Winged Colt of Casa Mia.* Related books: *Gentle Ben* (n); *Danger Dog,* by Lynn Hall; *The Secret Life of Dilly McBean,* by Dorothy Haas; see also listing with *Daisy Rothschild* (p).

MIRACLE AT CLEMENT'S POND
by Patricia Pendergraft
Putnam, 1987; Scholastic, 1988
Gr. 6 and up   242 pages
Three teens, having discovered an abandoned baby, deposit the child on the front porch of the town spinster—who thinks it is an answer to her prayers, a "miracle." When the rest of the town agrees, the pressure is on the three to confess their part. And the longer they delay, the deeper they sink. Rich with humor and deeply textured characters and families, the story is told in the colorful tongue of rural America. Related books: *A Blue-Eyed Daisy* (s); *Pinch,* by Larry Callen; *Cracker Jackson,* by Betsy Byars.

MR. POPPER'S PENGUINS
by Richard and Florence Atwater • Illustrated by Robert Lawson
Little, Brown, 1938; Dell, 1978
Gr. 2–4   140 pages
When you add twelve penguins to the family of Mr. Popper, the house painter, you've got immense food bills, impossible situations, and a freezer full of laughs. Extra-short chapters that will keep your audience hungry

for more. Related books: *Owls in the Family* (s); *The Story of Doctor Doolittle* (n); see also listing with *Daisy Rothschild* (p).

MRS. FISH, APE, AND ME, THE DUMP QUEEN
by Norma Fox Mazer
Dutton, 1980; Avon, 1982
Gr. 3–6   138 pages
Living with her homely but loving uncle (the manager of the town dump), Joyce is taunted unmercifully by her classmates. The walls she has built to resist such derision are beginning to weaken when help comes from a most unlikely source—Mrs. Fish, the "crazy" school custodian. For all its candidness in describing the cruelty of the peer group, the book also portrays the powerful effects of love as an anchor in the lives of three different people. Related books: *A Blue-Eyed Daisy* (s); *The Hundred Dresses* (s); *Sara Crewe* (s); *Gray Cloud,* by Charlotte Graeber.

MRS. FRISBY AND THE RATS OF NIMH
by Robert C. O'Brien
Atheneum (both), 1971
Gr. 4–6   232 pages
A fantasy–science fiction tale that can only be described as "unforgettable." A group of rats have become super-intelligent through a series of laboratory injections. Though it opens with an almost fairy tale softness, it grows into a taut and frighteningly realistic tale. More than a decade after its publication, the fiction of this book grows closer to fact; see December 27, 1982, issue of *Newsweek,* "The Making of a Mighty Mouse," p. 67; also "Human Immune Defenses Are Transplanted in Mice," *The New York Times,* September 15, 1988, p. 1. Sequel: *Racso and the Rats of NIMH,* by Jane L. Conly (Robert C. O'Brien's daughter). Also by the author: *The Silver Crown.* Related books: *Pearl's Promise* (n); *The Twenty-one Balloons* (n).

MY BROTHER SAM IS DEAD
by James Lincoln Collier and Christopher Collier
Four Winds, 1974; Scholastic, 1977
Gr. 5 and up   251 pages
In this award-winning historical novel, the inhumanity of war is examined at close hand through the experiences of one sharply divided Connecticut family during the Revolutionary War. Told in the words of a younger brother, the heartache and passions described here hold true for all wars in

all times, and the authors' balanced accounts of British and American tactics allow plenty of latitude for readers to come to their own conclusions. This book makes a good comparative study with *Rain of Fire* (n), in which a young brother is startled by the effect World War II had upon his brother. Regarded as leading figures in American historical fiction for children, the authors also have written an exciting trilogy that deals with the black experience during the same period; see *Jump Ship to Freedom* (n). Related books: *Otto of the Silver Hand* (n); *Sarah Bishop* (n); *The Fighting Ground,* by Avi; *So Far from the Bamboo Grove,* by Yoko Watkins.

MY SIDE OF THE MOUNTAIN
by Jean George
Dutton (both), 1959; 1975
Gr. 3–8   178 pages
A modern-day Robinson Crusoe in adolescence, city-bred Sam Gribley describes his year surviving as a runaway in a remote area of the Catskill Mountains. His diary of living off the land is marked by moving accounts of the animals, insects, plants, people, and books that helped him survive. See *Sarah Bishop* for comparative study. For experienced listeners. Also by the author: *Julie of the Wolves.* Related books: *The Cay* (n); *Hatchet* (n); *Gentle Ben* (n); *Incident at Hawk's Hill* (n); *Slake's Limbo* (n); and two excellent wilderness survival stories by Gloria Skurzynski: *Caught in the Moving Mountain* and *Trapped in Sliprock Canyon.*

NORTH TO FREEDOM
by Anne Holm
Peter Smith, 1984; Harcourt, 1974
Gr. 4 and up   190 pages
This is a magnificent and unforgettable book. Picture a twelve-year-old boy, raised in an East European prison camp, who remembers no other life. Suddenly the opportunity to escape presents itself, and he begins not only a terrifying odyssey across Italy, Switzerland, France, and into Denmark but also a journey into human experience. David must now deal with the normal experiences and knowledge that had been denied him in prison. Here are wondrous but confusing moments when he meets for the first time a baby, flowers, fruit, a church, children playing, a toothbrush. Meanwhile, he learns how to smile, the meaning of conscience, the need to trust. For experienced listeners. Related books: *The Long Journey* (n); *And Nobody Knew They Were There* (n); *No Promises in the Wind,* by Irene Hunt.

THE ORDINARY PRINCESS
by M. M. Kaye
Doubleday, 1984; Simon & Schuster, 1986
Gr. 2–5   112 pages
In a most unconventional but liberated fairy tale, we see a young princess who is marked by her fairy godmother with the gift of "ordinariness"— that is, straight hair, grayish-brown eyes, a freckled nose, awkwardness, and even an ordinary name: Amy. The princes are as uninterested in her as she is in them, to the point where she runs away and gets her first job in the kitchen of a neighboring kingdom. While the warm spoof lays to rest some old stereotypes, it also gives us a captivating princess. Related books: *The Maid of the North* (a); *The Dragon of Og,* by Rumer Godden; *Once Upon a Test: Three Light Tales of Love,* by Vivian Vande Velde; and *Seven Daughters and Seven Sons,* by Barbara Cohen (with Bahija Lovejoy); see also Fairy/Folk Tale listing in Anthology section of the Treasury.

OTTO OF THE SILVER HAND
by Howard Pyle
Dover, 1967 (paperback only)
Gr. 5–8   132 pages
First published in 1888 and written by one of the leading figures of American children's literature, this book is an ideal introduction to the classics. Set in the Middle Ages, the narrative spins the tale of a young boy's joy and suffering as he rises above the cruelty of the world. Though the language may be somewhat foreign to the listener at the start, it soon adds to the flavor of the narrative. For other medieval books, see listings with *Harald and the Great Stag* (p); related war books: *Good Night, Mr. Tom* (n); *Rain of Fire* (n); *So Far from the Bamboo Grove,* by Yoko Watkins.

PATH OF THE PALE HORSE
by Paul Fleischman
Harper, 1983
Gr. 6 and up   144 pages
More than one hundred years before Walter Reed discovered the cause of yellow fever, one-tenth of Philadelphia's population died of the disease. In this story, a fourteen-year-old boy is apprenticed to a doctor working in the heat of the epidemic, and we are given a fascinating view of the entangled worlds of myth and science in 1793. For experienced listeners. Also by the author: *The Half-a-Moon Inn* (s). Related book: *The Doctors,* by Leonard E. Fisher.

PEARL'S PROMISE
by Frank Asch
Delacorte, 1984; Dell, 1984
K–4   152 pages
Adventure, danger, heartache, tenderness, romance, and courage—all are woven tightly into this fast-moving novel about a pet-store mouse who promises her young brother that she will save him somehow from the snake that is about to make a breakfast of him. Fans of *Charlotte's Web* and *Stuart Little* will love the spunky Pearl, who gives us a study in courage and determination while at the same time allowing us a mouse's-eye view of the world. Related novels: *The Mouse and the Motorcycle,* by Beverly Cleary; *Mrs. Frisby and the Rats of NIMH* (n); *Stuart Little,* by E. B. White. For a listing of picture books on mice, see *Broderick* (p).

PEPPERMINTS IN THE PARLOR
by Barbara Brooks Wallace
Atheneum (both), 1980; 1985
Gr. 3–7   198 pages
When the newly orphaned Emily arrives in San Francisco, she expects to be adopted by her wealthy aunt and uncle. What she finds instead is a poverty-stricken aunt held captive as a servant in a shadowy, decaying home for the aged. Filled with Dickensian flavor, this novel has secret passageways, tyrannical matrons, eerie whispers in the night, and a pair of fearful but plucky kids. Related books: *The Case of the Baker Street Irregular* (n); *Prisoners at the Kitchen Table* (n); *Sara Crewe* (s); *The Wolves of Willoughby Chase* (n).

THE PINBALLS
by Betsy Byars
Harper, 1977; Scholastic, 1979
Gr. 5–7   136 pages
Brought together under the same roof, three foster children prove to each other and the world that they are *not* pinballs to be knocked around from one place to the next; they have a choice in life—to try or not to try. The author has taken what could have been a maudlin story and turned it into a hopeful, loving, and very witty book. Very short chapters with easy-to-read dialogue. For other books by the author, see *The Midnight Fox* (n). Related books: *A Blue-Eyed Daisy* (s); *The Girl with the Silver Eyes* (n); *Holding Me Here* (n); *Mrs. Fish, Ape, and Me, the Dump Queen* (n); *No Promises in the Wind,* by Irene Hunt.

PRISONERS AT THE KITCHEN TABLE
by Barbara Holland
Clarion, 1979
Gr. 3–6   122 pages
Two neighborhood friends (a timid boy and boisterous girl) are pitted against a bickering husband-and-wife kidnapping team, a creepy, secluded farmhouse, and a week of waiting—waiting for food, waiting for ransom, waiting for a chance to escape. Along with a nice blend of humor and suspense, the author provides us with an excellent study of character development. Your listeners will think twice before accepting a ride with strangers after hearing this story. Also by the author: *The Pony Problem; Creepy-Mouse Is Coming to Get You.* Related books: *The Girl with the Silver Eyes* (n); *The Half-a-Moon Inn* (s); *Missing,* by James Duffy.

RAIN OF FIRE
by Marion Dane Bauer
Clarion, 1983
Gr. 3–6   153 pages
Matthew's experiences in Japan during World War II have left him a different person, and no one is more affected than his kid brother, Steve. Matthew's talk of the shame and inhumanity in war confuses his twelve-year-old brother, who is looking for a war hero. When Steve's peers accuse Matthew of being a coward, Steve concocts heroic war stories in his defense—with near-tragic results. This is a powerful story, suggesting the seeds of warfare between nations often are sown first in backlots and alleyways among children. Matthew's recollections of Hiroshima will be etched in children's minds long after the book is read. Also by the author: *On My Honor* (s). Related books on the subject of war: *My Brother Sam Is Dead* (n); *Otto of the Silver Hand* (n); *The Bicycle Man,* by Allen Say; *Hiroshima No Pika,* by Toshi Maruki; *The Little Riders,* by Margaretha Shemin; *The Pushcart War,* by Jean Merrill; *Sadako and the Thousand Paper Cranes,* by Eleanor Coerr; *So Far from the Bamboo Grove,* by Yoko Watkins.

RAMONA THE PEST
by Beverly Cleary
Morrow, 1968; Dell, 1982
Gr. K–4   144 pages
Not all of Beverly Cleary's books make good read-alouds. She is a prolific writer for the early reader, but her books sometimes move too slowly to hold read-aloud interest. But that's not so with *Ramona the Pest,* which

follows the outspoken young lady through her early months in kindergarten. All children will smile in recognition at Ramona's encounters with the first day of school, show-and-tell, seat work, a substitute teacher, Halloween, young love—and dropping out of kindergarten. Long chapters can easily be divided. Early grades should have some experience with short novels before trying *Ramona*. The sequels follow Ramona as she and her family grow older and experience the challenges of modern life (like unemployment, Mom going back to work, after-school babysitters): *Ramona and Her Father; Ramona and Her Mother; Ramona Quimby, Age 8; Ramona Forever*. See also *Ramona: Behind the Scenes of a Television Show*, by Elaine Scott. Also by the author: *Dear Mr. Henshaw* (n); *The Mouse and the Motorcycle*. Related books: three by Janice Lee Smith—*The Kid Next Door and Other Headaches; The Monster in the Third Dresser Drawer*; and *The Show-and-Tell War*.

RASMUS AND THE VAGABOND
by Astrid Lindgren
Puffin (paperback only), 1987
Gr. 2–5   192 pages
Nine-year-old Rasmus was running away from his Swedish orphanage to look for a home when he met a remarkable tramp named Oscar. And though they hit it off immediately and greet one adventure after another, there lingers in Rasmus a hunger for something he can call a home. Related books: *Bella Arabella* (s); *Dear Mr. Henshaw* (n); *The Story of Holly and Ivy* (s).

ROBIN HOOD—PRINCE OF OUTLAWS
by Bernard Miles • Illustrated by Victor Ambrus
Macmillan Checkerboard, 1979
Gr. 3–6   124 pages
Of the more than 700 books written on the famous outlaw of Sherwood Forest, this is one of the most ambitious and most successful of contemporary efforts. Relying as much as possible on fact and personal observation of the historic English locale, the author has humanized Robin while retaining his medieval flavor. His updating of the language to nearer present-day usage brings the story within the listening bounds of children as young as third grade. The book's format is large and allows for brilliant full-color illustrations on every page. For experienced listeners. Also by the author and illustrator: *Favorite Tales from Shakespeare*. A perfect companion to this book is *Knights,* by Julek Heller and Deirdre Headon (Schocken), a comprehensive illustrated book on the traditions, heroes, and equipment as-

sociated with medieval times. For other medieval books, see listings with *Harald and the Great Stag* (p).

ROLL OF THUNDER, HEAR MY CRY
by Mildred Taylor
Dial, 1976; Bantam, 1978
Gr. 5 and up   276 pages

Filled with the life blood of a black Mississippi family during the Depression, this novel throbs with the passion and pride of a family that refuses to give in to threats and harassments by white neighbors. The story is told through daughter Cassie, age nine, who experiences her first taste of social injustice and refuses to swallow it. She, her family, her classmates and neighbors will stir listeners' hearts and awaken many children to the problems of minorities in our society. Winner of the Newbery Award. For experienced listeners. Other books in the series about the Logans: *Let the Circle Be Unbroken* (novel) and two short novels, *The Friendship* (s) and *Song of the Trees*. Also by the author: *The Gold Cadillac*. Related books: see listing with *Marching to Freedom* (s); *Philip Hall Likes Me, I Reckon Maybe,* by Bette Greene.

SARAH BISHOP
by Scott O'Dell
Houghton Mifflin, 1980
Gr. 5 and up   184 pages

Based on an actual historical incident, this is the story of a courageous and determined young girl who flees war-torn Long Island after her father and brother are killed at the outbreak of the Revolutionary War. In the Connecticut wilderness, she takes refuge in a cave where she begins her new life. It is a story of constant courage, as well as a historical account of a time that shaped our nation's destiny. *Sarah Bishop* makes an interesting comparative study with two other read-aloud novels dealing with children running away: *Slake's Limbo* (n) and *My Side of the Mountain* (n). Each approaches the subject from a different point in time but each poses the same question: Are any men or women really islands unto themselves? For experienced listeners. Also by the author: *Sing Down the Moon* (n); *The King's Fifth*. Related books: *Jump Ship to Freedom* (n); *My Brother Sam Is Dead* (n); *Toliver's Secret* (n); *Rain of Fire* (n).

THE SEARCH FOR DELICIOUS
by Natalie Babbitt
Farrar, 1969; Avon, 1974
Gr. 3–7   160 pages
Here is a small masterpiece: fantasy and the English language as they were meant to be written. After a nasty argument among the King, Queen, and their court over the correct meaning of the word "delicious," the Prime Minister's adopted son is dispatched to poll the kingdom and determine the choice of the people. The foolishness of man, his pettiness and quarrelsome nature are suddenly aroused by the poll: Everyone has a different personal definition of "delicious" and civil war looms. An excellent book about values that is guaranteed to challenge every child's sense of the word "delicious." Also by the author: *Tuck Everlasting* (n). Related books: *Chocolate Fever* (s); *The Ordinary Princess* (n).

THE SECRET GARDEN
by Frances Hodgson Burnett • Illustrated by Shirley Hughes
Viking, 1989; numerous paperback publishers
Gr. 2–5   240 pages
Few books spin such a web of magic about their readers (and listeners) as does this children's classic (first published in 1911) about the contrary little orphan who comes to live with her cold, unfeeling uncle on the windswept English moors. Wandering the grounds of his immense manor house one day, she discovers a secret garden, locked and abandoned. This leads her to discover her uncle's invalid child hidden within the mansion, her first friendship, and her own true self. For experienced listeners. Also by the author: *Sara Crewe* (s); *Little Lord Fauntleroy; A Little Princess; The Lost Prince*. Related books: *Peppermints in the Parlor* (n); *Understood Betsy* (n).

SIDEWAYS STORIES FROM WAYSIDE SCHOOL
by Louis Sachar
Avon, 1985 (paperback only)
Gr. 2–5   124 pages
Thirty chapters about the thirty-nine students who inhabit the thirtieth floor of Wayside School, the school that was supposed to be built one story high and thirty classes wide, until the contractor made a mistake. If you think the building is bizarre, meet the wacky kids on the top floor who keep you laughing and wondering what's coming next. Sequel: *Wayside School Is Falling Down*. Also by the author: *Johnny's in the Basement; Sixth-Grade Secrets; Someday Angeline; There's a Boy in the Girls' Bathroom*.

THE SIGN OF THE BEAVER
by Elizabeth George Speare
Houghton Mifflin, 1983; Dell, 1984
Gr. 3 and up   135 pages

This is the story of two boys—one white, the other Indian—and their coming of age in the Maine wilderness prior to the Revolutionary War. It is also an insightful study of the awkward relationship that develops when the starving boy is forced into teaching the reluctant Indian to read. A similar pioneer survival story for younger readers is *The Courage of Sarah Noble* (s). Also by the author: *The Witch of Blackbird Pond*. For related Indian books, see listing with *Where the Buffaloes Begin* (p).

SING DOWN THE MOON
by Scott O'Dell
Houghton Mifflin, 1970
Gr. 3–6   138 pages

Through the first-person narrative of a fourteen-year-old Navaho girl, we follow the plight of the American Indian in 1864 when the U.S. government ordered the Navahos out of their Arizona homeland and marched them 300 miles to Fort Sumner, New Mexico, where they were imprisoned for four years. Known as "The Long Walk," it is a journey that has since become a part of every Navaho child's heritage. The injustices and the subsequent courage displayed by the Indians should be known by all Americans. The novel also provides a detailed account of daily Indian life during the period. Short chapters are told with the vocabulary and in the style appropriate to a young Indian child. An updated view of Native Americans can be found in *Happily May I Walk: American Indians and Alaska Natives Today*, by Arlene Hirschfelder. Also by the author: *Sarah Bishop* (n). For related Indian books, see listing with *Where the Buffaloes Begin* (p).

SKINNYBONES
by Barbara Park
Knopf, 1982; Avon, 1983
Gr. 3–5   112 pages

Author Barbara Park is one of the freshest voices writing for middle-grade children. Her characters are far from lovable but they also are remarkably alive and interesting as they deal with losing ball games, moving, camp, or sibling rivalries. But best of all, they are funny; not cutesy or caustic, but genuinely and interestingly funny. Typical is Alex Frankovitch of *Skinnybones,* who is an uncoordinated smart aleck who throws tantrums; he's also a laugh a minute and if we'd had a choice of who we wanted sitting next to us in fourth grade, most would choose Alex. Sequel: *Almost Starring Skinnybones*. Also by the author: *Beanpole; Buddies; The Kid in the Red Jacket; Operation: Dump the Chump;* and *Don't Make Me Laugh,* an affecting, bittersweet novel on divorce. Related books: *Sideways Stories from Wayside School* (n); *"Hey, What's Wrong with This One?"* (s).

SLAKE'S LIMBO
by Felice Holman
Scribners (both), 1984; 1986
Gr. 5–8   117 pages
A fifteen-year-old takes his fears and misfortunes into the New York City subway one day, finds a hidden construction mistake in the shape of a cave near the tracks, and doesn't come out of the system for 121 days. The story deals simply but powerfully with the question: Can anyone be an island unto himself? It is as much a story of survival as it is a tale of personal discovery. This book makes an interesting comparative study with two other books which discuss running away, hiding, and personal discovery: *My Side of the Mountain* (n) and *Sarah Bishop* (n). For experienced listeners. Other related books: *Isaac Campion* (s); *Good Night, Mr. Tom* (n); *North to Freedom* (n).

SNOW-BOUND
by Harry Mazer
Dell, 1975 (paperback only)
Gr. 5–8   146 pages
Two teenagers, a boy and a girl, marooned by a car wreck during a severe snowstorm, fight off starvation, frostbite, wild dogs, broken limbs, and personal bickering in order to survive. An excellent example of people's lives being changed for the better in overcoming adversity. Adults should be advised of occasional four-letter words in the dialogue. Related books: *The Cay* (n); *Hatchet* (n); *My Side of the Mountain* (n); *The Sign of the Beaver* (n); *Flyaway,* by Lynn Hall.

SOMEONE IS HIDING ON ALCATRAZ ISLAND
by Eve Bunting
Clarion, 1984; Berkley, 1986
Gr. 7–10   136 pages
Here's a white-knuckle thriller for the reluctant reader but not for the faint of heart. When fourteen-year-old Danny incurs the wrath of a local street

gang, he flees in desperation to Alcatraz Island where he hopes to blend in with sightseers and lose the pursuing gang. Instead they trap him there for the night and the action turns chilling. Related books: *Death Run* (n); *Killing Mr. Griffin* (n); *Wolf Rider* (n).

THE STORY OF DOCTOR DOOLITTLE
by Hugh Lofting
Delacorte, 1988; Dell, 1988
K–4   156 pages
In recent years, Hugh Lofting's classic tales fell on hard times due to several regrettable racist references in two of his books. With the permission and cooperation of his family (who agreed the remarks were unfortunate but innocent of malice for the time—1920—when the books were originally published), the offending sections have been removed and the wonderful tales of the man who learned to talk with animals are again available. Other books in the series: *Doctor Doolittle's Circus; Doctor Doolittle's Caravan; Doctor Doolittle and the Green Canary; Doctor Doolittle's Post Office; Doctor Doolittle's Garden;* and *Doctor Doolittle in the Moon*. Related books: *Charlotte's Web* (n); *Mr. Popper's Penguins* (n).

A STRANGER CAME ASHORE
by Mollie Hunter
Harper (both), 1975; 1977
Gr. 4–7   163 pages
The handsome stranger who claims to be the sole survivor of a shipwreck off the Scottish coast is really the Great Selkie, come to lure the Henderson family's beautiful daughter to her death at the bottom of the sea. Here is a novel brimming with legend and suspense. Related books: *The Animal Family* (n); *The Crane Wife,* retold by Katherine Paterson; *The Selkie Girl,* by Susan Cooper.

TALES OF A FOURTH-GRADE NOTHING
by Judy Blume
Dutton, 1972; Dell, 1976
Gr. 3–5   120 pages
A perennial favorite among schoolchildren, this story deals with the irksome problem of a kid brother and his hilarious antics with his fourth-grade brother, Peter. Sequel: *Superfudge*. (Readers-aloud should be cautioned that this book deals with the question, Is there a Santa Claus?) Also by the

author: *Freckle Juice*. Related books: *Ramona the Pest* (n); *Skinnybones* (s) for a listing of Barbara Parks's books; *Toad Food and Measle Soup* and *Lucky Charms and Birthday Wishes,* by Christine McDonnell.

THANK YOU, JACKIE ROBINSON
by Barbara Cohen
Lothrop, 1986
Gr. 5–7   126 pages
Set in the late 1940s, this is the story of young Sam Green, one of that rare breed known as the True Baseball Fanatic and a Brooklyn Dodger fan. His widowed mother runs an inn and when she hires a sixty-year-old black cook, Sam's life takes a dramatic turn for the better. They form a fast friendship and begin to explore the joys of baseball in a way that the fatherless boy has never known. A tender book that touches on friendship, race, sports, personal sacrifice, and death. *Benny* is another Cohen book with an underlying sports theme; for other books by the author, see *The Carp in the Bathtub* (p). Related books: *The Cay* (n); *In the Year of the Boar and Jackie Robinson* (n). Related sports books: *Hang Tough, Paul Mather* (n); *Winning Kicker* (n); *Matt's Mitt,* by Marilyn Sachs.

TOLIVER'S SECRET
by Esther Wood Brady
Crown, 1976 (paperback only)
Gr. 3–5   166 pages
During the Revolutionary War, ten-year-old Ellen Toliver is asked by her ailing grandfather to substitute for him and carry a secret message through British lines. What he estimates to be a simple plan is complicated by Ellen's exceptional timidity and an unforeseen shift by the British. The book becomes a portrait of Ellen's personal growth—complete with a heart-stopping crisis in each chapter. Related books: *Call It Courage* (s); *The Long Journey* (n).

TUCK EVERLASTING
by Natalie Babbitt
Farrar, Straus (both), 1975; 1986
Gr. 4–7   124 pages
A young girl stumbles upon a family that has found the "Fountain of Youth," and in the aftermath there is a kidnapping, a murder, and a jailbreak. This touching story suggests a sobering answer to the question, What would it be like to live forever? For experienced listeners. Also by the author: *Search for Delicious* (n). Related books: the French short story

"The Magic Thread" in *Fairy Tales,* by Nikolai Ustinov; Ray Bradbury's short story "Hail and Farewell," contained in *Young Mutants,* edited by Isaac Asimov; *A Day No Pigs Would Die* (n); *On My Honor* (s); *A Taste of Blackberries* (s).

THE TWENTY-ONE BALLOONS
by William Pène du Bois
Viking, 1947; Puffin, 1986
Gr. 4–6   180 pages
Here is a literary smorgasbord; there are so many different and delicious parts one hardly knows which to mention first. The story deals with a retired teacher's attempts to sail by balloon across the Pacific in 1883, his crash landing and pseudo-imprisonment on the island of Krakatoa, and, finally, his escape. The book is crammed with nuggets of science, history, humor, invention, superior language, and marvelous artwork. Winner of the Newbery Medal. For experienced listeners. Be sure to have available either the January 1981 issue of *National Geographic* or *Volcano,* by Patricia Lauber, both of which offer a close-up view of the eruption on Mount St. Helens.

UNDERSTOOD BETSY
by Dorothy Canfield Fisher
Dell, 1987 (paperback only)
Gr. 2–6   211 pages
Written in 1917 by one of America's most celebrated writers, this is the classic story of a timid, almost neurotic orphan child (Betsy) being raised by her fearful and overprotective city-dwelling aunts. Then a family illness requires that the child be sent to live with "stiff-necked" rural relatives in Vermont and she must stand on her own two feet, do chores, and speak for herself—all of which causes a heart-warming metamorphosis. As a novel, even as a psychological or historical profile, the book is enormously successful. Related books: *Good Night, Mr. Tom* (n); *The Midnight Fox* (n); *Sara Crewe* (s); *The Secret Garden* (n).

US AND UNCLE FRAUD
by Lois Lowry
Houghton, 1984; Dell, 1985
Gr. 2–6   160 pages
Was Uncle Claude, Mom's vagabond black-sheep brother, really a world traveler? Had he really hidden Russian jewels in the house for his niece and

nephew? Or was he, as Dad suggested, a fraud? Did he rob the Leboff estate? This is one family's timeless story that brims with laughter, drama, and boundless affection. Also by the author: *Autumn Street.* Related books: *Ida Early Comes over the Mountain* (n); *Pinch,* by Larry Callen.

WEIRD HENRY BERG
by Sarah Sargent
Bantam, 1981 (paperback only)
Gr. 4–6   114 pages
Twelve-year-old Henry is content to play the role of class weirdo and family recluse until the family heirloom he inherited from his grandfather hatches into a dragon. That's when Henry begins to change. That is also the moment when the dragon's relatives in Wales send an emissary to Henry's hometown in search of the newborn member of the clan. Henry's subsequent adventures with Millie, the town's elderly eccentric, in pursuit of the dragon are filled with a happy blend of mystery, humor, and fantasy. Related books: *The Deliverers of Their Country* and *The Dragon Book,* by E. Nesbit.

WHERE THE RED FERN GROWS
by Wilson Rawls
Doubleday, 1961; Bantam, 1974
Gr. 3–7   212 pages
A ten-year-old boy growing up in the Ozark mountains, praying and saving for a pair of hounds, finally achieves his wish. He then begins the task of turning the hounds into first-class hunting dogs. It would be difficult to find a book that speaks more definitively about perseverance, courage, family, sacrifice, work, life and death. Long chapters are easily divided. Related books: *Bridge to Terabithia* (n); *A Day No Pigs Would Die* (n); *A Dog Called Kitty* (n); *The Dog Days of Arthur Cane* (n); *Lassie-Come-Home* (n); *Stone Fox* (s); *Foxy,* by Helen Griffith.

WINNING KICKER
by Thomas J. Dygard
Morrow, 1978
Gr. 6–8   190 pages
A hard-nosed football coach at the end of a long and successful career is jolted in his final season when a girl makes his high school team as a place kicker, potentially turning the season into a three-ring circus. In a companion novel, *Rebound Caper,* a high school boy, benched by his basketball coach, retaliates by joining the girls' team. The author offers a liberated

and sensitive view of the family, school, and community pressures that result. Sure to stir the interest of both sexes and make for lively discussion. Nobody writing teenage sports books today comes close to equaling Dygard. Also by the author: *Halfback Tough; Outside Shooter; Point Spread; Quarterback Walk-on; The Rookie Arrives; Running Scared; Soccer Duel; Wilderness Peril.*

THE WISH GIVER
by Bill Brittain
Harper (both), 1983; 1986
Gr. 4–8   181 pages
Into the town of Coven Tree comes a mysterious stranger who sets up a tent at the church social, promising wishes–come–true for fifty cents. Three young people in this tiny New England town find out the hard way that sometimes we'd be better off if our wishes didn't come true. There is lots of homespun merriment and fast-moving suspense here. Before reading the tale aloud, have your listeners write down a secret wish and hide it. After completing the book, have them rethink their wish. Also by the author: *All the Money in the World; The Devil's Donkey; Dr. Dredd's Wagon of Wonders; The Fantastic Freshman; Who Knew There'd Be Ghosts?* Related books: *Aladdin* (p); *Among the Dolls* (s); *Bella Arabella* (s); *The Dog Days of Arthur Cane* (n); *Tuck Everlasting* (n).

WOLF RIDER
by Avi
Bradbury, 1986
Gr. 7 and up
Subtitled *A Tale of Terror,* this is breathtaking, plausible, and nonstop reading. When fifteen-year-old Andy accidentally receives a random phone call from a man claiming he's killed a college coed, he discovers nobody believes him. When everyone writes it off as a prank, Andy sets out to find the anonymous caller in a race against death and the clock. Be sure to read *Wolf! Wolf!* (p) or any version of the "Boy Who Cried Wolf" tale before reading aloud this book. Also by the author: *Captain Grey, Emily Upham's Revenge;* and *The Fighting Ground.* Related books: *Death Run* (n); *Killing Mr. Griffin* (n); *On My Honor* (s); *Someone Is Hiding on Alcatraz Island* (n); *Flyaway,* by Lynn Hall.

THE WOLVES OF WILLOUGHBY CHASE
by Joan Aiken
Dell, 1987 (paperback only)
Gr. 3–6   168 pages
Here is Victorian melodrama in high gear: a great English estate surrounded by hungry wolves, two young girls mistakenly left in the care of a wicked, scheming governess, secret passageways and tortured flights through the snow in the dark of night. For experienced listeners. Sequels: *Black Hearts in Battersea; The Cuckoo Tree; Nightbirds on Nantucket; The Stolen Lake*. Related books: *Peppermints in the Parlor* (n); *The Secret Garden* (n); *Sara Crewe* (s).

THE (WONDERFUL) WIZARD OF OZ
by L. Frank Baum
Grossett, 1956; Puffin, 1983; Ballantine, 1985
Gr. 1–5   260 pages
Before your children are exposed to the movie version, treat them to the magic of this 1900 book many regard as the first American fairy tale, as well as early American science fiction. (Incidentally, the book is far less terrifying for children than the film version.) The magical story of Dorothy and her friends' harrowing journey to the Emerald City is but the first of fourteen books on the Land of Oz by the author. If your audience already has seen the movie, introduce them to one of the sequels: *Dorothy and the Wizard of Oz; The Emerald City of Oz; The Marvelous Land of Oz; Ozma of Oz; The Patchwork Girl of Oz; The Road to Oz*.

WORDS BY HEART
by Ouida Sebestyen
Little, Brown, 1979; Bantam, 1981
Gr. 5 and up   162 pages
A young girl and her family must summon all their courage and spirit in order to survive as the only black family in this 1910 Texas community. The child's spunk, her father's tireless patience, and the great faith in God he leaves with her make this an unforgettable book. For experienced listeners. The slow-moving first chapter can be edited with prereading. Sequel: *On Fire*. Related books: *Roll of Thunder, Hear My Cry* (n).

Poetry

THE BEST LOVED POEMS OF THE AMERICAN PEOPLE
Edited by Hazel Felleman
Doubleday, 1936
Gr. 3 and up   648 pages
As editor of the Queries and Answers page of *The New York Times Book Review,* Hazel Felleman was fully aware of the nation's tastes in poetry. By keeping track of the *Times*'s readers' poetry correspondence, she was able to compile the most often requested poems. Parents and teachers could not have been better served, especially when she arranged her anthology under various themes, thereby easing the burden of those who go in search of a poem to fit a particular child or occasion. Here are poems that tell a story (the best loved by children), poems of friendship, inspiration, home and motherhood, childhood, patriotism, humor, and animals. The book is usually shelved in the poetry section of your library; most of these 575 poems are for experienced listeners.

CASEY AT THE BAT
by Ernest L. Thayer • Illustrated by Barry Moser
Godine, 1988
Gr. 4 and up   32 pages
This description of a small-town baseball game and local hero is one of the most famous pieces in America's literary quilt. This centennial hardcover edition from Godine publishers includes Barry Moser's illustrations based on the uniforms and settings of the original period, though "Casey" is as topical today as it was in 1888. It also contains a ten-page afterword by poet and baseball enthusiast Donald Hall on the fascinating history of Thayer and his poem. Younger children may prefer the illustrations by Wallace Tripp in the Putnam paperback edition of the poem, for which he uses animal characters for the ball players. Be sure to treat your listeners to the lesser-known sequels offered by other poets through the years: "Casey's Revenge," by James Wilson, and "Casey: Twenty Years Later," by S. P. McDonald, both included in *The Best Loved Poems of the American People* (po).

THE CREMATION OF SAM MCGEE
by Robert W. Service • Illustrated by Ted Harrison
Greenwillow, 1987
Gr. 4 and up   30 pages

Once one of the most memorized poems in North America, this is still wonderfully funny and remains the best description of the sun's strange spell over the men who toil in the cold Arctic. After seeing this edition, it will be hard to hear the words ever again without seeing Harrison's brilliant art work. Two excellent collections of Service poetry: *Best Tales of the Yukon* (Running Press) and *Collected Poems of Robert Service* (Dodd). Related books: *Call of the Wild* (n); *Lost in the Barrens,* by Farley Mowat.

ELLA
by Bill Peet
See listing under *The Whingdingdilly* (p).

HONEY, I LOVE
by Eloise Greenfield • Illustrated by Diane and Leo Dillon
Harper (both), 1976; 1978
Pre-S.–3   42 pages
Here are sixteen short poems about the things and people children love: friends, cousins, older brothers, keepsakes, mother's clothes, music, and jump ropes. Set against an urban background, the poems elicit both joyous and bittersweet feelings. Related books: *Jelly Belly* (po); see also listing with *Regards to the Man in the Moon* (p).

A HOUSE IS A HOUSE FOR ME
by Mary Ann Hoberman • Illustrated by Betty Fraser
Viking, 1978; Puffin, 1982
Pre-S.–6   44 pages
On the surface this book is a rhyming picture book about the variety of dwelling places people, animals, and insects call home. Below the surface it is an ingeniously entertaining study of metaphor: "cartons are houses for crackers," "a rose is a house for a smell," "a throat is a house for a hum." Such imagination-expanding thoughts can be easily developed after the book is finished. Encourage the class or child to compile their own list of houses. Also by the author: *The Cozy Book; Yellow Butter Purple Jelly Red Jam Black Bread.* Related book: *A Little House of Your Own,* by Beatrice Schenk de Regniers.

IF I RAN THE ZOO
by Dr. Seuss
See page 174.

IF I WERE IN CHARGE OF THE WORLD AND OTHER WORRIES
by Judith Viorst
Atheneum (both), 1981; 1984
Gr. 3 and up   56 pages
If the meter or rhyme in these forty-one poems is occasionally imperfect, it is easily overlooked in light of their perfect pulse and timing. In prescribing these short verses "for children and their parents," this contemporary American humorist offers a two-point perspective: Children reading these poems will giggle, then recognize themselves, their friends and enemies, and think "That's really the way it is!" Parents will recognize in the poems the child they used to be. Witty, introspective, sometimes bittersweet poems on children's hopes, fears, and feelings. Also by the author: *Alexander and the Terrible, Horrible, No Good, Very Bad Day* (p); *I'll Fix Anthony; The Tenth Good Thing About Barney; Alexander Who Used to be Rich Last Sunday; My Mama Says There Aren't Any Zombies, Ghosts, Vampires, Creatures, Demons, Monsters, Fiends, Goblins, or Things; Rosie and Michael.*

JELLY BELLY
by Dennis Lee • Illustrated by Juan Wijngaard
Bedrick Blackie, 1985 (both)
Pre-S.–3   64 pages
Here are eighty-six original nursery rhymes and poems from Canada's favorite children's poet, covering a broad range of subjects and audiences, complete with double-page, color illustrations set in contemporary homes and schools, as well as urban and rural locales. Related books: *Honey, I Love* (po); *Read-Aloud Rhymes for the Very Young* (po); *Auntie's Knitting a Baby,* by Lois Simmie.

THE MIGHTY SLIDE
by Allan Ahlberg
Viking, 1988
Gr. 2–8   96 pages
As might be expected from the person who gave us *The Jolly Postman* (p), here are five off-beat tales told in narrative verse, some as long as twenty-four pages. There's a gigantic snow slide constructed on the playground during recess; the mysterious stranger who battles alligators; the girl who kept doubling (that's right—every time she woke she'd have another twin); the

husband-and-wife team of clothing thieves; and (best of all) the scary, hairy thing that lives under the school. There's a British flavor to some of the tales that adds an exotic flavor. If you like Roald Dahl, you'll love these poems.

MOTHER GOOSE, A TREASURY OF BEST LOVED RHYMES
See page 182.

THE NEW KID ON THE BLOCK
by Jack Prelutsky • Illustrated by James Stevenson
Greenwillow, 1984
K–4   160 pages
One of today's most prolific poets for children, Prelutsky has collected here more than 100 of his most outrageous and comical characters, wanting nothing more than to amuse and please children—which he does with a poem about the taken-for-granted blessings of having your nose on your *face* instead of in your ear, and the one about Sneaky Sue who started playing hide-and-seek a month ago and still can't be found. Also by the author: *The Baby Uggs Are Hatching; The Mean Old Hyena; Nightmares: Poems to Trouble Your Sleep; The Queen of Eene; Ride a Purple Pelican; The Snopp on the Sidewalk;* see also his *Random House Book of Poetry* (po) and *Read-Aloud Rhymes for the Very Young* (po).

NOW WE ARE SIX
by A. A. Milne • Illustrated by Ernest H. Shepard
Dutton, 1927; Dell, 1975
K and up   104 pages
This best-selling classic celebrates the dreams and nonsense of childhood in thirty-one narrative poems: stories of good children and naughty children; foolish kings, and imaginary friends. For experienced listeners. Also by the author: *The House at Pooh Corner; When We Were Very Young; Winnie-the-Pooh.*

THE RANDOM HOUSE BOOK OF POETRY FOR CHILDREN
Selected by Jack Prelutsky • Illustrated by Arnold Lobel
Random House, 1983
K–5   248 pages
In this, one of the best children's anthologies ever, poet Jack Prelutsky recognizes that the common language of all children is laughter and wonder. The 572 selected poems (from traditional as well as contemporary poets) are short—but long on laughter, imagery, and rhyme, and grouped around

fourteen categories that include food, goblins, nonsense, home, children, animals, and seasons. This is an excellent companion to his other anthology, *Read-Aloud Rhymes for the Very Young* (a); see also *New Kid on the Block* (po).

READ-ALOUD RHYMES FOR THE VERY YOUNG
Collected by Jack Prelutsky • Illustrated by Marc Brown
Knopf, 1986
Tod.–1   88 pages
Here are more than 200 little poems (with full-color illustrations) for little people with little attention spans to help both to grow. Related books: *Mother Goose* (p); *Whiskers and Rhymes,* by Arnold Lobel; and three volumes for infants and toddlers containing timeless finger/hand rhymes (complete with diagrams) collected and illustrated by Marc Brown: *Finger Rhymes; Hand Rhymes;* and *Play Rhymes.* For older children, see the Prelutsky collection, *Random House Book of Poetry* (po). Related book: *Side by Side* (po).

SIDE BY SIDE: POEMS TO READ TOGETHER
Collected by Lee Bennett Hopkins • Illustrated by Hilary Knight
Simon and Schuster, 1988
Pre-S.–2   80 pages
Teacher, poet, and anthologist Lee Bennett Hopkins assembles here traditional and contemporary poems to be read aloud to young children. Covering the seasons, holidays, animals, and lullabies, the fifty-seven poems also include several of the classic narratives for young children like "Poor Old Lady," "The House That Jack Built," and "A Visit from St. Nicholas." With Hilary Knight's double-page artwork, it is a superb book. Also by Hopkins: *Surprises; More Surprises; The Sky Is Full of Song;* and for adults, *Pass the Poetry, Please,* the definitive book on introducing poetry to children. Related books: *Read-Aloud Rhymes for the Very Young* (po); *Tomie dePaola's Book of Poems.*

SING A SONG OF POPCORN: EVERY CHILD'S BOOK OF POEMS
Selected by Beatrice Schenk deRegniers, Eva Moore, Mary M. White, and Jan Carr
Scholastic, 1988
K–5   160 pages
What distinguishes this volume from other excellent poetry collections (and from its previous smaller edition, *Poems Children Will Sit Still For*) is that

each of the nine sections has been assigned to a different Caldecott Award–winning illustrator, including Maurice Sendak, Trina Schart Hyman, and Arnold Lobel. Thus the sounds *and* sights of this book make it outstanding. Related book: *Tomie dePaola's Book of Poems.*

WHERE THE SIDEWALK ENDS
by Shel Silverstein
Harper, 1974
K–8   166 pages

This is, without question, the best-loved collection of poetry for children. (It sold one million copies during its first eight years in print.) When it comes to knowing children's appetites Silverstein is pure genius. The titles alone are enough to bring children to rapt attention: "Bandaids"; "Boa Constrictor"; "Crocodile's Toothache"; "The Dirtiest Man in the World"; "If I Had a Brontosaurus"; "Recipe for a Hippopotamus Sandwich." Here are 130 poems that will either touch children's hearts or tickle their funny bones. Silverstein's second collection of poems, *A Light in the Attic,* was the second children's book to make *The New York Times* best-seller list, where it remained for 186 weeks. The multi-talented Silverstein also has thirty-eight selections from *Sidewalk* on an exciting forty-minute cassette (Harper). Also by the author/illustrator: *The Giving Tree* (p); *Lafcadio, the Lion Who Shot Back* (s); *Who Wants a Cheap Rhinoceros?* Related books: *Jelly Belly* (po); *The New Kid on the Block* (po).

YOU READ TO ME, I'LL READ TO YOU
by John Ciardi • Illustrated by Edward Gorey
Lippincott, 1961; Harper, 1987
Gr. 1–4   64 pages

Of the thirty-seven poems by this critic-scholar-poet, every other one is written in a vocabulary that could be read by the average second-grade student. The others are meant to be read by the adult to the child. As always with Ciardi, the subject matter amusingly runs the gamut—from shark teeth and Halloween to "a checklist of things to think about before being born." When American schoolchildren were polled some years ago for their favorite poem, Ciardi's "Mummy Slept Late and Daddy Fixed Breakfast" topped the list; you'll find it here. Also by the author: *Doodle Soup; The Hopeful Trout and Other Limericks; I Met a Man.* Related book: *Auntie's Knitting a Baby,* by Lois Simmie.

Anthologies

AMERICAN BEAT
by Bob Greene
Atheneum, 1983; Penguin, 1984
Gr. 7 and up   301 pages
Here are eighty-eight stories (averaging five pages apiece) from one of today's most respected journalists, all having appeared originally either as newspaper or magazine columns. I consider them to be the best of their kind. These are true stories but not news stories. They are stories about people, and each is presented matter-of-factly by Greene the observer, leaving you to draw your own conclusions. Greene is a master at finding stories that highlight the human condition. He writes about people who inspire courage and respect—as well as those you will detest—people at home, in school, in business, in life and in death. The story entitled "Rush Week," one that should be heard in every junior and senior high, will give you an exact pulse on the book. Readers-aloud should preview each story before reading—a few deal with subject matter that may not be appropriate for your child or class. Also by the author: *Cheeseburgers*.

CLASSICS TO READ ALOUD TO YOUR CHILDREN
by William Russell
Crown, 1984
K and up   400 pages
Recognizing that not all great literature can be comfortably read aloud and that those classics that are suitable are spread out in separate volumes requiring hours of searching out, Russell has compiled in one book thirty-eight selections of the very best from poetry, fairy tales, myths, short stories and novels. The works are divided into three listening levels: ages 5–7; 8–10; 11–13, the last being works from Crane, London and Twain that can be enjoyed by sixty-year-olds as well. Each selection is prefaced with a brief paragraph about the story, an estimate of the reading time, and notes on any unusual vocabulary in the text. Most entries are complete in themselves; some excerpts are used from novels. Sequels: *More Classics to Read Aloud to Your Children* and *Classic Myths to Read Aloud*. Related books: *A Wonder Book* (a); *The World Treasury of Children's Literature* (a); *Fables from Aesop* (p); *The World's Great Stories* (a).

THE FABER BOOK OF NURSERY STORIES
Edited by Barbara Ireson • Illustrated by Shirley Hughes
Faber, 1984 (paperback only)
K–3   184 pages
A splendid collection of forty-two traditional fairy tales and contemporary stories by authors like Charlotte Zolotow and Ted Hughes, this is a perfect bedside book. All the tales are briefly told but not so they insult children's potential attention spans. Related book: *Stories for Under-Fives* (a).

Folk/Fairy Tale Collections

(The last decade has seen a proliferation of excellent folk/fairy anthologies. Here, with brief annotations, are a few of the best.)

ERIC CARLE'S TREASURY OF CLASSIC STORIES FOR CHILDREN
by Eric Carle
Orchard, 1988
K–4   154 pages
The best twenty-two stories from Carle's previous collections from Grimm, Andersen, and Aesop, complete with his colorful collages.

THE FAIRY TALE TREASURY
Collected by Virginia Haviland
Coward, 1972; Dell, 1986
Pre-S.–4   191 pages
Former head of the children's department at the Library of Congress, Haviland has collected thirty-two of the most popular tales of all time from Grimm, Andersen, Jacobs, and Perrault, with full-color art by Raymond Briggs. Other excellent collections by Haviland: *Favorite Fairy Tales Told Around the World; North American Legends*.

FAVORITE FOLKTALES FROM AROUND THE WORLD
Edited by Jane Yolen
Pantheon, 1986
Gr. 6 and up   498 pages
Here are excellent versions (unillustrated) of more than 150 classic tales

from forty different cultures, including a bibliographic genealogy on each tale, edited by one of today's most prolific children's authors. For experienced listeners.

HANS ANDERSEN'S FAIRY TALES (p)

HOUSEHOLD STORIES OF THE BROTHERS GRIMM (p)

THE MAID OF THE NORTH AND OTHER FOLK TALE HEROINES
by Ethel Johnston Phelps
Holt (both), 1981; 1983
Gr. 2 and up   174 pages
A collection of twenty-one fast-moving tales with witty, resourceful and confident heroines (not heroes) from seventeen different cultures. Also by the author: *Tatterhood and Other Tales* (feminist fairy tales). Related books: *Nice Little Girls* (p); *The Ordinary Princess* (n); *Sleeping Ugly,* by Jane Yolen; *The Tough Princess,* by Marty Waddell.

THE PEOPLE COULD FLY: AMERICAN BLACK FOLKTALES
by Virginia Hamilton
Knopf, 1985
Gr. 3–6   174 pages
Rich with the rhythm, energy, and humor of black culture, these twenty-four stories were kept alive by slave tellers and include Bruh Rabbit, Gullah, and freedom-trail adventures, illustrated by Caldecott winners Leo and Diane Dillon. Related book: *Tales of Uncle Remus* (a).

THREE BEARS AND 15 OTHER STORIES
by Anne Rockwell
Harper (both), 1975; 1984
Pre-S.–1   117 pages
A collection of famous tales, unthreatening but entertaining, profusely illustrated by the author.

THE WORLD'S GREAT STORIES
Retold by Louis Untermeyer
Evans, 1964
Gr. 5 and up   256 pages

Fifty-five great legends and moments in history in concise (about four pages each) but literate terms, told by a poet and master storyteller. The tales include Greek and Roman myths, the Arthurian legends, the Magna Carta, Marco Polo, William Tell, and the Pied Piper. Also by the author: *The Firebringer and Other Great Stories.* Related book: *Classic Myths to Read Aloud,* by William Russell, with a pronunciation guide for those difficult Greek names and places.

FREE TO BE YOU AND ME
Edited by Carole Hart, Letty C. Pogrebin, Mary Rodgers, and Marlo Thomas
Bantam, 1987
Pre-S.–3   116 pages

This is a liberated collection of stories, songs, poems, drawings, and photos aimed at encouraging children to the highest goals regardless of sex or race. With humor and sensitivity, many contemporary stereotypes are challenged and subdued here by a variety of authors for children, including Judy Blume, Lucille Clifton, Carol Hall, Betty Miles, Carl Reiner, Mary Rodgers, Shel Silverstein, Judith Viorst, and Arnold Lobel. A record of the book's songs is also available. Sequel: *Free to Be . . . a Family,* in which a variety of award-winning writers, artists, and photographers portray the diverse ways we form and live as families. For books related to *Free to Be You and Me,* see listing with *Nice Little Girls* (p).

LISTEN CHILDREN
Edited by Dorothy S. Strickland
Bantam, 1982 (paperback only)
K–5   122 pages

This short collection of black literature is a true anthology—managing to squeeze into its few pages little gems from poetry, myth and folklore, plays, speeches, and, surprisingly, biography. One seldom sees biography included in most literature collections, and the book is all the better for including moments from the lives of Rosa Parks, Wilma Rudolph, and Stevie Wonder. All the entries underline the black experience, but they also speak, of course, to the human condition. The selection from Maya Angelou's biography happens to be one of my lifetime favorites, and it is something that will touch every child. Related titles on the black experience: *Honey, I Love* (po); *The Stories Julian Tells* (s); *Wagon Wheels* (p); *The People Could Fly* (a).

PAUL HARVEY'S "THE REST OF THE STORY"
by Paul Aurandt
Doubleday, 1977; Bantam, 1978
Gr. 6 and up   234 pages
These collections of broadcaster Paul Harvey's five-minute radio show, "The Rest of the Story," are perfect for teachers and parents trying to win older students to the art of listening. Nearly all of these pieces deal with famous people past and present. The person's name is saved for the last few lines of the tale and serves as an O. Henry punch. The eighty-one stories average two pages in length. Other books in the series: *Destiny; More of Paul Harvey's "The Rest of the Story."* Another book of short anecdotal nonfiction—especially for history or social studies classes—is *Extraordinary Origins of Everyday Things,* by Charles Panati, the fascinating beginnings of 500 items we take for granted today, from chewing gum and ketchup to nursery tales and April Fool's Day.

RANDOM HOUSE BOOK OF HUMOR FOR CHILDREN
Selected by Pamela Pollack
Random House, 1988
Gr. 2 and up   309 pages
Here are thirty-four selections (mostly excerpts from widely acclaimed novels) from some of America's most famous writers and humorists—including Mark Twain, Beverly Cleary, Garrison Keillor, Judy Blume, T. H. White, Betsy Byars, Sid Fleischman, and James Thurber. Though each stands on its own, they are in excellent way to lure children into the author's complete work.

RICHARD KENNEDY: COLLECTED STORIES
by Richard Kennedy
Harper, 1987
Gr. 2 and up   270 pages
Outstanding among today's children's authors, Richard Kennedy assembles here sixteen of his best stories, published originally as picture books. (Thus for the price of one, you receive sixteen.) From simple to more complex (including a short novel, *Inside My Feet* [s]), they are always wittily original (and therefore difficult to categorize), have a fairy-tale quality, and are peopled with fools, innocent maidens, thieves, wily old men, leprechauns, outlaws, and crafty kids—as well as magic stones, music, and always love, life, and death. And with each, he offers a note on how he arrived at the story idea. Caution: "The Mouse God" story can be interpreted as less than complimentary toward organized religion.

SCARY STORIES TO TELL IN THE DARK
Collected by Alvin Schwartz • Illustrated by Stephen Gammell
Lippincott, 1981; Harper, 1983
Gr. 5 and up   112 pages
Dipping into the folk vaults of the past and present, the author presents twenty-nine American "horror" stories and songs guaranteed to make your listeners cringe. The text includes suggestions for the reader-aloud on when to pause, when to scream, even when to turn off the lights. The selections run the gamut from giggles to gore and average two pages in length. In addition, a source section briefly traces each tale's origin in the U.S. (Discretion is advised because of the subject matter.) Sequel: *More Scary Stories to Tell in the Dark*. Related book: *Nightmares*, by Jack Prelutsky.

STORIES FOR UNDER-FIVES
Edited by Sara and Stephen Corrin
Faber, 1974; Penguin (Canada only) 1979
Pre-S.–1   126 pages
This is one in a series of eight outstanding anthologies compiled by the Corrins, each collection aimed at a different age group, and drawing from classical as well as contemporary storytellers. As the age levels increase, the stories become longer and more complex. One of the best bargains for bedside or classroom anthologies. Also in the series: *Stories for Five-Year-Olds; Stories for Six-Year-Olds; Stories for Seven-Year-Olds; More Stories for Seven-Year-Olds; Stories for Eight-Year-Olds; Stories for Nine-Year-Olds; Stories for Tens and Over*. Also by the authors: *The Faber Book of Modern Fairy Tales; Pet Stories for Children*.

THE TALES OF UNCLE REMUS
Retold by Julius Lester • Illustrated by Jerry Pinkney
Dial, 1987
Gr. 1–6   151 pages
Just as captured slaves adapted their African folktales to a Southern locale, black author Julius Lester has moved them off the plantation and into the twentieth century without losing any of their wit, wisdom, or flavor. This celebrated black author has replaced Joel Chandler Harris's heavy dialect with a more contemporary and accessible Southern tongue in the mouth of an Uncle Remus who might be sitting on the front porch telling these forty-eight tales to his grandchild. Sequel: *More Tales of Uncle Remus*. Also by the author: *The Knee-High Man and Other Tales*. Related books: *Bo Rabbit*

Smart for True: Folktales from the Gullah, by Priscilla Jaquith; *Fables from Aesop* (a); *Foolish Rabbit's Big Mistake,* by Rafe Martin; *Mr. Monkey and the Gotcha Bird,* by Walter Dean Myers; *The People Could Fly* (a).

A TASTE FOR QUIET AND OTHER DISQUIETING TALES
by Judith Gorog
Philomel, 1982
Gr. 5 and up   128 pages
A dozen modern fantasy and fairy tales, always rooted in the familiar but giving rise to the bizarre and unexpected. Ranging from the short to the long, from eerie to tender, from human to supernatural, they are always thought-provoking. The short story "Those Three Wishes" will give you a good gauge of the book's contents. For experienced listeners. Related book: *Young Mutants,* edited by Asimov, Greenberg, and Waugh.

A WONDER BOOK
by Nathaniel Hawthorne
Airmont, 1966 (paperback only)
Gr. 4–8   160 pages
Fearing that the classical tone of the ancient myths would frighten future generations of children away from these great stories, Nathaniel Hawthorne produced this collection in 1851. Translating the classical language into modern romantic, he used a keen ear that was carefully tuned to children. Sadly, the book is not well-known by today's parents and educators.

The book is divided into six chapters, each treating a different myth. The stories are supposedly told by a college student to his cousins, and his conversations with them serve as transitions between the various tales. These conversations are the least successful and the least necessary parts of the book, and I recommend that you skip them entirely. For experienced listeners. Related books: *Classics to Read Aloud to Your Children* (a) and *Classic Myths to Read Aloud,* both by William Russell, with a pronunciation guide to those difficult Greek names; and *The World's Great Stories* (a).

THE WORLD TREASURY OF CHILDREN'S LITERATURE
by Clifton Fadiman
Little, Brown, 1984
Pre-S.–6   Two volumes (200 pages in each)
One of the most respected names in publishing, Fadiman has assembled the essential rhymes, poems, myths, fairy tales, and novels of children's literature. This is the Hall of Fame for children's books. Under one roof—

including much of the original art work—are *Madeline, Curious George, The Little House, Little Bear,* and *Peter Rabbit.* From the Brothers Grimm to Beverly Cleary—these volumes speak to the heart and soul of childhood.

ZLATEH THE GOAT AND OTHER STORIES
by Isaac B. Singer • Illustrated by Maurice Sendak
Harper (both), 1966; 1984
Gr. 3–6   90 pages
The magic of one of the world's great storytellers and winner of the Nobel Prize for literature is seen in these seven folk tales derived from the Eastern European Jewish oral tradition. The captivating blend of humor, fantasy, and deviltry in these stories has become a Singer trademark. For experienced listeners. Also by the author: *The Golem; The Power of Light; Stories for Children; Why Noah Chose the Dove.*

Notes

Introduction

1. *The Wall Street Journal,* July 30, 1987, p. 1.

2. *ISR (Institute for Socal Research) Newsletter,* Winter 85/86, "How Families Use Time," p. 3.

3. Hilary T. Holbrook, "Sex Differences in Reading: Nature or Nurture?," *Journal of Reading,* March 1988, pp. 574–76.

4. David Laband and Bernard Lentz, "The Natural Choice," *Psychology Today,* August 1986, pp. 37–43.

Chapter 1: Why Read Aloud?

1. Richard C. Anderson, Elfrieda H. Hiebert, Judith A. Scott, and Ian A. G. Wilkinson, *Becoming a Nation of Readers: The Report of the Com-*

mission on Reading (Champaign-Urbana, IL: Center for the Study of Reading, 1985), p. 23.

2. Ibid., p. 51.

3. Courtney B. Cazden, *Child Language and Education* (New York: Holt, Rinehart and Winston, 1972).

4. Psychologist Burton L. White interviewed in "Training Parents Helps Toddlers," *The New York Times,* October 2, 1985, p. C1.

5. George A. Miller and Patricia M. Gildea, "How Children Learn Words," *Scientific American,* September 1987, pp. 94–99.

6. Dolores Durkin, *Children Who Read Early* (New York: Teachers College Press, 1966). See also Anne D. Forester, "What Teachers Can Learn from 'Natural Readers,' " *Reading Teacher,* November 1977, pp. 160–66; Margaret M. Clark, *Young Fluent Readers* (London: Heinemann, 1976).

7. "Business Bulletin," *The Wall Street Journal,* January 3, 1985, p. 1.

8. Television Bureau of Advertising (477 Madison Avenue, New York, NY 10022), January 1988 report for 1987 viewing.

9. Harry F. Waters, "What TV Does to Kids," *Newsweek,* February 21, 1977, p. 63.

10. *USA Today,* December 5, 1986, p. 1D.

11. "A Tight Squeeze at Video Stores," *The New York Times,* May 1, 1988, p. C4.

12. *American Behavioral Scientist,* May–June 1986.

13. John Steinbeck, *The Acts of King Arthur and His Noble Knights* (New York: Farrar, Straus and Giroux, 1976), p. 3.

14. "As Kids' Books Proliferate, Quality Sometimes Suffers," *The Wall Street Journal,* June 23, 1988, p. 35.

15. *Literacy: Profiles of America's Young Adults* (Princeton, NJ: National Assessment of Educational Progress, 1987).

16. "Illiteracy Seen as Threat to U.S. Economic Edge," *The New York Times,* September 7, 1988, p. B8.

17. "Auto Mechanics Struggle to Cope with Technology in Today's Cars," *The Wall Street Journal,* July 26, 1988, p. 37.

18. "The Annual School Scoreboard," *USA Today,* February 26, 1988, p. 5D.

19. Izaak Wirszup, "Education and National Survival," *Educational Leadership,* December/January 1984, p. 6.

20. *Investing in Our Children: Business and the Public Schools* (New York: Committee for Economic Development [477 Madison Avenue, New York, NY 10022], 1985), p. 2.

21. Arthur N. Applebee, Judith A. Langer, and Ina V. S. Mullis, *Who*

Reads Best? (Princeton, NJ: National Assessment of Educational Progress/ ETS, 1988).

22. *Writing Report Card* (Princeton, NJ: National Assessment of Educational Progress, 1986).

23. *Literacy: Profiles of America's Young Adults* (Princeton, NJ: National Assessment of Educational Progress, 1987).

24. Diane Ravitch and Chester E. Finn, Jr., *What Do Our 17-Year-Olds Know?* (New York: Harper & Row, 1987).

25. Archie Lapointe, "The State of Instruction in Reading and Writing in U.S. Elementary Schools," *Phi Delta Kappan,* October 1986, pp. 135–38.

26. "Companies Cite Poor Skills in Entry-Level Applicants," *The New York Times,* July 4, 1987, p. 29.

27. "Business Teaching 3 R's to Employees in Effort to Compete," *The New York Times,* May 1, 1988, p. 1; "Defect Rate 50% from USA Schools," *USA Today,* October 27, 1987, p. B1.

28. Barbara Bush, in remarks to literacy volunteers in Wyoming County, NY, in 1982.

29. "The Paperback Evolution," *The New York Times Book Review,* January 10, 1982, p. 7. Statement by Ronald Busch, former president of Pocket Books.

30. Remarks by Jonathan Kozol, director of National Literacy Coalition, in Boston, reported in *Marketing News,* May 13, 1983, p. 18.

31. Book Industry Study Group, Inc., "The 1983 Consumer Research Study on Reading and Book Purchasing," a summary report presented at the Library of Congress, April 11, 1984.

32. Terry Ley, "Getting Kids into Books: The Importance of Individualized Reading," *Media and Methods,* March 1979, p. 22–24.

33. 1987 Roper Organization report for Television Information Office; also *presstime,* American Newspaper Publishers Association, September 1987.

34. "We Daydream About One Life, Live Another," *USA Today,* May 13, 1986, p. 1. (Based on the D'Arcy Masius Benton & Bowles survey.)

35. Applebee, et al., *Who Reads Best?,* p. 42.

36. "New Theory on Reading Goes Awry," *The New York Times,* October 9, 1985, pp. C1, 21.

37. Archie Lapointe, "State of Instruction," p. 136.

38. Nigel Hall, *The Emergence of Literacy* (Portsmouth, NH: Heinemann, 1987), pp. 77–78.

39. Anderson et al., *Becoming a Nation of Readers,* pp. 75–76.

40. Richard C. Anderson, Linda Fielding, and Paul Wilson, "Growth in Reading and How Children Spend Their Time Outside of School," *Reading Research Quarterly,* Summer 1988, pp. 285–303.

41. Jean Chall and Catherine Snow, "Families and Literacy: The Contribution of Out-of-School Experiences to Children's Acquisition of Literacy—Final Report," Harvard School of Education, 1982, ERIC No, ED 234 345.; H. Holbrook, "Teachers Working with Parents," *Language Arts* 62 (1985): 897–901.

42. From the workbook accompanying *Skylights* (Boston: Houghton Mifflin, 1981), p. 21.

43. Richard Allington, "If They Don't Read Much, How They Gonna Get Good?" *Journal of Reading,* October 1977, pp. 57–61. See also: Richard Allington, "Sustained Approaches to Reading and Writing," *Language Arts,* September 1975, pp. 813–15.

44. Bruno Bettelheim, *The Uses of Enchantment: The Meaning and Importance of Fairy Tales* (New York: Knopf, 1976), pp. 3–6.

45. Robert Penn Warren, "Why Do We Read Fiction," *The Saturday Evening Post,* October 20, 1962, pp. 82–84.

46. Anthony Manna and Sue Misheff, "What Teachers Say About Their Own Reading Development," *Journal of Reading,* November 1987, pp. 160–68.

47. Edward B. Fiske, "Eight-Year Study of Public Schools Finds Chronic Problems in System," *The New York Times,* July 19, 1983, p. 1.

48. *Time,* February 1, 1988, pp. 52–58.

49. Betty S. Heathington and J. Estill Alexander, "Do Classroom Teachers Emphasize Attitudes Toward Reading?," *The Reading Teacher,* February 1984, pp. 484–88.

50. Selected by the International Reading Association in 1987 as one of the year's ten outstanding dissertations; Maryellen Smith Cosgrove, "Reading Aloud to Children: The Effects of Listening on the Reading Comprehension and Attitudes of Fourth and Sixth Graders in Six Communities in Connecticut," unpublished doctoral dissertation, University of Connecticut, 1987.

Chapter 2: When to Begin Read-Aloud

1. These remarks were made during a half-hour interview (September 3, 1979) with Dr. Brazelton conducted by John Merrow for *Options in Education,* a co-production of National Public Radio and the Institute for Educational Leadership of George Washington University.

2. Marjory Roberts, "Class Before Birth," *Psychology Today,* May 1987, p. 41; Sharon Begley and John Carey, "The Wisdom of Babies," *Newsweek,* January 12, 1981, pp. 71–72.

3. Dorothy Butler, *Cushla and Her Books* (Boston: The Horn Book, 1980).

4. Martin Deutsch, "The Disadvantaged Child and the Learning Process," in *Education in Depressed Areas,* ed. A. Harry Passow (New York: Teachers College Press, 1963), pp. 168–78.

5. Vera Propp, "All Babies Are Born Equal" (21 Bartlett Lane, Delmar, NY 12054).

6. Jerome Kagan, "The Child: His Struggle for Identity," *Saturday Review,* December 1968, p. 82. See also: Steven R. Tulkin and Jerome Kagan, "Mother-Child Interaction in the First Year of Life," *Child Development,* March 1972, pp. 31–41.

7. Further examples of "concept-attention span" can be found in Kagan, "The Child," p. 82.

8. These two became the seminal studies for read-aloud research: Dolores Durkin, *Children Who Read Early* (New York: Teachers College Press, 1966), and Margaret M. Clark, *Young Fluent Readers* (London: Heinemann, 1976). See also: Anne D. Forester, "What Teachers Can Learn from 'Natural Readers,' " *Reading Teacher,* November 1977, pp. 160–66.

9. *The New York Times,* March 22, 1959, p. D9.

10. Miriam Martinez and William H. Teale, "Reading in a Kindergarten Classroom Library," *The Reading Teacher,* February 1988, pp. 568–72.

11. John Holt treats this concept at length in his essay "How Teachers Make Children Hate Reading," *Redbook,* November 1967.

12. Richard C. Anderson, Elfrieda H. Hiebert, Judith A. Scott, and Ian A. G. Wilkinson, *Becoming a Nation of Readers: The Report of the Commission on Reading* (Champaign-Urbana, IL: Center for the Study of Reading, 1985), p. 51.

13. Robert Coles, "Gatsby at the Business School," *The New York Times Book Review,* October 25, 1987, p. 1; "There's a Lot to Be Learned from Literature, Owners Find," *The Wall Street Journal,* May 20, 1985, p. 29; see also Robert Coles, *The Call of Stories: Teaching and the Moral Imagination* (Boston: Houghton Mifflin, 1989).

Chapter 3: The Stages of Read-Aloud

1. Grace B. Martin and Russell D. Clark III, "Distress Crying in Neonates: Species and Peer Specificity," *Developmental Psychology* 18:1 (1982): 3–9.

2. Otto Friedrich, "What Do Babies Know?" *Time,* August 15, 1983, pp. 52–59.

3. Nancy Rubin, "Learning How Children Learn from the First Moments of Life," *The New York Times Winter Survey of Education,* January 10, 1982, Section 13, pp. 36–37.

4. "New Evidence Points to Growth of the Brain Even Late in Life," *The New York Times,* July 30, 1985, p. C1.

5. "Rapid Changes Seen in Young Brain," *The New York Times,* June 24, 1986, p. 17.

6. "The Experience of Touch: Research Points to a Critical Role," *The New York Times,* February 2, 1988, p. C17.

7. Linda Lamme and Athol Packer, "Bookreading Behaviors of Infants," *The Reading Teacher,* February 1986, pp. 504–9; Michael Resnick, Jeffrey Roth, Patricia Aaron, Jack Scott, William Wolking, Janet Larsen, and Athol Packer, "Mothers Reading to Infants: A New Observational Tool," *The Reading Teacher,* May 1987, pp. 888–94.

8. "Talking to Baby: Some Expert Advice," *The New York Times,* May 1987, p. C20.

9. Bess Altwerger, Judith Diehl-Faxon, and Karen Dockstader-Anderson, "Read-Aloud Events as Meaning Construction," *Language Arts,* September 1985, pp. 476–84.

10. Dorothy White, *Books Before Five* (Portsmouth, NH: Heinemann, 1984), p. 2.

11. David Yaden, "Understanding Stories Through Repeated Read-Alouds: How Many Does It Take?," *The Reading Teacher,* February 1988, pp. 556–60.

12. Bruno Bettelheim, *The Uses of Enchantment: The Meaning and Importance of Fairy Tales* (New York: Knopf, 1976), pp. 17–18.

13. "Preventing Summer Learning Losses," *The Harvard Education Letter,* June 1988, pp. 5–7; Barbara Heyns, *Summer Learning and the Effects of Schooling* (New York: Academic Press, 1978).

14. Kornei Chukovsky, *From Two to Five,* trans. Miriam Morton (Berkeley, CA: University of California Press, 1963), pp. 7, 9.

15. David Crystal, *Listen to Your Child* (New York: Penguin, 1986), pp. 16–18.

16. Joannis K. Flatley and Adele D. Rutland, "Using Wordless Picture Books to Teach Linguistically/Culturally Different Students," *The Reading Teacher,* December 1986, pp. 276–81; Donna Read and Henrietta M. Smith, "Teaching Visual Literacy Through Wordless Picture Books," *The Reading Teacher,* May 1982, pp. 928–52; J. Stewig, *Children and Literature* (Chicago: Rand McNally, 1980), pp. 131–58.

17. Miriam Martinez and William H. Teale, "Reading in a Kindergarten Classroom Library," *The Reading Teacher,* February 1988, pp. 568–72; see also Gail Heald-Taylor, "Predictable Literature Selections and Activities for Language Arts Instruction," *The Reading Teacher,* October 1987, pp. 6–12; Lynn K. Rhodes, "I Can Read! Predictable Books as Resources for Reading and Writing Instruction," *The Reading Teacher,* February 1981, pp. 511–18.

18. Eli M. Bower, "The Magic Symbols," *Today's Education* 57 (January 1968): 28–31. See also: Vincent R. Rogers, "Laughing with Children," *Educational Leadership,* April 1984, pp. 46–50.

19. Richard Abrahamson, "An Analysis of Children's Favorite Picture Storybooks," *Reading Teacher,* November 1980, pp. 167–70. *Children's Choices* is an annual publication of the International Reading Association in conjunction with the Children's Book Council. To order a copy, see Chapter 6.

20. "Finding New Ways to Make Geography Exciting," *The New York Times,* August 3, 1988, p. B6.

21. Mary Budd Rowe, "Wait Time: Slowing Down May Be a Way of Speeding Up!," *Journal of Teacher Education* 37:1 (1986).

22. For kindergarten statistics, "New York Chancellor Seeks to Broaden Teachers' Roles," *The New York Times,* August 22, 1988, p. 1; third-child statistics, see Harold Hodgkinson, *All One System* (Washington, DC: Institute for Educational Leadership, 1985).

23. William F. Coughlin, Jr., and Brendan Desilets, "Frederick the Field Mouse Meets Advanced Reading Skills as Children's Literature Goes to High School," *Journal of Reading,* December 1980, pp. 207–11.

24. Patricia Greenfield and Jessica Beagles-Roos, "Radio vs. Television: Their Cognitive Impact on Children of Different Socioeconomic and Ethnic Groups," *Journal of Communications,* Spring 1988, pp. 71–92.

25. Robertson Davies, *One Half of Robertson Davies* (New York: Viking, 1977), p. 1.

26. Edgar Allan Poe short story "The Fall of the House of Usher."

27. Daniel N. Fader and James Duggins, Tom Finn, and Elton B. McNeil, *The New Hooked on Books* (New York: Berkley, 1976), pp. 95–96.

28. Donald Barr, "Should Holden Caulfield Read These Books?," *The New York Times Book Review*, May 4, 1986, p. 1.

29. Katherine Paterson, "National Book Award Acceptance," *The Horn Book*, August 1979, pp. 402–3.

30. Bernice E. Cullinan, with Mary K. Karrer and Arlene M. Pillar, *Literature and the Child* (New York: Harcourt Brace Jovanovich, 1981), p. 250.

31. Miriam E. Wilt, "A Study of Teacher Awareness of Listening as a Factor in Elementary Education," *Journal of Educational Research*, April 1950, pp. 626–36.

32. Fred Hechinger, "About Education," *The New York Times*, May 11, 1988, p. Y22.

33. Penelope Laurans, "News, the Scores . . . and a Poem," *The New York Times*, September 3, 1988, Op Ed page.

34. Arthur Schlesinger, Jr., "Advice from a Reader-Aloud-to-Children," *The New York Times Book Review*, November 25, 1979.

35. Stephen Krashen, "Comic Book Reading and Language Development," a monograph from Abel Press, P.O. Box 6162, Station C, Victoria Station, BC, Canada V8P 5L5; Emma Halstead Swain, "Using Comic Books in Teaching Reading and Language Arts," *Journal of Reading*, December 1978, pp. 253–58. See also: Larry Dorrell and Ed Carroll, "Spider-Man at the Library," *School Library Journal*, August 1981, pp. 17–19.

Chapter 5: Read-Aloud Success Stories

1. *Mademoiselle*, December 1984.

2. Joyce L. Epstein, "Parents' Reactions to Teacher Practices of Parent Involvement," *Elementary School Journal* 86:3 (1986): 277–94.

3. Louise Sherman, "Practically Speaking: Have a Story Lunch," *School Library Journal*, October 1986, pp. 120–21.

4. Jill Locke, "Pittsburgh's Beginning with Books Project," *School Library Journal*, February 1988, pp. 22–24.

5. "An Expert Urges Multiple Reforms," *The New York Times*, July 7, 1983, p. C1.

6. Peter Cohen, James Kulik, and Chen-Lin Kulik, "Educational Outcomes of Tutoring: A Meta-Analysis of Findings," *American Educational Research Journal* 19:2 (1982); *The Harvard Education Letter*, March 1987.

7. For information, write: Read-Aloud Delaware, P.O. Box 25249, Wilmington, DE 19899.

8. For information, write: Read-Aloud West Virginia, P.O. Box 8472, South Charleston, WV 25303-0472.

Chapter 6: Home and Public Libraries

1. Dolores Durkin, *Children Who Read Early* (New York: Teachers College Press, 1966). See also: Anne D. Forester, "What Teachers Can Learn from 'Natural Readers,' " *Reading Teacher,* November 1977, pp. 160–66.

2. Jeanne Chall and Catherine Snow, *Families and Literacy: The Contribution of Out-of-School Experiences to Children's Acquisition of Literacy,* National Institute of Education, 1982, ED 234 345.

3. Donald Bissett, "The Amount and Effect of Recreational Reading in Select Fifth-Grade Classes," unpublished doctoral dissertation, Syracuse University, 1969; see also: Miriam Martinez and William Teale, "Reading in a Kindergarten Classroom Library," *The Reading Teacher,* February 1988, pp. 568–72.

4. Richard Anderson, Linda Fielding, and Paul Wilson, "A New Focus on Free Reading: The Role of Trade Books in Reading Instruction," in *Contexts of School Based Literacy,* ed. T. E. Raphael (New York: Random House, 1986).

5. John Updike, "A Few Words in Defense of the Amateur Reader," *The New York Times Book Review,* February 14, 1984, p. 13.

6. "State Journal," *Education Week,* October 12, 1988, p. 12.

7. "Reading Rainbow," an excellent series, is noncommercial, PBS.

8. Anthony Brandt, "Literacy in America," *The New York Times,* August 25, 1980, p. 25.

9. Pete Hamill, "D'Artagnan on Ninth Street: A Brooklyn Boy at the Library," *The New York Times Book Review,* June 26, 1988, p. 48.

Chapter 7: Television

1. Television Bureau of Advertising (477 Madison Avenue, New York, NY 10022), January 1988 report for 1987 viewing.

2. "Incentives for Inmates: Television Sets in Cells," *The New York Times,* April 4, 1988, p. B3.

3. According to 1981 Gallup Poll on TV viewing on school nights.

4. "National Report on College-Bound Seniors, 1988," The College Board, 888 Seventh Avenue, New York, NY 10106.

5. Paul Copperman, *The Literacy Hoax: The Decline of Reading, Writing, and Learning in the Public Schools and What We Can Do About It* (New York: Morrow, 1980), p. 166.

6. Herbert London, "What TV Drama Is Teaching Our Children," *The New York Times,* August 23, 1987, p. 23.

7. California Department of Education, "Student Achievement in California Schools, 1979–80 Annual Report" (P.O. Box 271, Sacramento, CA 96802).

8. M. Morgan and L. Gross, "Television and Educational Achievement and Aspiration," in *Television and Behavior: Ten Years of Scientific Progress and Implications for the Eighties,* ed. D. Pearl, L. Bonlithilet, and J. Lazar (Rockville, MD: NIMH, 1982).

9. Rosemarie Truglio, Aletha Huston, and John Wright, "The Relation Between Children's Print and Television Use to Early Reading Skills," Center for Research on the Influences of Television on Children, Department of Human Development, University of Kansas, 1988.

10. "Zapping of TV Ads Appears Pervasive," *Wall Street Journal*, April 25, 1988, pg. 29.

11. Donald Hayes and Dana Birnbaum, *Developmental Psychology* 16:5 and 17:2. See also: *Psychology Today,* June 1982, pp. 78–79.

12. Meg Schwartz, "Broadcasting Books to Young Audiences," *RE:ACT,* Spring/Summer 1980, p. 19. Mr. Rushnell's remarks were made at a symposium co-sponsored by Action for Children's Television (ACT) and the Library of Congress Center for the Book. *RE:ACT* is a nonprofit journal published by ACT.

13. Neil Postman, *Teaching as a Conserving Activity* (New York: Delacorte, 1980), pp. 77–78.

14. "Myths, Men, & Beer," booklet available from AAA Foundation for Traffic Safety.

15. Jackie S. Busch, "TV's Effects on Reading: A Case Study," *Phi Delta Kappan,* June 1978, pp. 668–71.

16. Wilbur Schramm, Jack Lyle, and Edwin B. Parker, *Television in the Lives of Our Children* (Stanford, CA: Stanford University Press, 1961).

17. Michael Liberman, "The Verbal Language of Television," *The Journal of Reading,* April 1983, pp. 602–9.

18. Patricia Greenfield and Jessica Beagles-Roos, "Radio and Television: Their Cognitive Impact on Children of Different Socioeconomic and Ethnic Groups," *Journal of Communication,* Spring 1988, pp. 71–91.

19. Frank Mankiewicz and Joel Swerdlow, *Remote Control: Television and the Manipulation of American Life* (New York: Times Books, 1978), pp. 6, 15–72.

20. "Why TV Won't Let Up on Violence," *The New York Times,* January 13, 1985, Section 2, H-1, 25.

21. "TV 'Family Hour' Rated Most Violent," *USA Today,* September 11, 1986, p. 1.

22. Postman, *Teaching as a Conserving Activity,* p. 208.

23. Mankiewicz and Swerdlow, *Remote Control,* p. 6.

24. Linda S. Lichter and S. Robert Lichter, *Crooks, Conmen and Clowns* (Washington, DC: Media Institute of Mental Health, 1982; Earle Barcus, *Images of Life on Children's Television: Sex Roles, Minorities, and Families* (New York: Praeger, 1983).

25. "NBC's Head Says TV Viewers Spurn Quality Shows," *The New York Times,* September 30, 1984, p. 1.

26. Bob Keeshan's remarks were made during an interview on September 24, 1979, with John Merrow for *Options in Education,* a co-production of National Public Radio and the Institute for Educational Leadership of George Washington University.

27. Milton Goldman and Sandra Goldman, "Reading with Close-Captioned TV," *Journal of Reading,* February 1988, pp. 458–61.

28. John Leo, "How the Hostages Came Through," *Time,* February 9, 1981, p. 52; Gregg W. Downey, "Keough Ponders the Lessons of Captivity," *Executive Educator,* May 1981, pp. 24–29.

29. Further evidence can be found in Alexander Dolgun's autobiographical account of his role as a "storyteller" for 129 Soviet prisoners in a tiny labor cell. See Alexander Dolgun, with Patrick Wilson, *Alexander Dolgun's Story: An American in the Gulag* (New York: Knopf, 1975), pp. 138–49.

30. Marie Carbo, "Teaching Reading with Talking Books," *Reading Teacher,* December 1978, pp. 267–73.

Chapter 8: Sustained Silent Reading: Reading-Aloud's Natural Partner

1. Richard Anderson, Linda Fielding, and Paul Wilson, "Growth in Reading and How Children Spend Their Time Outside of School," *Reading Research Quarterly,* Summer 1988, pp. 285–303.

NOTES

2. John I. Goodlad, *A Place Called School: Prospects for the Future* (New York: McGraw-Hill, 1984), p. 107.

3. Robert A. McCracken, "Instituting Sustained Silent Reading," *Journal of Reading,* May 1971, pp. 521–24, 582–83.

4. Anderson et al., "Growth in Reading," p. 152.

5. Edward Fry and Elizabeth Sakiey, "Common Words Not Taught in Basal Reading Series," *The Reading Teacher,* January 1986, pp. 395–98.

6. Kenneth S. Goodman, Yvonne Freeman, Sharon Murphy, and Patrick Shannon, *Report Card on Basal Readers* (New York: Richard Owen, 1988); see also Kenneth S. Goodman, "Look What They've Done to Judy Blume!: The 'Basalization' of Children's Literature," *The New Advocate* 1:1 (1988): 29–42.

7. Harriet Tyson-Bernstein, *A Conspiracy of Good Intentions* (Washington, DC: Council for Basic Education, 1988); Gilbert T. Sewall, "American History Textbooks: Where Do We Go from Here?," *Phi Delta Kappan,* April 1988, pp. 553–57; William Bennett, *Our Children and Our Country* (New York: Simon & Schuster, 1988).

8. Jeanne Jacobson, "I Couldn't Read This Week Because My Mother Was Busy," *Journal of Reading,* March 1988, pp. 496–97.

9. S. Jay Samuels, "Decoding and Automaticity: Helping Poor Readers Become Automatic at Word Recognition," *The Reading Teacher,* April 1988, pp. 756–60.

10. *Becoming a Nation of Readers* (Champaign, IL: Center for the Study of Reading, 1985), p. 119.

11. Mark Sadoski, "An Attitude Survey for Sustained Silent Reading Programs," *Journal of Reading,* May 1980, pp. 721–26.

12. Richard Allington, "If They Don't Read Much, How They Gonna Get Good?," *Journal of Reading,* October 1977, pp. 57–61.

13. Michael H. Kean, Anita H. Summers, Mark Raivetz, and Irvin J. Farber, "What Works in Reading?: Summary and Results of a Joint School District/Federal Reserve Bank Empirical Study in Philadelphia," The School District of Philadelphia: ERIC Report ED176216, May 1979, p. 8, of Document Résumé.

14. Martha Efta, "Reading in Silence," *Teaching Exceptional Children,* Fall 1978, pp. 12–24.

15. Robert A. McCracken and Marlene J. McCracken, "Modeling Is the Key to Sustained Silent Reading," *Reading Teacher,* January 1978, pp. 406–8. See also: Linda B. Gambrell, "Getting Started with Sustained Silent

Reading and Keeping It Going," *Reading Teacher,* December 1978, pp. 328–31.

16. For program details, write: *Book It!* Program, P.O. Box 2999, Wichita, KS 67201.

Chapter 9: How to Use the Treasury

1. Jacques Barzun, *Teacher in America* (Garden City, NY: Doubleday, 1954), pp. 60–62, 136.

Bibliography

Adler, Mortimer. *Paideia Problems and Possibilities*. New York: Macmillan, 1983.

———. *The Paideia Proposal: An Educational Manifesto*. New York: Macmillan, 1982.

Anderson, Richard C., Elfrieda H. Hiebert, Judith Scott, and Ian A. G. Wilkinson. *Becoming a Nation of Readers*. Champaign-Urbana, IL: Center for the Study of Reading, 1985.

Applebee, Arthur N., Judith A. Langer, and Ina V. S. Mullis. *Who Reads Best?* Princeton, NJ: National Assessment of Educational Progress, 1988.

Ashton-Warner, Sylvia. *Spearpoint: "Teacher" in America*. New York: Vintage, 1974.

Atwell, Nancy. *In the Middle: Writing, Reading and Learning with Adolescents*. Portsmouth, NH: Heinemann, 1987.

Barcus, Earle. *Images of Life on Children's Televison: Sex Roles, Minorities, and Families*. New York: Praeger, 1983.

Barr, Donald. *Who Pushed Humpty Dumpty? Dilemmas in American Education Today*. New York: Atheneum, 1971.

Barzun, Jacques. *Teacher in America*. Garden City, NY: Doubleday, 1954.

Bennett, William. *Our Children and Our Country*. New York: Simon & Schuster, 1988.

Bettelheim, Bruno. *The Uses of Enchantment: The Meaning and Importance of Fairy Tales*. New York: Knopf, 1976.

———, and Karen Zelan. *On Learning to Read*. New York: Knopf, 1982.

Butler, Dorothy. *Babies Need Books*. New York: Atheneum, 1980.

———. *Cushla and Her Books*. Boston: The Horn Book, 1980.

Cass-Beggs, Barbara. *Your Baby Needs Music*. New York: St. Martin's, 1980.

Cazden, Courtney B. *Child Language and Education*. New York: Holt, Rinehart and Winston, 1972.

Chukovsky, Kornei. *From Two to Five*. Translated by Miriam Morton. Berkeley, Calif.: University of California Press, 1963.

Clark, Margaret M. *Young Fluent Readers*. London: Heinemann, 1976.

Coles, Robert. *The Call of Stories: Teaching and the Moral Imagination*. Boston: Houghton Mifflin, 1989.

Committee for Economic Development, Research and Policy. *Investing in Our Schools: Business and the Public Schools*. Washington, DC: Committee for Economic Development, 1985.

Copperman, Paul. *The Literacy Hoax: The Decline of Reading, Writing, and Learning in the Public Schools and What We Can Do About It*. New York: Morrow, 1980.

Crystal, David. *Listen to Your Child*. New York: Penguin, 1986.

Cullinan, Bernice E., ed. *Children's Literature in the Reading Program*. Newark, DE: International Reading Association, 1987.

———, with Mary K. Karrer and Arlene M. Pillar. *Literature and the Child*. New York: Harcourt Brace Jovanovich, 1981.

Davies, Robertson. *One Half of Robertson Davies*. New York: Viking, 1977.

Dodson, Fitzhugh. *How to Father*. Los Angeles: Nash, 1974.

———. *How to Parent*. Los Angeles: Nash, 1970.

Dolgun, Alexander, with Patrick Wilson. *Alexander Dolgun's Story: An American in the Gulag*. New York: Knopf, 1975.

Durkin, Dolores. *Children Who Read Early*. New York: Teachers College Press, 1966.

Egoff, Sheila, G. T. Stubbs, and L. F. Ashley, eds. *Only Connect: Readings on Children's Literature*. Toronto: Oxford, 1969.

Elkind, David. *The Hurried Child: Growing Up Too Soon Too Fast*. Reading, MA: Addison-Wesley, 1981.

———. *Miseducation: Preschoolers at Risk*. New York: Knopf, 1987.

Fader, Daniel N., James Duggins, Tom Finn, and Elton B. McNeil. *The New Hooked on Books*. New York: Berkley, 1976.

Fadiman, Clifton and James Howard. *Empty Pages: A Search for Writing Competence in School and Society*. Belmont, CA: Fearon Pitman and the Council for Basic Education, 1979.

Glazer, Susan Mandel. *Getting Ready to Read*. Englewood Cliffs, NJ: Prentice-Hall, 1980.

Goodlad, John I. *A Place Called School: Prospects for the Future*. New York: McGraw-Hill, 1984.

Goodman, Ken. *What's Whole in Whole Language?* Portsmouth, NH: Heinemann, 1986.

Goodman, Kenneth, Yvonne Freeman, Sharon Murphy, and Patrick Shannon. *Report Card on Basal Readers*. New York: Richard Owen, 1988.

Graves, Donald, and Virginia Stuart. *Write from the Start*. New York: Dutton, 1985.

Hall, Nigel. *The Emergence of Literacy*. Portsmouth, NH: Heinemann, 1987.

Hayden, Torey L. *One Child*. New York: Putnam, 1980.

Hearne, Betsy. *Choosing Books for Children: A Commonsense Guide*. New York: Delacorte, 1981.

Herndon, James. *How to Survive in Your Native Land*. New York: Simon & Schuster, 1971.

Hirsch, E. D., Jr. *Cultural Literacy: What Every American Needs to Know*. Boston: Houghton Mifflin, 1987.

Hopkins, Lee Bennett. *Pass the Poetry, Please!* New York: Harper & Row, 1987.

Kimmel, Margaret Mary, and Elizabeth Segal. *For Reading Out Loud!* New York: Delacorte, 1988.

Kobrin, Beverly. *Eyeopeners! How to Choose and Use Children's Books About Real People, Places, and Things*. New York: Viking, 1988.

Larrick, Nancy. *A Parents' Guide to Children's Reading*. 4th ed. New York: Bantam, 1975.

Mankiewicz, Frank, and Joel Swerdlow. *Remote Control: Television and the Manipulation of American Life*. New York: Times Books, 1978.

McCracken, Robert A. and Marlene J. *Reading Is Only the Tiger's Tail*. Kimberley, BC: Classroom Publications, 1985.

Mussen, Paul Henry, John Janeway Conger, and Jerome Kagan. *Child Development and Personality*. 4th ed. New York: Harper & Row, 1974.

National Commission on Excellence in Education. *A Nation at Risk: The Imperative for Educational Reform*. Washington, DC: U.S. Department of Education, 1983.

Passow, Harry A., ed. *Education in Depressed Areas*. New York: Teachers College Press, 1963.

Paulin, Mary Ann. *Creative Uses of Children's Literature*. Hamden, CT: Library Professional Publications, 1982.

Postman, Neil. *Amusing Ourselves to Death*. New York: Viking, 1985.

———. *The Disappearance of Childhood*. New York: Harper & Row, 1982.

———. *Teaching as a Conserving Activity*. New York: Delacorte, 1980.

Prescott, Orville. *A Father Reads to His Children: An Anthology of Prose and Poetry*. New York: Dutton, 1965.

Ravitch, Diane, and Chester E. Finn, Jr. *What Do Our 17-Year-Olds Know?* New York: Harper & Row, 1987.

Reed, Arthea J. S. *Comics to Classics: A Parent's Guide to Books for Teens and Preteens*. Newark, DE: International Reading Association, 1988.

Ross, Eden Lipson. *The New York Times Parents' Guide to the Best Books for Children*. New York: Times Books, 1988.

Rudman, Masha. *Children's Literature: An Issues Approach*. New York: Longman, 1984.

———, and Anna M. Pearce. *For Love of Reading: A Parent's Guide to Encouraging Young Readers from Infancy Through Age 5*. Mt. Vernon, NY: Consumers Union, 1988.

Rutstein, Nat. *"Go Watch TV!"* New York: Sheed and Ward, 1974.

Sabine, Gordon, and Patricia Sabine. *Books That Make a Difference*. Hamden, CT: Library Professional Publications, 1983.

Schramm, Wilbur, Jack Lyle, and Edwin B. Parker. *Television in the Lives of Our Children*. Stanford, CA: Stanford University Press, 1961.

Simon, Sidney B., Leland W. Howe, and Howard Kerschenbaum. *Values Clarification: A Handbook of Practical Strategies for Teachers and Students*. Rev. ed. New York: A & W, 1978.

Sizer, Theodore R. *Horace's Compromise: The Dilemma of the American High School.* Boston: Houghton Mifflin, 1984.

Sloan, Glenna Davis. *The Child as Critic.* New York: Teachers College Press, 1975.

Smith, Frank. *Insult to Intelligence.* New York: Arbor House, 1986.

———. *Understanding Reading.* 3rd ed. New York: Holt, Rinehart and Winston, 1982.

Steinbeck, John. *The Acts of King Arthur and His Noble Knights.* New York: Farrar, Straus and Giroux, 1976.

Stewig, J. *Children and Literature.* Chicago: Rand McNally, 1980.

Taylor, Denny, and Dorothy Strickland. *Family Storybook Reading.* Portsmouth, NH: Heinemann, 1986.

Theroux, Phyllis. *Night Lights: Bedtime Stories for Parents in the Dark.* New York: Viking, 1987.

White, Dorothy. *Books Before Five.* Portsmouth, NH: Heinemann Educational Books, 1984.

Wiener, Harvey S. *Talk with Your Child.* New York: Viking, 1988.

Winn, Marie. *The Plug-in Drug.* New York: Penguin, 1977, 1985.

———. *Unplugging the Plug-in Drug.* New York: Penguin, 1987.

Yolen, Jane. *Touch Magic.* New York: Philomel, 1981.

Subject Index

attention span, 26–27, 63
author week, 62, 81–82

Becoming a Nation of Readers,
    1–2, 10–11, 36, 88
bed lamp, 29–30
bedtime, 50–51
Bettelheim, Bruno, 13, 49, 55
bookrack, 29
book(s)
    bedtime, 50–51
    chapter, 62–63
    Children's Choices, 58
    classic, 60–61, 64, 67–69
    comic, 77–78
    controlled vocabulary, 53–
        54

cost-savers, 101–6
fairy tale, 55–57
favorite, 48–49
as gifts, 88–89, 111
joke (humor), 54–55
movies made from, 83–84
ownership, 29
predictable, 52–53, 153–
    154
readership, 7–8
recorded, 134–38
reviewing sources, 51–52,
    104–6, 153–263
textbooks vs. tradebooks,
    142–43
wordless, 52–53, 154–56
Brandeis University, 37

Brazelton, T. Berry, 20, 23
Bruna, Dick, 46
Butler, Dorothy, 21

Cambridge University, 36–
    37
cereal boxes, 114–15
Charlotte's Web, 63–64
Chicago Public Schools, 10
child care, 27–28
Coles, Robert, 37–38
Cosgrove, Maryellen, 17–18
Cushla and Her Books, 21

Dahl, Roald, 39–40
Delaware, Read-Aloud, 94–
    95

Dr. Seuss, 53–54
dropout rate, school, 5–6
Durkin, Dolores, 28

Eisner, Michael, 131
Elkind, David, xxi
ESL (English as second language), 52–53

fairy tale, 55–57
  feminist, 56
  parodies, 58

geography enrichment, 58–59
Georgia kindergartners, 11

Harvard Business School, 37–38
Hopkins, Lee Bennett, 77
"hurried" children (superbabies), xxi–xxiii, 23–24

illiterates, 52–53, 104, 137, 143
incentive (reading) programs, 146–47
infant
  attention span, 26–27, 44
  hearing, 42
  imitation, 42

Keeshan, Bob, 128
kindergarten students, 11, 63

library, 97–115
  cards, 109, 111
  classroom, 100–1
  cost-savers, 101–6
  home, 47–48, 97–100
  public, 22, 106–11
listening comprehension, 2, 24–25

McCloskey, Robert, xvi
McCracken, Robert and Marlene, 141, 145
magazines, 8, 102–3
Michener, James, xxvi–xxvii
"Mister Rogers," 120–21
Mother Goose, 43
Murphy, Deborah, 32–33

National Inquirer, The, 8
nonfiction, 17, 51–52, 98–99, 102–3, 156–57

O'Neill, Thomas P., Jr., 14–17
Oxford University, 37

parent
  and attention span, 63
  fast-track, xxi–xxiii
  fathers, xv, xxii–xxiv, 82–83
  illiterate, 52–53, 104, 137, 143
  teenage, 60
  time with child, xxii, 23–24
  working, xxii
peer learning, 93–94
Peet, Bill, 62
Pizza Hut's Book It!, 146
poetry, 72–77
  children's preferences in, 74
  memorization of, 75–76
prisons, 7, 118
Pusey, Nathan, 33

readers, early fluent, 28
Reader's Digest, 39
reading
  adolescents and, 67–68, 70–71, 103
  advertising, 3–4, 9
  business and, 6–7, 16, 37–38, 75, 90–91, 94, 109, 115
  comic books, 77–78
  comprehension, 2, 24–25
  delinquents and, 7, 67–68
  ethics and, 37–38
  experience and, 49–50
  eyesight and, 29–30
  incentive programs, 146–147
  level
    emotional vs., 65–66
    listening vs., 30–31, 63–64
    social vs. 66–68
  newspaper, 7–8, 69
  promoting, 86–96, 107–15
  purpose of, 13–14
  reading to, see reading aloud
  recreational, 11–12, 50, 139–47
  remedial, 12
  in school, 141
  scores
    adult, 7–8
    student, 5–7
  sports and, xxiii–xxiv, 9–10
  summer, 50
  workbooks, 9–10, 35–36

writing ties to, 6, 28
  see also nonfiction; sustained silent reading
reading aloud
  across the curriculum, 36–40, 58–59
  adolescents and, 36–40, 59–61, 66–72
  anthologies, 69
  bonding and, 25–26, 31–32, 43–44
  California and, 10–11
  censorship and, 66–67, 71
  clergy and, 112–13
  disadvantaged child and, 23
  Dos, 79–83
  Don'ts, 83–85
  during school lunch, 89–90
  dyslexia and, 24
  guest readers for, 16, 87, 90–91
  infants and, 19–23, 41–49
  in utero, 20–21
  language arts and, 34–35
  lists of books for, 87, 104–6, 108, 153–262
  Michigan and, 10–11
  middle grades and, 17–18
  newspapers, 69
  pediatricians and, 113–14
  by peers, 93–94
  primary grades and, 52–59, 61–66
  principals and, 14–16, 34–35, 89, 91–92
  promotions
    in clinics, 92–93
    by libraries, 107–11
    by states, 10–11, 94–96
  purposes of, 2–4, 9–11, 13–18
  questions and, 59, 84
  research, 1–2, 17–18, 28, 36, 136–37
  spelling and, 35–36
  sustained silent reading and, 33–34, 139–47
  writing and, 35–36
"Reading Rainbow," 34, 121

Secret Garden, The, 30–31
Silverstein, Shel, 73
Steinbeck, John, 5
story (as teacher), 37–38
sustained silent reading, 33–34, 91–92, 139–47

Becoming a Nation of Readers and, 143
in the home, 147
procedures, 141–42
research, 141, 144–45

teaching, purpose of, 33
television, 116–38
    addictive nature of, 118, 126
    as babysitter, 119, 126
    as classroom subject, 133–34
    close-captioned, 131–32
    distorting reality, 127–28
    imagination and, 124

informational vs. entertainment, 120–21
language development and, 122–24
newspapers vs., 123
parents and, 128–34
as "plug-in drug," 118
reading vs., 121–28
role models, 119–20, 126–127
school scores and, 119, 120–24
thinking and, 123
"turn-off" campaigns, 133
viewing, 4, 8, 117
violence and, 125

"zapping," 122, 125
thinking, critical, 59, 75–76
Tintin, 77–78
TV Guide, 8

video cassette recorder (VCR), 4–5
vocabulary development, 21–28, 51, 122

Warren, Robert Penn, 14, 58
West Virginia, Read-Aloud, 95–96
word of mouth (influence), 86

Author-Illustrator Index
to the Treasury

Italics are for illustrator only; * after page number gives location of a group of books by an author or illustrator.

Adler, David, 159
Aesop, 166, 257
Ahlberg, Allan, 165, 166, 174, 177*, 199, 252
Ahlberg, Janet, 165, 174, 177*, 199
Aiken, Joan, 182, 249*
Alexander, Lloyd, 210
Alexander, Martha, 155, 178, 197*
Alexander, Sue, 184, 185
Aliki, 166, 196
Allard, Harry, 164, 181*, 193*
Allsburg, Chris Van, 165, 187, 188*
Ambrus, Victor, 239

Ammon, Richard, 205, 221
Andersen, Hans Christian, 169*, 194, 229, 257
Angelou, Maya, 259
Anno, Mitsumasa, 167
Archambault, John, 169, 179, 185, 198
Ardizzone, Edward, 158*, 160*
Arkin, Alan, 180
Arnold, Tedd, 185
Asch, Frank, 178, 237
Asimov, Isaac, 246, 262
Atwater, Richard and Florence, 233
Aurandt, Paul, 260*
Avi, 235, 248*

Babbitt, Natalie, 241, 245
Baker, Olaf, 198
Balian, Lorna, 159*
Bang, Molly, 155, 164*, 169, 174, 179, 187
Banks, Lynne Reid, 229
Barrett, Angela, 170
Barrett, Judi, 162*
Barrett, Ron, 162
Bauer, Caroline Feller, 196
Bauer, Marion Dane, 212, 238
Baum, Arline and Joseph, 199
Baum, L. Frank, 249*
Beasley, Roberta, 188
Bellairs, John, 221*

Bemelmans, Ludwig, 180*
Benchley, Nathaniel, 197, 198
Bennett, Jack, 229, 233
Bennett, Jay, 223
Bethancourt, T. Ernesto, 224
Birdseye, Tom, 185, 190
Birkett, Rachel, 169
Bishop, Claire H., 195, 215
Bjork, Christina, 182
Blake, Quentin, 154, 173, 185
Blathwayt, Benedict, 211
Bloom, Lloyd, 184
Blos, Joan, 187
Blume, Judy, 244, 259, 260
Bolognese, Don, 197
Bond, Felicia, 175
Booth, Jerry, 166
Bowers, Kathleen Rice, 169
Bradbury, Ray, 246
Brady, Esther Wood, 245
Branley, Franklyn M., 167, 177
Brenner, Barbara, 197
Briggs, Raymond, 156, 189, 257
Brink, Carol Ryrie, 217, 219
Brittain, Bill, 248*
Brothers Grimm, 172*, 194, 257, 263
Brown, Marc, 159, 183, 254*
Brown, Margaret Wise, 154, 169
Brown, Ruth, 175
Bruna, Dick, 156, 169, 191*, 196
Bulla, Clyde Robert, 170, 197, 209*, 213, 214
Bunting, Eve, 169, 184, 186, 196, 243
Burch, Robert, 218, 228
Burkert, Nancy Ekholm, 230
Burnett, Frances Hodgson, 213*, 229, 241*
Burningham, John, 159
Burton, Virginia Lee, 170, 177, 179, 180*
Byars, Betsy, 207, 214, 227, 233*, 237, 260

Callen, Larry, 204, 227, 233, 247
Cameron, Ann, 213, 214*, 230
Carle, Eric, 154, 155, 183, 196*, 257
Carlstrom, Nancy W., 174

Carr, Jan, 254
Carrara, Larry, 164
Carrick, Carol, 166, 183, 184, 185, 186, 191*
Carrick, Donald, 160, 170, 182, 185, 191*
Caselli, Giovanni, 156, 157
Catling, Patrick Skene, 221
Caudill, Rebecca, 204
Cauley, Lorinda B., 170
Cerf, Bennett, 159*
Chorao, Kay, 161
Chrisman, Arthur Bowie, 195
Ciardi, John, 255*
Cleary, Beverly, 222, 237, 238*, 260, 263
Clifford, Eth, 207*, 221
Clifton, Lucille, 184, 197, 206, 211, 259
Coerr, Eleanor, 160, 197, 238
Cohen, Barbara, 161*, 226, 236, 245
Cohen, Marsha, 188
Cohen, Miriam, 165*
Cohn, Janice, 184
Cole, Bruce, 171, 183, 187
Collier, Christopher, 231, 234
Collier, James Lincoln, 231, 234
Collington, Peter, 155
Collodi, Carlo, 217
Cone, Molly, 223
Conly, Jane L., 234
Conrad, Pam, 227
Cooney, Barbara, 181, 215
Cooper, Susan, 165, 187, 244
Corcoran, Barbara, 232
Corrin, Sara and Stephen, 261*
Coville, Bruce, 171, 211
Crane, Walter, 172
Creswell, Helen, 203
Cruz, Ray, 157

Dahl, Roald, 173, 205, 206, 217, 222, 230*
Dalgliesh, Alice, 205
Day, Alexandra, 155
DeJong, Meindert, 228
Delaney, A., 154, 179
Delton, Judy, 159
dePaola, Tomie, 155, 166, 177*, 181, 184, 185, 186, 189, 193, 198, 212
deRegniers, Beatrice Schenk, 251, 254

Devlin, Wende and Harry, 163*
Dillon, Barbara, 200
Dillon, Diane and Leo, 251, 258
Dr. Seuss, 158, 159, 174*, 179, 181, 185, 189, 190, 196, 251
Dougherty, James, 196
Douglas, Barbara, 176
Douglass, Frederick, 211
Duffy, James, 238
Duncan, Lois, 231
Duntze, Dorothee, 170
Dupasquier, Philippe, 155, 158, 172, 179, 195
Duvoisin, Roger, 187
Dygard, Thomas J., 247*

Eastman, P. D., 153, 180
Eckert, Allan W., 228
Eckstein, Joan, 160
Ehrlich, Amy, 170
Eisenberg, Lisa, 159
Elholm, Nancy, 173
Elliott, Dan, 196
Ellis, Anne, 180
Emberley, Barbara, 167
Emberley, Ed, 154, 155, 167
Estes, Eleanor, 207

Fadiman, Clifton, 262
Faulkner, Matt, 158
Feldman, Thea, 180
Felleman, Hazel, 250
Fisher, Dorothy Canfield, 246
Fisher, Leonard E., 236
Fitzgerald, John D., 226*
Flack, Marjorie, 153, 180
Fleischman, Paul, 206, 236
Fleischman, Sid, 216, 227*, 260
Flora, James, 162, 183
Forman, Michael, 173
Fosburgh, Liza, 203
Fowles, John, 182
Fox, Mem, 154, 186, 189
Fraser, Betty, 251
Freeman, Don, 161, 163*
French, Michael, 223
Friedrich, Priscilla and Otto, 163
Fritz, Jean, 196, 198, 229
Fuchshuber, Annegert, 187

Gackenbach, Dick, 171*
Gag, Wanda, 181*
Galdone, Paul, 154, 165, 175, 193*

Gallico, Paul, 224
Gammell, Stephen, 198, 261
Gannett, Ruth S., 211
Gardiner, John R., 214
Garfield, Leon, 167, 208, 220, 222
George, Jean, 235
Gerstein, Mordicai, 159, 184
Gibbons, Gail, 196
Gibson, Michael, 170
Giff, Patricia Reilly, 209
Gillham, Bill, 174, 188
Ginsburg, Mirra, 169
Gipson, Fred, 222
Gleit, Joyce, 160
Godden, Rumer, 161, 213, 215, 236
Goldin, Barbara, 189
Goodall, John S., 154, 155, 157*
Gorbaty, Norman, 188
Gorey, Edward, 190, 255
Gorog, Judith, 262
Graeber, Charlotte, 234
Graham, Margaret B., 171
Grahame, Kenneth, 212
Gramatky, Hardie, 179
Gray, Catherine and James, 185
Greene, Bette, 215, 240
Greene, Bob, 256
Greenfield, Eloise, 251
Griffith, Helen V., 169, 223, 228, 232, 247
Grimm Brothers, 172*, 194, 257, 263
Guilfoile, Elizabeth, 202
Gwynne, Fred, 159

Haas, Dorothy, 225, 233
Hall, Katy, 159
Hall, Lynn, 208, 219, 223, 225, 227, 231, 233, 244, 248
Haller, Danita, 198
Halpern, Joan, 161
Hamilton, Virginia, 258
Handford, Martin, 199
Harrison, Ted, 250
Hartley, Deborah, 177, 186
Harvey, Brett, 197
Harvey, Paul, 260
Hauman, George and Doris, 178
Hautzig, Esther, 162
Haviland, Virginia, 198, 257*
Hawkins, Colin and Jacqui, 154

Hawthorne, Julian, 232
Hawthorne, Nathaniel, 221, 262
Headon, Deirdre, 239
Heide, Florence Parry, 190*
Heller, Julek, 239
Hergé, 195*
Hermes, Patricia, 207
Hest, Amy, 169
Hildebrandt, Tim and Greg, 182
Hill, Eric, 154, 174, 199*
Hines, Anna, 176
Hirschfelder, Arlene, 242
Hoban, Lillian, 196
Hoban, Russell, 185
Hoban, Tana, 174
Hoberman, Mary Ann, 251*
Hodges, Margaret, 170, 213
Holland, Barbara, 238
Holm, Anne, 235
Holman, Felice, 243
Hooks, William H., 182
Hopkins, Lee Bennett, 254*
Howe, John, 190
Howell, Lynn and Richard, 185, 199
Howker, Janni, 208
Hughes, Shirley, 156, 159, 166*, 174, 176, 191, 257
Hughes, Ted, 208, 257
Hunt, Irene, 218, 235, 237
Hunter, Edith Fisher, 221
Hunter, Mollie, 244
Hutchins, Pat, 155
Hyman, Trina Schart, 172, 173, 179, 255

Innocenti, Roberto, 217
Irving, Washington, 190
Ivimey, John, 154
Iwasaki, Chihiro, 170

Jacobs, Joseph, 193, 257
Jacques, Brian, 232
Jaquith, Priscilla, 167, 168, 262
Jarrell, Randall, 173, 218
Jeffers, Susan, 170
Jeschke, Susan, 173
Johnson, Annabel and Edgar, 225
Joosse, Barbara, 171
Jorgensen, David, 170, 216
Joyce, William, 166, 174, 183
Jukes, Mavis, 160, 185

Kalas, Sybille, 164
Kaye, M. M., 236
Keats, Ezra Jack, 189*
Kellogg, Steven, 161, 166, 176*, 183
Kelly, Jeffrey, 214, 226, 227
Kennedy, Richard, 207, 260
Khalsa, Dayal Kaur, 169
Kimmel, Eric, 189
Klingsheim, T. B., 164
Knight, Hilary, 199
Konigsburg, E. L., 224
Koontz, Robin, 154
Kovalski, Maryann, 154
Krahn, Fernando, 154, 155
Krasilovsky, Phyllis, 182
Krauss, Ruth, 179
Kunhardt, Dorothy, 186
Kunhardt, Edith, 186
Kunnas, Mauri, 189

L'Amour, Louis, 229
Larrecq, John, 161
Lasker, Joe, 170
Lauber, Patricia, 246
Lawson, Robert, 192, 233
Leaf, Munro, 192
Le Cain, Errol, 157
Lee, Alan, 182
Lee, Dennis, 252
Lee, Robert C., 226
Lee, Virginia, 215
Lent Blair, 195
Leonni, Leo, 187
Leslie-Melville, Betty, 164
Lester, Julius, 261*
Levine, Ellen, 197
Levinson, Nancy, 196
Levinson, Riki, 197, 216
Levitin, Sonia, 181
Levoy, Myron, 216
Levy, Elizabeth, 184
Lewis, C. S., 232*
Lewis, Naomi, 157, 167, 170
Lindgren, Astrid, 182, 185, 239
Lindgren, Barbro, 188*
Lionni, Leo, 167, 168*
Lobe, Mira, 177
Lobel, Arnold, 167, 168*, 172, 183, 253, 254, 255, 259
Locker, Thomas, 160
Lofting, Hugh, 244*
London, Jack, 219

Lord, Bette Bao, 229
Lord, John, 162
Louie, Ai-Ling, 182, 195
Lovejoy, Bahija, 236
Lowrey, Janette S., 188*
Lowry, Lois, 246

McCleery, William, 217
McCloskey, Robert, 158, 180*, 227
McCully, Emily, 155, 169
McCurdy, Michael, 219
MacDonald, George, 182, 190
McDonald, S. P., 250
McDonnell, Christine, 245
McGovern, Ann, 211
McKie, Roy, 159
McKissack, Patricia, 179
MacLachlin, Patricia, 204, 219
McLerran, Alice, 183
McMillan, Bruce, 174
McMurtry, Stan, 209, 211
McPhail, David, 158, 172*, 179, 196, 200
McSwigan, Marie, 216
Magorian, Michelle, 225
Mahy, Margaret, 166, 183, 206
Manes, Stephen, 202*
Marshall, James, 164*, 166, 177, 181, 193
Martchenko, Michael, 194
Martin, Bill, Jr., 153, 169, 179, 185, 198
Martin, Charles, 179
Martin, Rafe, 167, 262
Maruki, Toshi, 238
Mayer, Marianna, 192
Mayer, Mercer, 154, 155, 157, 171, 179, 180, 192*, 200
Mazer, Harry, 243
Mazer, Norma Fox, 234
Meltzer, Milton, 211
Mendoza, George, 192
Merrill, Jean, 238
Mikolaycak, Charles, 169, 189
Miles, Bernard, 239
Miles, Miska, 186, 198
Milne, A. A., 253*
Milton, Joyce, 211
Minarik, Else Holmelund, 178*
Moeri, Louise, 189
Monjo, F. N., 197, 205

Moore, Elaine, 169, 177
Moore, Eva, 211, 254
Moore, Lilian, 165
Morey, Walt, 219, 224
Morris, Willie, 225
Mosel, Arlene, 154, 195
Moser, Barry, 250
Mowat, Farley, 212, 251
Munsch, Robert, 194*
Murphy, Jim, 223
Murphy, Shirley, 179
Myers, Bernice, 177
Myers, Walter Dean, 168, 262

Nelson, Vaunda, 169, 186
Nesbit, E., 182, 247
Newman, Robert, 220*
Nilsson, Ulf, 163
Noble, Trinka Hakes, 165
Norman, Howard, 186
Norton, Mary, 211, 229
Numeroff, Laura, 161, 175

O'Brien, Robert C., 234
O'Dell, Scott, 240, 242
Olson, Arielle North, 160
Oram, Hiawyn, 200
Ormerod, Jan, 155, 156, 169, 188*
Ormondroyd, Edward, 161, 176
Oxenbury, Helen, 188*

Palin, Michael, 182, 208, 211
Panati, Charles, 260
Parish, Peggy, 158*, 165, 174
Park, Barbara, 242*, 245
Parker, Kristy, 172
Parkin, Rex, 183
Parks, Gordon (photographer), 230
Patent, Dorothy, 198
Paterson, Diane, 196
Paterson, Katherine, 165, 218, 244
Patterson, Francine, 164
Paulsen, Gary, 220, 226
Pearce, Philippa, 160
Peck, Robert Newton, 213*, 222
Peet, Bill, 160, 179, 180, 186, 200*, 251
Pendergraft, Patricia, 233
Pène du Bois, William, 201, 204, 246

Peppé, Rodney, 154, 176
Perrault, Charles, 211, 257
Peters, Lisa, 183
Peterson, John, 210*
Phelps, Ethel Johnston, 258
Phillips, Louis, 160
Pinkney, Jerry, 261
Pinkwater, Daniel, 196
Piper, Watty, 178, 182
Pittman, Helena, 179
Pope, Joyce, 156
Porte, Barbara Ann, 160, 184
Postma, Linda, 211
Potter, Beatrix, 162
Prater, John, 155
Prelutsky, Jack, 253*, 254, 261
Purdy, Carol, 196
Pyle, Howard, 236

Rabe, Berniece, 165, 185
Rawls, Wilson, 247
Rayner, Mary, 194
Reeves, James, 166
Retan, Walter, 179, 180
Rettich, Margret, 160
Rey, H. A., 163*
Rice, Eve, 169
Richler, Mordecai, 209
Robart, Rose, 154, 175
Robinson, Barbara, 203
Robinson, Charles, 215
Rockwell, Anne, 173, 174, 203, 258
Rofes, Eric, 215
Rogasky, Barbara, 172, 173, 216
Rogers, Jean, 166, 196
Root, Phyllis, 182, 200
Rose, Elizabeth and Gerald, 202
Ross, Tony, 177, 205
Roth, Arthur, 220
Russell, William, 256*, 259, 262
Rylant, Cynthia, 186, 204*

Sachar, Louis, 241*
Sachs, Marilyn, 203, 245
Salassi, Otto, 218
Sargent, Sarah, 247
Say, Allen, 238
Scarry, Richard, 174
Schatell, Brian, 159
Schertle, Alice, 169
Schindler, S. D., 167
Schoenherr, John, 186
Schubert, Dieter, 156, 176

Schwartz, Alvin, 158, 159, 193, 261
Schwartz, Amy, 169
Schwerin, Doris, 169, 174
Scott, Elaine, 239
Sebestyen, Ouida, 249
Seibel, Fritz, 158
Seidler, Tor, 212, 223
Selden, George, 220
Seligson, Susan, 173
Sendak, Maurice, 154, 178, 185, 200*, 255, 263
Service, Robert W., 219, 250*
Seuling, Barbara, 154
Seuss, Dr., 158, 159, 174*, 179, 181, 185, 189, 190, 196, 251
Sharmat, Marjorie, 185, 202
Shaw, Charles, 154
Shemin, Margaretha, 216, 238
Shepard, Ernest H., 212, 253
Shulevitz, Uri, 187
Silverstein, Shel, 168, 183, 209, 255*, 259
Simmie, Lois, 252, 255
Simmonds, Posy, 173, 195
Simont, Marc, 229
Singer, Isaac Bashevis, 161, 189, 216, 263*
Skurzynski, Gloria, 220, 235
Sleator, William, 202, 223
Slote, Alfred, 226
Small, David, 187
Smith, Doris B., 215
Smith, Janice Lee, 239*
Smith, Robert K., 169, 205, 223
Snyder, Carol, 216
Snyder, Zilpha K., 211
Speare, Elizabeth George, 242
Sperry, Armstrong, 204
Spier, Peter, 155, 166, 174, 186*, 189, 190
Stanley, Diane, 181
Steig, William, 161, 193*, 217
Stepto, Michele, 176
Steptoe, John, 182
Stevens, Carla, 177, 207
Stevens, Harry, 154, 175
Stevens, Kathleen, 158

Stevenson, James, 165, 169, 189, 197*, 253
Stone, Irving, 219

Talbert, Marc, 215
Taylor, Judy, 161
Taylor, Mark, 179
Taylor, Mildred, 197, 206*, 240*
Taylor, Theodore, 220
Tenggren, Gustaf, 188
Thayer, Ernest L., 250
Thiele, Colin, 160, 212
Thomas, Jane Resh, 184
Thompson, Brian, 174
Tresselt, Alvin, 177
Tripp, Wallace, 250
Troughton, Joanna, 198
Tsuchiya, Yukio, 160
Turkle, Brinton, 155, 157, 158, 165, 171, 172, 194*

Udry, Janice M., 182
Ungerer, Tomi, 180
Ustinov, Nikolai, 190, 246

Van Allsburg, Chris, 165, 187, 188*
Velde, Vivian Vande, 185, 236
Vesey, A., 177
Vincent, Gabrielle, 155
Viorst, Judith, 157*, 184, 252*, 259
Vipont, Elfrida, 154, 175
Vivas, Julie, 189
Vogel, Ilse-Margaret, 215, 218
Voigt, Cynthia, 219

Waber, Bernard, 173*, 176
Waddell, Martin, 177, 197, 258
Wadsworth, Olive, 154
Wagner, Jane, 230
Wahl, Jan, 176, 200
Wakefield, Pat, 164
Wallace, Barbara Brooks, 237
Wallace, Bill, 160, 223*
Walsh, Jill Paton, 179, 197, 210
Walter, Mildred P., 187
Ward, Lynd, 155, 160, 190

Watkins, Yoko, 225, 235, 236, 238
Weisgard, Leonard, 205
Weiss, Leatie, 165
Wells, Rosemary, 165, 188*
White, E. B., 211, 220, 237
Whitfield, Philip and Ruth, 156
Whitlock, Susan, 171
Whitman, Sally, 165
Wijngaard, Juan, 252
Wilbur, Richard, 161
Wildsmith, Brian, 160
Wilhelm, Hans, 184
Wilkie, Katharine, 221
Williams, Garth, 220
Williams, Jay, 192, 213, 231
Williams, Linda, 154, 171, 176
Williams, Margery, 216
Williams, Vera B., 162, 169
Willis, Val, 157, 165, 183
Wilson, James, 250
Wilson, Maurice, 166
Winter, Jeanette, 169
Winter, Paula, 155
Winthrop, Elizabeth, 161, 185
Wojciechowska, Maia, 207
Wolitzer, Hilma, 229
Wolkstein, Diane, 190
Wood, Audrey, 158, 161, 171, 184*
Wood, Don, 161, 171, 184
Wright, Betty, 202
Wyeth, N. C., 190

Yashima, Taro, 165, 185, 195
Yektai, Niki, 199
Yolen, Jane, 160, 169, 172, 177, 185, 186*, 195, 257, 258
Young, Ed, 155, 156, 167

Zacharias, Thomas and Wanda, 199
Zelinsky, Paul O., 172, 173
Zhitkov, Boris, 173
Ziefert, Harriet, 188, 199*
Zion, Gene, 171*, 180
Zolotow, Charlotte, 172, 177, 184, 186, 201*, 257
Zwerger, Lisbeth, 170, 211